MW01491301

Journey
to the Edge
of the Sky

A journal of missionary flying and
experiences in Alaska and Africa

Les Paul Zerbe

Alaska's far north flying chaplain

© 2008 by Les Paul Zerbe. All rights reserved
Visit us at: www.FarNorthFlyingChaplain.com

Printed by Calvary Publishing
A Ministry of Parker Memorial Baptist Church
1902 East Cavanaugh Road, Lansing, MI 48910.
www.CalvaryPublishing.org

No part of this publication may be reproduced, stored
in a retrieval system or transmitted in any way by any
means—electronic, mechanical, photocopy, recording or
otherwise—without the prior permission of the copyright
holder, except as provided by USA copyright law.

All Scriptures are taken from the King James Bible.
ISBN # 978-0-9802043-0-8

Calvary **FOR BAPTISTS BY BAPTISTS**
PUBLISHING
CP
KJV

A ministry of Parker Memorial Baptist Church
1902 East Cavanaugh Road • Lansing, Michigan 48910
Phone: 517.882.2112 • Fax: 517.882.2317

www.calvarypublishing.org

DEDICATION

This book is dedicated to my children and grandchildren to preserve for them my flying and hunting stories. May their lives be as full and enjoyable as mine has been;

And to Jane, my wife of forty years, who has tirelessly labored in editing and typing these pages and who went from the frying pan (Africa) to the freezer (Alaska) with me.

ACKNOWLEDGEMENTS

Thanks to the following people for their assistance:

Tom Furse, Janice McKay and Katie Duffett for typing;
Dr. Tom Furse, for his encouragement to complete my writing.
Shirleen Philpot, for her enthusiasm after reading a very rough first draft;
Liller Burke, who encouraged me to keep writing and helped greatly in the editing of these pages.

TABLE OF CONTENTS

*"When once you have tasted flight,
you will forever walk the earth
with your eyes turned skyward,
for there you have been, and there
you will always long to return."*

-- Leonardo da Vinci

JOURNEY TO THE EDGE

OF THE SKY

INTRODUCTION

How is it possible to bring order out of a fading memory? I will begin at the beginning, like the African weaverbird; just pick an interesting tree and start somewhere. After much patient weaving, I'll be able to call it finished.

But, there are a hundred places to start, a thousand names and places that I recall all in a second. A bank teller refers to a ledger; a seaman to a tide book; a pilot to his logbook. That is where I shall begin.

From the first time I caught a sparrow and tied a note to his leg, flight intrigued me. The sparrow departed for the unknown, with such speed and in such freedom - I knew I would one day duplicate him.

I, Les Paul Zerbe, have flown my bush plane in all the states except Hawaii, and have flown in Canada, Africa, Mexico, the Bahamas and through the Caribbean Islands to St. Thomas. Most of my 20,000 hours of flight time has been in Africa and Alaska.

GRANDPA'S JOURNEY –1913

This account begins in Russia with my Grandpa "Bill" Zerbe. Providence is one of the most interesting parts of our human experience. Grandpa "Bill" Zerbe, out of necessity, began this journey to the edge of the sky. The longing for freedom is the drumbeat of every human heart, in every nation, in every man, for all time. Had it not been for grandpa, and his yearning to explore the meaning of the word "freedom," this book could not be written. What caused him to leave Europe in 1913, to go so far, to endure great hardships, to forsake family? Some of the answers may have gone to the grave with him, but my journey began with his.

Grandpa Bill Zerbe rented a room and slept in a thatched roof house in a German community in Poland, "because de r-r-rent vas cheaper," but he went across the border to work at a brick factory in Hamburg, Germany, because there were no jobs in Poland. He was concerned about being conscripted into the Russian army when the Russians were moving in, so Wilhelm, at age 20, fled to the U.S. -- to the "promised land"-- with his brother Ferdinand, three years older. Bill paid his way with money borrowed from his brother Henry, who had immigrated earlier and started a mechanic shop in South Dakota. Born in 1893, William Zerbe did not know the exact day of his birth, but needed a date for his immigration papers, so the captain of the ship marked September 16th as his birthday.

Bill and Ferd rode a train to South Dakota, and began working for farmers in the area shucking corn by hand. They used two-thumbed gloves because the thumbs wore out so quickly. Over time, their grips became like steel.

Then Bill joined the US army during WWI, although he was not yet a citizen. When he was sworn into the army, at the same time he became a U.S. citizen. "I only raised my hand vonce," he said. Here he was a German in a war against Germany. His assignment was to take care of the cavalry horses stateside.

"Why get captured by the Russians and have to fight for them as a German slave?" was his rationale.

Bill acquired some horses in South Dakota and some wagons and took a train to North East Montana to the small town of Oswego to find homestead land. They went north from there up Wolf Creek, making their way up the prairie in an area with no road. He found his land, staked the corners and dug in a side of a hill a two story soddy, in which he and two other bachelors lived. His horses lived on the bottom, the people on the top. Bill kept cows as well as horses under his sod home in the dugout area to help heat the house. He had discovered coal in a nearby hill on the homestead, but "one horse gives 15,000 BTU's per hour, you know." Bill would say that he "loved to feed the animals when they do so well," but of course the smells of the horses were nothing new to him, and there was no woman in his life as yet.

Bill used three horses to pull a one bottom plow and began farming wheat. His first tractor was a steel-wheeled one on which the engine ran so slowly that Bill would say "the engine would pop over and then you could go eat breakfast before the second pop!" I still own some of the old leather bridle systems and one of his early saddles.

Now these three bachelors had no social lives--what kind of social life can you have with perhaps one person per twenty square miles? The German Mennonites had built a school first and used the building also as a church. Bill was a Lutheran, but there was no Lutheran church around. The Mennonites around him spoke German, so he went to their church—it didn't matter. It was the only place to find social contacts.

Then someone moved close in and homesteaded next to Bill, one Marie Redekopp, whose name in Russian meant "red top." Marie had come from Patrowka, Russia, to Canada, and then due south to homestead her own property, settling right next to Bill. Like all homesteaders, she had to sleep every night on her eighty acres for a year. The bachelors hired Marie to cook for them, and she would walk half a mile one way to cook at their place each day. Bill and Marie were soon married in the school house-church and began to develop the ranch, beginning by building a large barn with a hayloft.

The Dust Bowl and the Depression came and there was no crop from 1929 to 1939. Many farmers moved out, but Bill stuck it out, when nothing grew on the prairie, barely living off the cattle. He would cut green thistles to feed the animals supplemented with some corn and wheat. Bill bought land for seven to ten cents per acre. From 1939 to 1945, the crops were so good that Bill could have retired. He became a very progressive farmer, purchasing a new 1940 Minneapolis Moline tractor with rubber tires, fenders front and rear, and a heated cab.

Such was the life of the best of the best of immigrants that ever sought freedom. He loved and served America, learned her language, developed her lands, asked no one for anything, became a success, raised a family of four sons and two daughters and maintained his love for God every day. It would seem to me that in life, a man like Grandpa was not appreciated as much as he should have been, but in his death, all of us looked back and wondered, "How did they do it?"

Grandpa was no mere man; he couldn't have been. He raised a fine Christian family with six children, one of whom was my father, a missionary pilot of some forty years. Grandpa could persevere. When I was a young lad, "a little white black boy," having been raised in Africa, grandpa had to teach me the white man's ways from ground zero. When I was six years old, I could drive a farm tractor by myself, and by the age of eleven, I was driving wheat trucks all day like Jehu! I also learned to milk cows.

THE COW THAT WON – 1951

One day on the farm, grandpa decided we needed a new milk cow. The consequences of this decision were soon to be found out. He and I located a range Hereford, a wild beast she was, but she looked like a milker. With much effort, we got her into the corral, then the barn, and finally, through the temptation of oats, got her head in the stanchion. Once this head-locking device clamped her head fast, I at once believed a cow could jump over the moon.

When the milking stool and bucket came into her sight, another more rigorous dance ensued. Then, the hobbles were summoned and secured on the cow's hind legs. With the milk bucket now in place under the business end of the cow, her hind feet went high and came down in the bucket. Two lariat ropes were then fastened to her hind feet and tied straight back. Once again, as the stool and milk bucket approached, the cow's front legs came back and kicked me into the gutter, a place directly behind the cow containing "recycled grass." This most unhappy experience led grandpa to decide more ropes were needed, so the front legs were tied forward. Once I was under the cow and secure in the comfort of the ropes, the cow simply fell over on me. The dismal sensation that I was getting a whippin' by this cow was short lived as grandpa fetched another rope. Not savvy in cowboy ways, I was not sure where you could attach another rope to a cow. I soon found out, as grandpa ran this rope under the cow's belly and tied it off to the ceiling. Now the cow could not fall on me! Grandpa was teaching me the valuable lesson of never giving up.

Now, very secure in the knowledge that we had won, the milking began. Two squirts of milk in the bucket were accompanied by two "cow pies" that covered the cow's tail. That tail became the most formidable weapon as she wrapped it around my head, again and again. Since I was no longer able to see, grandpa got another rope. This one stretched the cow's tail straight back! The dribble of milk we had to show for our efforts helped us decide that this cow had won! Perseverance and using every available resource was the lesson learned. Actually, the cow taught this lesson better than grandpa! Another lesson learned: there are some things in life best left for a better cowboy. A "cow whisperer" somewhere may be more successful!

THE AFRICAN CONNECTION – MID 1940'S

There is the saying about "the chip off the old block." A clear progeny of Russian-German extract was my father, Ludwig Zerbe. My father was the best in this earth of preachers and pilots, preaching the Word with clarity and pioneering the idea of flight in a Piper J-3 Cub to the heart of West Africa. He was honest with himself and all others and afraid of nothing, it seemed.

Those early pioneers could never be replaced because the earth they trod would have to be brought back to its original state. Dad's father had gone West after the first World War and lived in a stick and sod house, and my dad and mom went to Liberia, West Africa, also to live in a stick and mud house in the village of Zondo in the Bassa tribe area. The house was primitive, with a hard dirt floor, thatch roof, and a wood stove for cooking.

Dad had received his flying lessons from Mr. Piper himself in the middle '40's in Lockhaven, Pennsylvania, the location of the Piper Aircraft Factory. Mr. Piper instructed his men to have the plane--a new Piper J-3 Cub with 65 hp--ready for dad, fueled, rolled out of the hangar, and to hand prop it when he was ready to fly.

Mr. Piper thought dad needed a total of 52 hours of flying experience to be ready for Africa and told dad that he would charge him one dollar per hour for the fifty-two hours. When dad went to pay him the $52, Mr. Piper rounded it off to $50! Dad's flying was so inexpensive that his experience did not really represent "the Good Ol' days"—it was actually better than the "Good Ol' Days"!

He was one of the first missionary pilots in all of West Africa. To be "the first" in any undertaking of this magnitude is sheer folly to most, insanity to others. When Dad flew a 65 horse power Piper Cub, its fabric sometimes patched with bed sheets, with 12 gallons of total fuel, every flight begun became an epic journey. No radio or navigation facilities existed, but mother's gray hairs soon did, as she would wait in the rainy season for weeks for dad's return from flights that were supposed to be one day in length.

The real pilots, the pioneers, lived then, not now. But the pioneer spirit is that which must be part and parcel of a missionary's life. Those who fear the jungle, the desert, snakes, cold, and hot, need not apply. Most mission fields are no land for the timid. The pioneer is one who will go in the direction of his fears, like Jonah after being spewed out on the shore, or Moses crossing the Red Sea. I'm convinced the pioneer spirit can be passed down from generation to generation. If your family doesn't have it to pass down, you may acquire the pioneer spirit only with great difficulty through trial and error. It's much easier to be afraid of the unknown than to pursue it. That's why I wear cowboy hats and boots-- I don't want to forget that Grandpa Zerbe trained horses for Uncle Sam's army as a grateful new immigrant. His "can-do" spirit was everywhere.

Those early days of flying were a pleasure, born out of necessity. A 250-mile trek through the jungle one-way was not all that uncommon. Steaming hot humid days spent under the canopy, eating freshly killed monkeys, trying to avoid Filaria-ridden swamps,[1] the overturned dugout canoe, the soldier ants hidden on the trail that made you bleed with every bite, the Gabon viper[2] and green mamba[3] on the trail ready to strike, all could take

---

[1] Filaria is a long, threadlike roundworm that lives as a parasite in the bodies of human beings and animals. Filariae The *larvae* (young worms) are born alive. They can be seen in the blood near the body surface of the *host* (the animal in which the larvae live). When a bloodsucking fly or mosquito bites an infected person, it takes up the larvae with the blood. The larvae develop in the mosquito's or fly's head near the mouth. Then when the insect bites another animal, the larvae enter the wound and infect a new host. *Worldbook Online*

[2] Gabon viper is an extremely venomous, ground-dwelling snake found in tropical forests of central Africa. It is the heaviest venomous snake in Africa, weighing 8 kg (18 pounds), and it grows to a length of 2 metres (about 7 feet). The Gabon viper also possesses the longest fangs of any snake, measuring up to 4 cm (1.6 inches) long. *Britannica Online.* As a blood-poisoning viper, the venom turns into nerve poison in later stages and, depending on the size of the victim, can kill within 18 hours.

their toll, but these early missionaries did not flinch. God had made certain promises to them and they believed. But, the airplane changed all this like the metamorphosis from an ugly slow caterpillar to a butterfly. What would previously take two weeks on foot, now took two hours.

Missionaries are some of the most important people in the world. They alone, in understanding the power of God, were the only outside element that made real change in the heart of Africa. The executive of a big company is an important person. His time is valuable. He flies in a $35,000,000 jet because he is important and needs speed and flexibility to be a wise steward of his time. It costs more than getting there in a Chevy or a bus, but it's worth it. Those early missionaries in Africa deserved, needed and used their $3,500.00 pair of wings to the fullest.

When I first tasted Africa at around age three, it tasted like roasted termites, snail soup, rice, greens, peanut oil, lots of hot pepper, smoked monkey legs, giant frog legs and crocodile tail-- all enjoyed in the company of my little black friends. Back then, you see, I was a "little white black boy" and fond of everything they were. The thought of piano lessons that my mother insisted on in those early years could not compete with hunting and bird catching with these young masters of the jungle. To be with them was to develop a sixth sense of my surroundings, to decipher the thoughts of the animals, and fine tune a sense of survival.

But, our villages of Zondo and Tappita were areas of existence very small in comparison to the continent. Beyond the trackless jungle are villages still sleeping, unknown to other men or what they might do to them. History shows these people, relatively untouched by the white man, are still unaware of a world outside their own. White men's wars are fought on the edges of

---

[3]The two varieties --Green mamba & black mamba, members of the Cobra family but not hooded, are the dreaded snake species of Africa. They are considered one of the most dangerous snakes known. Not only are they highly venomous but it is aggressive. They are one of the world's fastest moving snakes, and victims have little chance to escape from a bite, as the venom is highly neurotoxic. SurvivalIQ.com.

Africa. The white man can carry a rifle and hand grenade several hundred miles inland, and he is still on the outside, looking in. Africa, it seems, doesn't change on a whim.

Since ancient history, the white man has tried through various means to penetrate the "dark heart" of Africa. David Livingston painted a very "dark heart." Several colonial powers have since tried to reform that "dark heart" through geopolitical reformation with little or no success. Even the earlier of New Testament churches founded in Africa has not left any legible trace. It would seem that whatever power would rumble through Africa, whatever piece of land changes masters from time to time, in the end, Africa lies and will lie, like a great unmolested giant who refuses to be awakened by the bickering of noisy empires.

There are so many Africas, as many Africas as there are books about Africa. When Solomon wrote "of the making of many books there is no end," he must have been looking forward to those trying to acquaint us with Africa. My Africa was not the safari, the great game preserves, or the great desert. My Africa, the western hump part of, primarily, Liberia and Ivory Coast, is mystic. It is wild; it is a sweltering inferno; a place of unnoticed tribes of those who have not yet invented the wheel; of some twenty-eight tribes and language groups that live in an area the size of Ohio. It is a photographer's paradise, but it is a place to get stomach worms just by breathing dust in the air; where 200 inches of rain fall in six months; and the desert sand storms 10,000 feet thick and 2,000 miles away, find residence in the farthest crevice in your kitchen cupboard.

It is a place where the average tribesman, who says he believes in God, still proclaims the devil has more power than God since they have seen what he can do; where the witch doctor's trial by ordeal may be as accurate as our present day jury systems; where government officials who go to work each day in white shirt and tie still eat human flesh as part of ritualistic sacrifice to stay in power; a place where I found a man one day, as I was flying down the beach, who had his heart cut out of him. It was said that if a father "had a strong heart for hunting," his son having eaten his father's heart, would also distinguish himself in the same way.

It is a place of raging diseases like malaria, filaria, sleeping sickness, AIDS, lassa fever and leprosy to mention a few. It's a place of uncounted numbers of poisonous snakes, of scorpions and spiders the size of a wrestler's hand and twice as deadly; of one species or another at constant odds, one always trying to eat the other. Some evenly matched, and in the case of a human being catching, roasting and eating thousands of termites, not so evenly matched. Africa is what you will and it withstands all interpretations. Like Alaska, you either love it or hate it. To a lot of people including myself, it was just home, and it was hardly ever really dull.

ZONDO, LIBERIA, WEST AFRICA—1948

My father, Ludwig Zerbe, found this village—Zondo from his lofty perch in a Piper J3 Cub. The fuel tank held only 12 gallons of gas and a cork supported wire protruded through the gas cap to indicate how many explosions were still remaining in the heart of this flying machine that barely carried two. There were no maps or electronics for aeronautical guidance, just watch and compass and the Lord God of heaven. It was truly a "Journey to the Edge of the Sky," because once beyond the six gallon mark, there was no returning to more pleasant surroundings, only the jungle swallowing you as a crocodile would a frog, only to be found at the resurrection by God Himself. Since God doesn't need a radio to talk to you, this early plane had none.

Our family flew into Zondo and made it our home for four years, the little yellow Piper Cub parked next to the mud- stick, thatched-roof house. Because of no radios or instruments, mother would spend two or three weeks wondering where dad was. It was always supposed to be a one or two day trip that turned into weeks of bad weather. We wouldn't know if he was dead or alive until he arrived. All we had to comfort us was an African talking gray parrot and the friendly natives who would ask questions, such as "Why is the plane so big here and so small when it's in the sky."

In the rainy season, we couldn't see because of the rain or fog, in the dry season because of the "harmattan", i.e. a cloud of fine sand blowing from the Sahara desert that filled the atmosphere, or because of the smoke from the annual burning of the farmlands in the "slash and burn" farming method, as the Africans cut the rain forest and then burned it.

My father was the best in this earth of preachers and pilots, preaching the Word with clarity and pioneering the idea of flight in a Piper J-3 Cub to the heart of West Africa. He was honest with himself and all others and afraid of nothing, it seemed. Those early pioneers could never be replaced because the earth they trod would have to be brought back to its original state. Dad's father had gone West after the first World War and lived in a stick and sod house, and my dad and mom went to Liberia, West Africa, also to live in a stick and mud house in the village of Zondo in the Bassa tribe area. The house was primitive, the walls made from sticks set in the ground, then covered with thick mud. It had a hard dirt floor, thatch roof, and a wood stove for cooking. After a few weeks of "rustic" living, disaster struck.

One evening, Mom tucked my baby sister and me, a lad of around three, into bed; then my parents walked next door to a prayer meeting in another missionary's house. They joined in prayer with two other couples and several single lady missionaries, who proudly signed their names with the title "O.M." —Old Maid. During the prayer time, one of the old maids raised her eyes and glanced out the window to see flames on the thatch of our house. While my sister and I were sleeping, a spark from the wood stove (which had made this hot house even hotter) found its way to the dry palm branch roof. My baby sister Sheryl and I were unaware of the burning thatch roof falling in on our mosquito nets.

My dad and Missionary Bob Smith were the first to reach the house, running into the flaming structure to rescue us. Then they ran back to grab whatever possessions they could salvage—a box of sermon notes that had been painstakingly prepared over hours and hours of study, and a few things that could be reached in those frantic twenty minutes before the house burned to the ground.

My sister and I were barely saved from the fire. We lost all the family treasures and my glasses. They were priceless, and my only pair in Africa! No one had thought to grab them from their place in the room. We would have to order another pair all the way from the United States, which would take months with the slowness of the mail in those days, but our lives were spared.

The next day while looking around the burned area, an African man spied something in the grass at the edge of the jungle—my glasses! The nearest that anyone could figure was that, as the house burned, Bob Smith was throwing things out of the house as fast as he could. One such item was the curtains in the bathroom. On the way out the window, the curtains must have snagged my glasses. Wonders and miracles never cease!

Our next home was better. Termites worldwide are scorned and poisoned, but not in many parts of Africa, where they are a tasty treat when toasted over a fire. Their 20-foot high mounds could be smashed and mixed with water and molded into excellent bricks with which to make a home. My dad hired strong young men to chop and dig the termite hills and to mix the adobe clay and water into mud. Then they mixed the mud with their feet, stomping and squishing until smooth, and shaped bricks in a wooden mold. Drying in the sun for several days produced a brick almost impervious to rain. The termites would need to find a new home-- probably the new brick one we had just built from theirs!

Africa has a way of stealing time from you even though the native quite literally doesn't know what time is! He is not reminded or governed by calendar or watch; neither does he know how old he is. No written records exist, and he lost count of his birthdays several rice farms ago. Each day is simply a new "challenge" of the present need, and if it can wait till tomorrow, it will.

TAPPI –THE FORT -- 1950'S

My father made West Africa hum, not only with his constant building and fixing things, but was a pioneer in the Mid-Liberia Baptist Bible Institute in the village of Tappita, where we moved for our second term, as well as a church planter and the best of aviators. When he finally left Africa, the black people came and sat on his front porch and wept because their "lawyer" was leaving them. He was a true friend to them all, from the president to the leprosy patient and had even defended these humble Christians in the courts on occasion.

Then there was Mom, Agnes Lorraine, and like many of us, preferred her first name not be used. She is a wonderful woman--a classy dresser any man would be proud to be seen with, a fastidious housekeeper, and a real chef in the kitchen. In the early days with no refrigeration, she could fix Spam (this stands for "small pieces of animal meat") in about fifty different ways, and it would be gourmet. Meals were served on a table made pretty with a tablecloth or placemats and flowers.

We ate "native" at least every other day, which wasn't bad by any standard. An example of this would be "country chop" a delicious dish combining chicken (fresh caught with a worm in its beak and butchered) fried in palm oil or palm butter (a derivative of the red palm nut) to which was added finely chopped collard greens, okra, and eggplant, all cooked together and served on a bed of white rice with hot peppers on the side. A glass of sweet Southern tea would complement the homemade from scratch cake she had baked for the dessert. Then there were those homemade gooey cinnamon rolls each Sunday morning that would put any bakery out of business had there been any competition.

The laundry was always done and even the underwear ironed. Her house looked like a professional interior decorator had come through, beautifully accented with local arts and crafts or things she had made, working with what she had on hand in the jungle, which often wasn't very much. Yet she was the absolute realist, telling us in later years not to spend any money on a prospective female if you could not be sure she was wife material to begin with.

Her husband, my dad, Ludwig Zerbe, would sometimes fly away on a mission in that 65 horsepower J-3 Piper Cub holding 12 gallons of gas, expecting to return the same day, but would not return for two weeks or more. This was during the rainy season and before the mission had purchased any radio or other form of communication. Mom would not know if he was down in the jungle of equatorial Africa or just waiting out weather.

In one year at Tappita, Mom herself killed thirteen poisonous snakes in our house, some with her high-heeled shoe. Another snake crawled around her feet while she was at the table writing letters. Mom stood up and moved the chair onto the serpent's back just behind its head, pinning it to the floor; then proceeded to kill it with a blow. On another occasion, as she was rinsing out the dust in the tub in preparation for running us a bath, a snake slithered up the drain into the tub.

And the incessant moving! Maybe frequent moves were suitable for the apostle Paul, but they were not the best for a missionary wife. So many things were left behind. Not just things, but people and memories – all these were behind her, not like part of a life, but like a whole life lived and ended.

These and much more would have sent the average woman fleeing for her mother's skirts, but not this one. Her motto probably, although not voiced, was "never hope more than you can work." And after that, work and hope.

And in those early days of my childhood life at Tappita in the 1950's, I was a little white "black boy," destined to be one of them, to be part of another world, their world. A boy does not speak as a man or project as a man. He becomes like whom he associates with, and I was innocently white and proud to be a native. What I did not know of and did not want to know of race and color and class, I learned soon enough, as I grew to see each man put sovereignly into a slot of time and place.

One day on furlough, I could be just another white kid throwing baseballs, while another day would find me in darkest Africa shooting a homemade sling at a bird or a rat. My little black friend in front of me on the trail to our hideout in the jungle was a good friend, but in time, the handclasp will be shorter, the eyes will not meet so readily, the smile not so eager on his face. Though the path was for a while the same, later on he would walk behind me, when once in the simplicity of our youth, we walked together. As we grew older, we would come to understand that only the teachings of Christ would keep us as equals and lifelong friends.

But when we were eight and nine and ten years old, we walked, played, worked, schemed, and built things that didn't surprise us, but did surprise all others. We knew we were hunters, starting of course with small things we could get with a stick or spear or slingshot. You could eat little things if you were a little white-black boy, and little things, such as small birds with feathers and all, would find their place in some corner of mom's neat kerosene refrigerator. I was saving them until we had enough "meat" to make a meal in our hideout in the bush. But Mom threw my catch away, not agreeing to this usage of her clean fridge.

We had our home away from home, a place of miniature independence, our very own little hideout in the jungle, where no one could find or stop our inventions in progress. Back then, I made 25 cents a week mowing our grass to keep the snakes down near the house. I took great delight in finding a snake in the grass and in maneuvering the running lawn mower down on top of him. Generally, it was against my policy to fertilize the grass, but this was our exception.

But the 25 cents a week allowance gave us young warriors and hunters real power. At a Lebanese shop in downtown Tappita and I would buy raw gunpowder, and in those days, 25c would buy enough to be creative with it. Oh, gunpowder--that enslaves some and sets others free! We learned early on at around eight or nine years of age that gunpowder would change the way we hunted, although too young to buy, hold, or own weapons legally. So we set out to make our own weapons. We figured too many critters were getting away from our slingshots and bows-and-arrows, and we must upgrade our weaponry. A shotgun would be the weapon of choice.

We found in a storage shed, a left over piece of copper tubing used for plumbing a house. Then we ran into the jungle to chop down a worthy tree with our machetes, which were made from melted down old car springs by a native blacksmith. Back at the hideout, we would fashion a stock to hold the barrel of copper tubing. It was simple to make, but testing it would require some skill and precision and eventually the throwing away of the first prototype barrel.

We first hammered one end of the copper tubing flat and bent that end over. Then we drilled a hole there of 1/8" diameter and screwed it to the homemade stock. We wrapped the rest of the copper tubing to the stock with bailing wire. Then just ahead of the bent-over section of the copper tubing, we drilled another 1/8" hole and glued a matchbox striker to the stock near this hole. We then poured gunpowder down the barrel as you would a musket, then tamped in a tight rag behind the powder. Next, we loaded the barrel with a few small nails, rocks, or ball bearings for the shot. Last, we tamped in another rag tightly to hold everything together like a crude shot gun shell.

We were ready to light it off. We learned that the charge would go off as long as we held the match to the gunpowder hole while the hot sulphur of the match head was burning. It worked! We had made our own shotgun!

We experimented by adding powder in increasing increments to get the most effective load. When the barrel pressure started to expand and crack the soft copper tube, we backed off on the powder charge a bit and installed a new copper barrel. (Although we were careful, looking back over the years, it's amazing that we didn't hurt or kill ourselves doing this.) At 50 yards, we could blow holes all through a piece of tin roofing, so we extended our line of weapons to pistols and a canon made of steel pipe that would put a golf ball through the door of a car.

Once we knew we were in control and not dead ourselves, we let Dad and Mom know of our achievements by setting off the cannon right next to the house. (Until my dad read this story, he had no idea of the extent of my exploits in experimentation making this gun.) To the best of my memory, I can't remember what happened next, so it must have been somehow uneventful, our genius having shown through enough to circumvent the whipping we should have received. I think they saw that we were no fools, but mere dreamers, black and white dreamers of the highest caliber for our age and circumstance. Only Huckleberry Finn could have possibly surpassed us, and I thought we made all his adventures seem mundane.

This was a new thing. Ours was a very young world, eager for gifts and inventions – and this was one. The gunpowder exploding was a sound that was to me like a white light prying through closed eyes of adulthood, disturbing slumber they did not want disturbed. My black friend and I liked life too much to be patient with risks or death. We learned what every dreaming child needs to know – that no horizon is so far that you cannot get above or beyond it. Our jungle hideout was kept a secret because we could easily despair of man, but find poetry in a babbling stream or an ocean of 150 ft. tall trees. We knew we could have treated doomsday with a wink, and I think we did.

THE WITCH DOCTOR'S BREW -- 1953

The witch doctor is a powerful figure in this small country and the average man feared him. Possessed by demonic powers, he could seemingly work magic and miracles. One day five hunters went into the bush to hunt and one did not return. A search party found his body, shot in the back at close range with what had to be one of the other two hunter's weapons. The other hunters were brought to Tappi and a three-day trial by ordeal would follow. My father and I attended the proceeding, two white specks in a sea of black faces, all shoulders touching, all sweating, and all intent on the witch doctor's doings. My dad shared his account of what we saw:

The hunt was at night using carbide "miner's" lamps attached with a head band to spot the deer's eyes and the gun sight. Five hunters went out from the same village, and four returned, none of which acknowledged shooting the fifth after a search party found the body. In due time, the hunters were brought before the American-educated District Commissioner in the District Courthouse. For lack of any scientific examination available, the commissioner declared that the suspects be tried by ordeal.

A witch doctor was summoned and the trial date was set. My father and I attended the proceeding, two white specks in a sea of black faces, all shoulders touching, all sweating, and all intent on the witch doctor's doings.

Perhaps because of our presence, (although he himself probably was confident of the witch doctor's ability) the Commissioner required him to prove his power before trying these men for murder. This understood, the Commissioner took a ring off his finger and gave it to his aide with the public announcement that this soldier was to take four volunteers outside, one at a time and to hide the ring in the clothing of one of them at random.

Then, being given the go-ahead for the trial, the witch doctor immediately proceeded to build a fire on the cement floor in the center of the courtroom with fagots of wood, boy scout fashion. After the fire had burned for an hour or two and enough ashes were available, he took the ashes and poured them out in a ten-foot circle around the fire, which he kept on stoking for his further use. He then ordered a tall bucket of cold water and three buckets of wet sand brought in, setting the water inside, but near the edge of the circle and pouring out the sand in a heap beside the water.

Now he was ready. He explained to the Commissioner and to all of us curious onlookers how he would find the man who had the ring. He stood the four men used in this mock trial in a row just outside of his domain -- the circle of ashes. The fire by now had a substantial heap of live coals under the flames. The witch doctor placed his machete into his fire, leaving it there long enough so that every observer would be convinced that the metal was hot enough to brand even the tough hide of a hippo. This done, he placed the machete into the bucket of water to cool it and then thrusting it all the way to the wooden handle into the pile of wet sand. He left it there while he explained that this instrument of justice once heated very hot, then thoroughly cooled would again of itself turn as hot as it was when it was first withdrawn from the fire when he touched it to the forearm of the "guilty" one-of-the-four.

I must describe the "judge's" attire. He was wearing a lady's black wool winter coat (probably a donation originally given through an American welfare organization) and a light brown fur cap commonly seen in pictures of Siberian men - this at midday near the Equator and standing beside a fire for hours! On with the show! Now came the moment everyone had been eagerly awaiting.

He took the machete out of the sand, waving it in nondescript fashion over his head, the meanwhile calling upon his gods to identify the "culprit" to him. He approached the four men lined up outside of his circle and stroked their extended bare forearms slowly with the machete. The first three men felt no harm. This meant that the fourth one MUST be the one who had the ring. When the machete touched his arm he jerked back, probably because he realized he was the only one left, and the witch doctor declared him to be in possession of the ring. He was wrong, however, another produced it.

We were stunned to hear the Commissioner announce that he would give the "arbiter" another chance to prove his dark power. But this time he would personally choose four men out of the audience and the whole process would be resumed - this time his wrist watch would be given to be secretly hidden in the clothing of one of the four,

"Stand-ins." More wood was put on the fire, and in much longer time than it takes to tell, the entire bizarre process was repeated with the same result. This time the whole courtroom laughed the unsuccessful imposter to scorn, and he left with a sheepish smile on his face, leaving the mess on the courtroom floor behind. After restoring order in the court, the Commissioner announced that he would search for another witch doctor and in cooperation with him would set another trial date!

Several months later a witch doctor had been hired and the "suspects" were brought to district headquarters for a second trial by ordeal. The Assistant Secretary of Interior happened to be visiting from Monrovia, the capitol, and out of respect to him, he was given the dubious honor of presiding over this trial. Protocol required the four suspects to come before him to introduce themselves. One of the men, whose name was Kpa, when he gave his name, said this: "Your honor, Mr. Secretary, I am a Christian and no longer believe in the power of the witch doctor as I once did (in fact he had been a practicing Christian for a number of years and was highly respected in the region), so I affirm before you and my God that I did not kill the man in question; I therefore ask to be excused from this ordeal, although I am willing to stand in judgment in a regular court of law."

To seek to prove the sincerity of Kpa's confession to be a follower of Christ, the Secretary asked him one questions "How many wives do you have?" (It was a well-known fact that sincere believers were monogamous - a radical departure from that which was the norm in that society.) Kpa answered with a conviction born of reality; "Your honor, I have only one." This plainly caught the Secretary so much by surprise that he engaged in a brief whispering session with the Commissioner seated beside him and then came back with this pronouncement without explaining the reason for it: "You will be required to stand trial by the witch doctor this time, but I promise you that you will never need to do so again."

The secretary did not require proof of this witch doctor's power of discernment, as the commissioner had done in the first attempt to find the killer.

This uncivilized referee had a different modus operandi than the first one. He built a fire outdoors near the back door of the courthouse, in which he also heated his machete. He stood the four men in a row near his operation, being careful to place Kpa on his far right. In a black iron kettle he had a "brew" that appeared to be a mixture of palm oil and various leaves and herbs. With his hand he applied a generous layer of this stuff to the right shins of the four, explaining to those who were observing that when he took his heated machete out of the fire, he would strike it over the prepared shins; the innocent would not be burned, but the guilty would suffer a blistering burn. I stood within six feet of the witch doctor with no one in front of me, determined to detect any sleight of hand that might be observable, knowing from long experience the hostility these devil-worshipers had for Christians. My vigil was rewarded. This imposter took his machete directly out of the fire, and with one quick stroke, he brought that instrument down on each of the men's legs. The first three were not affected, but when he came to Kpa he brought that iron down his leg, and then with a sawing motion under pressure and as fast as you can blink your eye near his ankle he rubbed through the "insulation" and the subject received a serious burn.

Kpa-was pronounced guilty by the pretender and was sentenced by the Secretary to undetermined term in the jail, which was located on the courthouse grounds. Since the Liberian government did not feed the prisoners, Kpa's family was forced to move from their village and take up residence with others near the jail so his wife could cook and bring food daily to her imprisoned husband.

Six months after this the Secretary of Interior himself came to spend some time with the District Commissioner in our town in order to look into some of the more difficult and frustrating cases. I was allowed to have a private audience with him at his place of residence after hours and took the occasion to tell him Kpa's story from beginning to end as I had observed it and to appeal for his release. He graciously promised that he would hear the case before he left town.

The next day he sent soldiers to summon any and all who had any knowledge of the case to come in without hesitation. When all were present, he painstakingly questioned all who volunteered to testify and concluded that session by ordering Kpa's immediate release for lack of verifiable evidence against him. Two soldiers brought Kpa before the Secretary to hear his verdict.

While all this was going on, more than a hundred Christians were on their knees, in the Tappi Baptist Church a half mile from the courthouse. I drove up the hill where the church stood just in time to see them rushing out of the church to embrace their persecuted brother.

With father's follow-up appeal to higher government officials, a new law was passed that no Christian would have to participate in a trial by ordeal. The soldiers were then sent to arrest the other man who had retreated to his hut some distance away. Upon their arrival and knowing his unpleasant end, the killer asked to go in his hut and get some of his clothes to take to jail. Instead, he put his twelve gauge shotgun in his mouth and pulled the trigger with his toe. It would seem that this would be the end of the matter, but it wasn't. The soldiers tied his body to a pole, brought him to our front yard at 4 AM, and unceremoniously dumped him there, to prove to all that justice had been done.

Father's flashlight, however, revealed the man to be still barely breathing. The next day the nurses grafted skin from his leg to his face which had lost an eye, an ear, and part of his skull. After quite some time, this disfigured but alive murderer became a convert to Christianity. Feeling that he had suffered enough, the community commuted any further sentence. Earnest Hemingway once said, "the world is a nice place and worth fighting for." I guess I agree with this last half of his statement, and the first half on occasion. Hope always persists beyond reason; else, we all would have given up long ago.

DOING BUSINESS THE OLD FASHIONED WAY – 1957-59

Part of my life was, as you know, spent with Grandpa with the cow that won, and with good Aunt Fern and Uncle Paul, who didn't deserve me. These were missionary furlough times and sometimes I would find myself on the farm with grandpa. A farm has a life of its own and demands work, early rising and inventiveness. A young man in his early teens on the farm would of course drive, build, and wield the pitch fork and shovel. He would learn welding, cattle driving and branding, and fixing all manner of broken equipment in a vast variety of ways, baling wire being his best fix-it companion, as duct tape had not yet been invented. I was always looking for ways to make a sport of the work and creative entertainment when there was time for it.

On Sundays, we attended the Mennonite Brethren church. These were progressive Mennonites, who had all the modern appliances and machinery of that day, whose only clear distinction to the visitor was that the men and the women sat in opposite sections of the church. The formal-ity and quietness in the church service was considered the right way to worship, but it put some folks to sleep.

There was one older gentleman, a very nice man really, who went to sleep each time the preacher stood up to preach. I questioned that if he could sleep in the service, why couldn't I? I noticed that at the end of every service, at the benediction, he would stand up in perfect timing with the rest of the congregation. His timing intrigued me so much that, as a very young lad, I studied this behavior. I soon discovered that the pew he sat on was uneven, and when people stood up, it wiggled the bench enough to awaken him.

One day in the middle of the preacher's sermon, I shook the bench with some rigor, and the gentleman stood to his feet with bowed head, eyes still closed due to praying or to the sandman. I was sure it was the latter.

My buddies and I, being somewhat mischievous, or should I say about average in this department, saw opportunity for laughs and adventure in almost anything. What is more inviting to an adventuresome soul than an outhouse on the prairie in Mennonite Country? The outhouse, usually a public sentinel on the prairie, would remain uninhabited until some community meeting. Who of us had not either pushed an outhouse over or admired someone who did? "Doing business the old fashioned way in the lonely outhouse could **not** be tolerated!

When a fellow believes something and believes it strongly enough, he can make an inanimate object like an outhouse come alive. After careful observation, we agreed that most people, especially women, believe there is a strong possibility of something—anything—living in the outhouse where it can't be seen. We figured it was our business to help cement that innate fear, and make their worst fears become a reality. Old Job of the Bible after all had said, "The thing that I greatly feared has come upon me." But on second thought, and to be honest, I don't think we were trying to apply Scripture to excuse our mischievous deeds; we were just plain mischievous!

I'm sure that in any sport or hunt, the anticipation of what might happen is about as important as what actually happens. If the truth be known, if people concentrated on the really important things in life, there would be a shortage of fishing poles! Most people's lives are so boring, that they need a lift once in a while, something to startle, to bring an exclamation point to their lives. They need something that makes them realize that life could be short and to be careful with the life they have. Could an outhouse teach all of these lessons? Of course!

Remember too that the whole world loves a maverick, and the whole world wants the maverick to achieve something nobler than simple rebellion. What we did to teach the generally bored mainstream of Mennonites of the prairie was not really rebellious, but simply a way of removing for a time the boredom from our own lives. All this, of necessity, must be said; else, you think we were the worst of humanity to ever tinker with an outhouse or anyone's life. After all, variety is the spice of life, and doing business the old fashioned way in an old fashioned outhouse on an old fashioned prairie setting, just begged for some attention.

Like putting instructions on the internet on how to make an atomic bomb, it is with great fear and trepidation that I make this trade secret known to all those who would wreak havoc with outhouses. You must first find an outhouse and a public gathering where great numbers of bored people are simply wishing to do business the old fashioned way. There are only a few tools and items that you will need. A hand drill with about a quarter inch drill bit, a small stick, a cup hook, several rubber bands and a few chicken feathers. The most important piece of equipment is a fishing pole with about five hundred yards of line.

Putting the tools to work, first drill quarter inch holes in the sides of the outhouse, just below the seat level on both sides. Then run the fishing line through one hole, passing under the seat area, and through the hole on the other side. Next, tie a small stick to the end of the line where the fish hook would normally be, so that the line cannot come back through the outhouse. Screw the cup hook into the underside and to the back of the seat area. Then attach chicken feathers to the fishing line, directly under the center of the outhouse hole and give the line some slack. Loop a rubber band around the line next to the feathers, and then pull the loose end of the band back over the cup hook. When the fishing line is slack, the rubber band pulls the feathers out of sight into the abyss, where in fact some people think a gremlin lives, just waiting for its chance to strike and bite.

To make the sport successful, unreel the fishing line, as you move the fishing pole about five hundred yards away, or wherever you can conceal yourself behind available cover. With slack in the line, you await your first bored victim. Timing here is important as one must be quite sure the outhouse victim is actually sitting down as opposed to standing up. We, therefore, concluded that there were more bored women than men.

Once sure of someone sitting in the outhouse, you pitch back the fishing rod with some vigor, as though setting a hook in the mouth of a hard to catch fish. The slack in the line is gone, and, generally speaking, so is the occupant of the outhouse, as the chicken feathers have just tickled his or her behind! As the outhouse is coming apart, the door flying open with a bang, the occupant tries to escape.   Besides releasing all boredom, new languages were released from the lips, and new oaths were added to the English and German languages! With slack in the line, the gremlin chicken feathers pull back out of sight under the outhouse seat, ready to relieve someone else's boredom.

I now think that this would be classified as terrorism that transforms life, and a form of it that makes innocent lives a little miserable. Of course, some of my friends who played these kinds of practical jokes on me deserved to visit this outhouse.   The algebra teacher should have been made to live there. He deserved special treatment, so we soaked the feathers in honey for an "added touch."   You would think he could put two and two together, but he never caught us, and it was too private a matter to broadcast. It was surely a miracle that I passed algebra on this Mennonite prairie.

MY BEST PIECE OF MISSIONARY EQUIPMENT

In 1966, my dad had participated in a missionary conference at Miller Road Baptist Church, in Garland, Texas, and had brought me a catalog from Garland Bible College, a small school the church had started, which offered a course in missionary aviation.   That September I drove my very new looking, metallic blue, 1957 Chevy Bel Air two-door hardtop, with chrome mag wheels, and four on the floor to Texas, pulling behind a trailer with my '64 650 BSA Lightning Rocket motorcycle. Each machine had a distinct personality of its own, of course, but the Smitty muffler made the '57 Chevy sound like a motorcycle on steroids!   They both had a decal visible which read –"Loud pipes save lives – Jesus saves souls." But their conversation with their owner was somewhat limited, loud, yes, but only guttural. There is a lot of maintenance ahead with "wheels" like mine and with women.

I wanted to learn to fly, but I also wanted to have fun. I looked around the school, but none of the girls made an impression on me. Too bad, it'd be a good year to study. Then at lunch that day, the door opened and a tall brown-haired local gal came in to greet her returning student friends. Her smile was like someone had turned on the lights in a dark room. She almost glowed with the joy of the Lord. She not only greeted her friends, she greeted all us strangers too! Perhaps it was the Texas sun messing with my mind, but I think it was her bubbly personality, her ability to hold conversations on several topics, and avoidance of too much makeup that caught my attention. I decided right then that I would court this young lady. Yep, it'd be a good year at college!

Jane Sparling wanted to be a missionary in Africa, and I had lots to tell her about Africa. I charmed her with the stories of my childhood that I have shared in this book. By Christmas, we had looked at rings and had set a date--June 29, 1968. I did not learn to fly that year at school, but I had gained what senior missionaries Karl and Marion Luyben called the "best piece of missionary equipment" of all—a gracious wife. My interests went from my mother to this girl who was willing to follow me—as Sarah did Abraham-- to Liberia, West Africa, and eventually to Alaska—from "the frying pan to the freezer!"

As my helpmeet, she has busied herself in a ministry of hospitality (having shared food and lodging with many), using her gift of teaching in Bible classes of children or ladies and as a substitute at the Christian school, working with the deaf, office work for our newsletters and bookkeeping. Jane has used her strong voice to sing in the choir and ensembles, to teach Bible stories to children, and to speak out about her faith. Incidentally, she is probably responsible for Wal-Mart's coming to Fairbanks, having written a letter to the company describing in glowing terms Fairbanks' market and need of a store. She has personally designated April 27, 2004, (the day the store opened here), as "Wal-Mart Appreciation Day." All of this is in addition to being a wonderful mother to our four children and to "keeping the home fires burning" in my many absences.

THE EDGE OF THE SKY – 1973

T. D. Brown, my instructor when I was learning to fly was a WWII vet, who was dedicated to my educational experience, knowing I would be going to Africa with a "fresh ticket" (which is really just a license to learn). He knew that I would be in Africa with a mere forty hours of flying time under my belt. Very soon I would be buzzard bait. Thanks to his exacting teaching, T.D.'s students had an excellent record of safety, and he would teach me well.

Dead-stick landings were real--the engine shut down, not to be restarted. I would then have to glide that Piper Super Cub to a field, road or nearby airport. No mistakes were allowed in these exercises. He had prepared me for surprises -- trees and hot density altitudes and greasy generators. Just when I had learned the stall and was thinking quite highly of myself, he would spin the craft to show that there was still more to learn. He would never rob me of the opportunity to make mistakes, to learn that "pride goeth before a fall." Pride makes a pilot hurry when he doesn't have to be hurried; it makes him forget the gas cap, the seat belt hanging outside the door, the fuel selector on the wrong tank. Pride can lead a pilot to become seriously attached to the "get-home-itis" syndrome.

Everything the authors said in flying manuals was good, I guess, sound and sane, but they went on the theory that truth is rarer than platinum, and that if it became easily available, the market for it would become destitute, and gems of eternal value would be sold at a premium. The government, through the Federal Aviation Administration, had proven once again how an easier task could be made more difficult. It was a joy to get early coffee and fly with T. D. because he made the complicated seem simple. I learned what every dreamer needs to know--that no horizon is so far that you cannot go beyond it and that you could "journey to the edge of the sky" and beyond. This I learned early in my flight training and from parents who took me to Africa.

T. D. Brown taught, beyond the simple mechanics that go with flying, those things that don't lend themselves well to words—

intuition and instinct. His instruction, though simple, was not easy, though he was more capable than any aircraft he flew. Intuition and instinct are still mysterious, but things a good pilot must possess. Soon all pilots possessing these best of qualities will be a sunset in passing history. This era of great pilots, possessing the homing qualities of the pigeon, is all but vanishing, nudged aside by the march of electronic inventive genius. Computers, they say, are the wave of the future, but it's not the same as the art of flying in the past.

My father was of the early school, a purist with a watch and a compass, who lived through thousands of hours of flying to prove his school was sufficient. If someone has not already said it, I will say that he was a great man and missionary pilot who never achieved greatness. This will not only be trite, but wrong. He was a great man who never achieved arrogance. Something more must come from one so strong and gifted, and it did. There was never a more careful pilot, nor yet a more gifted and casual one. His confidence never shrank beside the bullying roar of his loud-propped plane. He wasn't a tall man, but he had a quiet-convincing manner that made him look bigger than any job he ever held and more capable than any craft he ever flew.

Dad's job was to pioneer new routes, to probe the innards of Africa, seeking footholds for the future. His process of flying the Gospel--"the good news" of Christ's salvation--and spiriting the message with wings were a most successful combination. More often than not, he took off from Zondo or Tappita, Liberia, flying over country as unused to wheels as it was to wings, with no more than a modest expectation that there might be a place to land at the end of the flight. He had the knack, knew all the tricks, and had what those thick books call "sensory perception." He was also his own mechanic, with an almost holy reverence for the hymn of purring pistons, grinning often through a thicket of wires and motor mounts. Most days to him were flyer's days, the snout of his Super Cub like a sentinel watching from an open hangar, watching eternally for a square of sky lonely for clouds. Dad was no fool, but was at least a romantic with stick and rudder.

In some ways this was passed down to several of dad's offspring, including my younger brother Steve and myself and my daughter Carol. Thirty-two years after I learned to fly, Carol became interested in flying at age seventeen. I promised Carol that if she wanted to would take flying seriously, I would help her all the way. She would not have to do anything around the house—no sweeping, mopping, dishes, or dusting—not anything, except her own laundry. But she could not have any friends over or go to their house either. She would "eat" and "drink" and "sleep" aviation for six weeks. She agreed and won her private license in six weeks, flew a Cessna 185 with me that summer and built time in the high performance airplane flying missionaries.

Almost immediately, Carol began training for her instrument rating. Her check ride with the examiner was notable. It was thirty degrees below zero outside, dark and snowing. The Beech Musketeer's heater was totally inadequate. The examiner always turns off all the instrument lights in the cockpit to simulate an emergency, so this check ride was no exception. The FAA rules say that a pilot flying instruments at night must have a flashlight aboard which Carol had complied with. But I know that a "flash light" is just that—it often flashes and the light goes out. I had given Carol my Mini-Mag light just in case her light went out. Yes, her light did go out. When the examiner turned off all the cockpit lights, Carol simply put my small light in her teeth and continued the check ride. The examiner remarked that it was one of the best check rides ever that he had given.

After earning her commercial license in one week at a specialty school, Carol was hired by Peninsula Airways in Anchorage at age 20. She helps me with missionary flying from time to time. Thus far she is the only one of my children to learn to fly.

There were several other Zerbe kin who also learned to fly—Uncle Otto and his sons (my cousins) Neil—a Navy F-14 Tomcat aviator-- and Grant, who flies a Bonanza A36, a Super Cub, and a Piper Pawnee crop duster. I attribute this to Grandpa Zerbe and the blood line. We are all romantics, I think you could say. There's a kind of magic in the soul of a romantic that makes the world a more interesting, gentler, more bearable place. A romantic has a belief in the face of any difficulty in the possibility of miracles and wonders and a sense of valuing beauty for its own sake.

Belief can be a powerful thing as can a suggestion, and so sometimes a romantic can actually make seemingly impossible feats come true. Maybe it's because all the flying Zerbes understand as all romantics do, that with all the pain and ugliness the world is capable of dishing out, it is important to persevere--to know and remember and experience beauty in as many dimensions as possible. It's the belief that once we fly, all the air other mortals breathe is merely air!

There is something that a Super Cub or Cessna 185 whispers to a romantic in soft, gentle, irresistible tones and somehow captures our hearts. And like all romantics who fall head over heels in love, they then do whatever it takes to make sure the objects of their attention are safe, sound, and continued valuable companions. Of course it's been said, "All lovers are fools." So perhaps all of us pilots and mechanics are fools after all. Fools, romantics, saints.....who bring dreams to life and help keep the sky from becoming merely air!

When my father left Africa, I tried to take his place, probably with mixed success. Then I too, because of revolution, needed to "let my basket over the wall" and depart--leaving its geography and people to determine their own fate, as we all must do.

WHEN YOU'RE RIGHT, YOU'RE RIGHT! -- 1975

In some 20,000 hours of flying, I have lifted the plane's wheels from terra-firma thousands of times, but I have never felt gravity overcome without knowing the exhilaration and uncertainty of my first flight. It was a hot, steamy, smoggy day in Rockwall, Texas, that day of my first solo cross-country. The 90-

horse power Super Cub climbed easily and settled in level flight, visibility almost nil in the moisture-laden smog.

A WWII Corsair, flying aerobatics out of Paris, Texas appeared out of nowhere, nose to nose. Our closing rate of 550 mph and one half mile visibility gave no time for careful assessment, only instinctive corrective actions on the part of both of us. We both made right knife edge turns and the greasy bodies of both planes passed about 200 feet apart. I was at the correct attitude and on a flight plan, but this reminded me of the Burma Shave signs I used to see on the Montana prairies--"close shave." This was a "Burma Shave" moment.

On another occasion some years later, I was flying a Cessna 185 on a clear night from Luster, Montana to Pensacola, Florida. Around 10 P.M., over Chicago on radar, the blinking lights of many jumbo jets in the area seemed to be coming at me from every direction. I flew at 10,500 feet until I was beyond radar range, and air traffic control handed me back to my two eyeballs for safe clearance.

Immediately, I tuned to the radio frequency for that segment of airspace and listened in to center and a conversation with a Boeing 747 who was evidently descending in radar control for Chicago. I put two and two together, and woke up all my sleeping passengers. They were still rubbing their eyes when I noticed a red light and two whites coming toward me at an alarming closure rate. I simply reached for my landing light switch, blinked them off and on once, the other pilot did the same. I went up about 100 feet, the large jet passing so close I could see the people reading their magazines. We were both legal - he in his descent, I in my altitude, and both so close to disaster.

I have since concluded that most flights can be lonely, but lonely or not, each flight is still free from the curse of boredom. My logbook under remarks simply indicated a close call with a 747 and that a change in underwear would be appropriate at the next fuel stop!

To my father Ludwig and me, the plane was always a beast of burden, and we always asked it to do more than its designer had imagined. My father, when flying his trusty yellow

Piper Cub in Liberia, W. Africa, was involved in modifying this plane, designed to carry one passenger in modest comfort, into a plane that could carry a missionary family of seven quite uncomfortably. This involved widening the fuselage and adding a padded board resting on supports along the sides of the original seat. In this way two thin adults or larger children could sit on the seat originally designed to carry one, with two more sitting on the padded board above the regular seat. It was like sitting on the laps of the passengers in the original seat, except that the padded board did not actually touch their lap. It wasn't piggy back, but piggy lap.

Before these four passengers climbed on board, three small children were stuffed into the baggage compartment. Then certain items such as beds, play cribs, etc. would be tied to the outside of the fuselage. The pilot would terminate this "test flight with human guinea pigs" approximately half way down the runway should the plane not want to fly well. A pilot with nerves of steel and knowing his steed well can do this.

Not one of the missionaries he or I flew in thousands of hours of flight was ever killed or injured from 1948 till the present. Between pilots and passengers in these remote parts of the world, there exists a kind of guild, a sincere trust of passenger to pilot, without charter and without bylaws. It demands no requirements save the passengers trust that the pilot had an understanding of the wind, the compass, the weather, the rudder and fair fellowship. It's the kind of trust men once must have put with Columbus, as he searched for the drop off point. We were our own pilot, weatherman, mechanic and navigator as well. It is a challenge equal to Lindbergh's, only mostly unreported.

To the average person who has never experienced the soul of Africa, its different views of integrity and courage, the slow pulse of life; unless steeped from childhood in its endless even beat, he could never hope to experience it as I did as a child. To be able to soar above Africa put me in another dimension. At the end of each flight, which had released me from the heat felt below the jungle and from all the dust and smells, the dream of flight and detachment was suddenly gone upon landing. I was aware once again of the mundane realities of growing grass and swirling dust, the slow plodding of men who walk ten feet in front of their burden carrying wives, and the enduring patience of rooted trees. Temporarily, freedom has been restricted again; the wings that even a moment ago were no less than the eagles, are metal once more, inert and heavy.

The pilot is the "man of the hour"--the contact with the outside world. I would be welcomed and treated to cookies and tea. Wherever the pilot lands, it seems he must have news of some other place, some larger circumstance. The plane then and its pilot are necessary to add dimension to these mundane earthbound folks; it insures and introduces a measure of sanity. All were lonely for news from Sua Koko. And those in Sua Koko want the news from Monrovia, and so on.

THE SELLING OF THE "FIRST WIFE" – 1975

For the most part, we as a majority are law-abiding citizens of the realm. If I ever wander off the path of righteousness, however, it will not be gold or fine clothing that enticed me, but more likely, I think, the irresistible contours of a fine Harley Davidson. The noise she makes when under stress makes even the least appreciative look up, wondering, "Who is enjoying himself now? It is the sound of a WWII fighter plane, having lost seven of her nine cylinders, reincarnated, but minus the wings.

On this morning in June, another motorcycle made in Milwaukee, Wisconsin, had come to my attention. It belonged to a young man, wanting to get married, but the Harley he owned had been his "wife" up to the present. He had put everything into that bike until he had no money left. This first wife must go for the second. "Such is life. Why aren't two wives possible?" he quips.

"Husbands and wives, like fishermen," I tell him, "often brag about the ones that got away and complain about the ones they caught."

He wanted $6,500 for his "first wife," explaining to me that he had much more in "her" in purchased accessories. I weighed the situation, agreeing that any form of lipstick would not make her prettier, and told him I couldn't spend that much money on a "slightly used wife." He could sell "her" to another. The desperation mounted in his eyes and voice, as his second wife-to-be looked on listening and analyzing. I said I would think about it and left him wondering how I could just walk away from such a fine "filly."

My banker cooperated and gave me twenty-one new, crisp one hundred dollar bills. I made my way back to the "war zone" and managed to find the owner, his fiancée and future mother-in-law sitting on the porch. Staring at the Harley, the fiancée insisted that the "first wife" go before she would take up residence. It was made quite clear to the poor chap that his choices were limited; he must choose a red-blooded wife over one with gasoline in her veins. In this setting I joined them and spread the twenty-one new bills out on the card table, weighing the poor lad's primal instincts. Now with two women staring him down, the deal was done. He cried, I'm sure, as the sound of his "first wife" faded into the distance.

That Harley rode fine and looked even better. <u>My</u> first wife really didn't mind that I had acquired her. I rode that fine filly for a whole year, until I was ready to move to Africa as a missionary pilot. I parked that fine piece of machinery on the driveway for sale and waited only about two hours until I had a bite. A young high school graduate he was, but not too "swift" between the ears. "How much for the Harley?" he wanted to know. "She's expensive, as she should be," I replied. "I'll take $6,500 firm!"

"That's too much for my blood," he exclaimed, "but I'd sure like to ride out to the Snake River Canyon and watch Evil Knievil jump the Snake River Canyon Gorge."

My next move was none too subtle. I started the Harley and let it idle after a couple revs. You could see the young man formulating his dreams of the trip across America on this fine machine, the whole world seeing and hearing that he had arrived.

"I'm a trader." I solemnly told him. "I'll trade anything of value worth $6,500 for this machine."

"Well, I've got this car" he said, "Brand new, 6,000 miles, a 1976 Chevy Monte Carlo, loaded. How much boot money would you give me for it," he asked?

"It's the other way around," I told him, tongue in cheek. "It will cost you boot money!" He traded the car straight across for the Harley, then I sold the car two days later for $6500, making $4,400 profit. It was enough to buy our tickets to Africa. I cried a tear as that famous, patented sound faded around the bend. I made a vow that someday I would ride a Harley from Key West, Florida, to Prudhoe Bay, Alaska, perhaps treating my body to enough punishment to say a final good bye to two wheels. I'll never know till I've tried it, but it should be done, that I do know.

There is a way to make any trip a standard outing, just A to Z--no fanfare, no excitement or reward. And there is a way to make any journey a new adventure under the sun. It's not just that you get there; it's how you got there. It almost seems unjust to the rest of mankind, those who have been bound to pedestrian cultures past, to have missed the joy of flying as it has developed in just a few decades. Only gravity, the mechanic's greasy hands, and the oil on the hanger floor serves to remind us that we to are tethered to the earth.

We dig oil wells, reduce oil to flame, harness its power behind a propeller, and we fly; but we have not conquered the air. Nature still presides in all her dignity, permitting us only to study and respect her forces. But by nature a sailor must sail, and a flyer must fly.

STOP THAT GOAT FROM KICKING ME IN THE BACK! -- 1977

Men and machines seem to, at some point, be pushed beyond the limit. One such trip found me behind the controls of the Cessna 180 on a flight from Tappita, Liberia to Sua Koko.

The plane was really a four place, but this day we made it a seven place. After I loaded the baggage compartment, five passengers climbed into the plane. I required that they hold all their suitcases, purses and umbrellas on their laps to make room for the 100 pound bag of rice on the floor between the legs of the people in the middle seats. Then there was a live goat in the baggage area, all tied up "securely" with ropes tightly holding him in place.

Somewhere during the flight, the goat got claustrophobia and got his back legs free. He then began to kick the rear passenger in the back in protest to his cruel and unusual fate. He would kick and the passengers would scream, but there were only tall trees and jungles below. Landing for some goat relief was not in our near future, only futile pleas for help and laughter from the pilot.

There is no twilight in West Africa. Night tramps on the heels of day in short order and covers the expanse the day recently held in darkness. Sounds of those things that live in the sun are exchanged for the song of the fruit bat and the thud of the rhinoceros beetle flying into my window screen. This flight with the goat would end at precisely this time in West Africa. The passengers, more than willing to have goat stew for supper, were obliged once more to chase and catch the goat upon his freedom from the ropes. He had earned his freedom as he vanished in the dark.

TIME AND THE SUN -- 1977

The elephant tail still hangs on my Alaska wall, a stark reminder of an elephant hunter, time, and the sun. The elephant hunter was the son of the chief called David Tappi. He was a fearless hunter of the jungle who once killed an elephant three days walk from the village. Having cut off the tail and come the distance to inform the village with his proof in hand, the village set off to retrieve the beast. Let's see, that's three days walk to the village, one day for the village to get ready, three days to walk back, one day to cut the elephant up and four days to walk back! That's "time" in the sun--the sun of Africa!

One cannot imagine the fine quality of the elephant as it arrived without any dignity in the village. No drum beating needed. No clapping or chanting. No announcement was needed to inform the old men and ladies that the people were back. The gentle moisture laden breeze was all that was needed to herald their arrival. The elephant had announced his own morbid arrival and etched it on my memory forever.

Africa truly is different. There really is nothing that is familiar on these shores to the average American. The smells, people, customs, means of travel, animals, music, insects, roads, rivers, refinements, the equations of the quality of life, are unrecognizable to the Western man as anything familiar. He is a visitor, a temporary fly speck on the African landscape. But a polite visitor is always welcome.

TWO FLIGHTS FROM GEHENNA -- 1977

Certain people are repelled by even the thought of snakes. Mambas, pythons, Gabon vipers and some of their kind have frequently popped into my life, either on treks through the forest or when, as a child, I climbed trees or visited my jungle hideout seeking small adventure.

Once, as a child, in a dark kerosene lit house, I stood on a very poisonous snake while waiting to tell my father good night. My thought was that I had misplaced the rubber part of my sling shot and that I would have to take it to my room, or my mother, a meticulous housekeeper even with a dirt floor in Africa, would throw it away the following day. The same house produced thirteen snakes in the first year that my mother herself killed.

While I have learned to avoid snakes and have even, I think, developed a sixth sense of their presence, I feel I could if necessary, still face a mamba or a spitting cobra with greater calm, than I could face a human being bathed in the atmosphere of stench and sickness, surrounded by oozing sores and impending death.

The call came in on our now modern WW II Bomber surplus radio that I would need to fly a leprosy patient to the colony for lepers. The depth of the fanged bite of the viper is about 1 ½ to 2 inches deep, but the thought of having to fly this contagious leper profoundly repulsed me to the heart. The only thing close is the flight when I was compelled to fly to a village to fly out a dead chief's body who had been honored in the village and tropical sun for five days. The plane never seemed to smell the same after that.

DON'T YOU DARE KISS ME! -- 1978

The bush woman arrived out of the mist, three days walk from her village with a young lad about ten years old on her back. On her head were all her earthly belongings, which included no money. She came from so deep in the rain forest, very little if any money existed in her village. The distinction of her arrival is the fact that her son was unconscious, and no one spoke her language. It was the first time she had seen a white man, an airstrip with mown grass, a motorbike, a jeep, a radio, a watch, or sunglasses, and people with clothes on the upper half of their bodies.

We scurried to find someone who understood her language and after some time were rewarded. The boy, a typical African poster child with bony limbs and an extremely protruding stomach, was barely breathing. This exhausted bush woman explained that her witch doctor had not helped her son, and she had heard of "the white woman healing power." We informed her that our nurses could not help her son; that they would have to get into the plane and fly 30 minutes to the nearest hospital.

It took some time just to get her to approach the door of this strange looking contraption, much less get into it. We finally got her into the middle row of seats, sitting directly behind the pilot's seat. The unconscious son was lifted in beside her. Because I knew these natives could be very unpredictable and succumb to reckless abandon once a loved one has gone to another shore, I brought out a rope to tie around her waist in addition to the seat belt. To have a white man tying her into a strange object that she has been told will soon be flying in the air like the vulture, was too much for her. In her culture, one would only be tied so securely if they were to be severely punished or delivered to a place of punishment.

The young lad was still unconscious and barely breathing, like an old steam locomotive that has run out of fire. I knew it was time to go. Once the engine fired and I uttered a quick prayer, the bush woman began to wail in earnest, tugging with all her might on the rope and seat belt. Fortunately, I had the presence of mind to tie the knot behind her back, and it held fast. As the plane shuddered and advanced down the runway under full throttle, her wails could be heard well above the engine. Not wanting to see her death coming, she had covered her eyes with her hands. Her son was unaware of anything.

This day in the rain forest during the rainy season, when we receive 200 inches of rainfall in six months, was typical. The solid layer of clouds lay only 300 feet above the forest canopy, with wisps of clouds touching the taller 150 foot high trees from time to time. Flying these conditions on a day with no stress inside the plane would be difficult enough. Navigation, which usually meant following a compass heading for many hours and minutes, would be complicated since I was compelled to zig and zag around the clouds that met the trees. I had to calculate the time in my head and use the compass to make sure I returned back on track after the zig and zag. One of my missionary passengers had fondly called me a name which stuck--"Zig Zag Zerbe. I never once had failed to find my destination.

At such low altitudes, the villages could only be seen when directly above them; so my "dead reckoning" had to be dead on! It was like finding a tick on a long haired dog! When I couldn't find a village where it was supposed to be, I would fly a precise pattern that always worked for me:

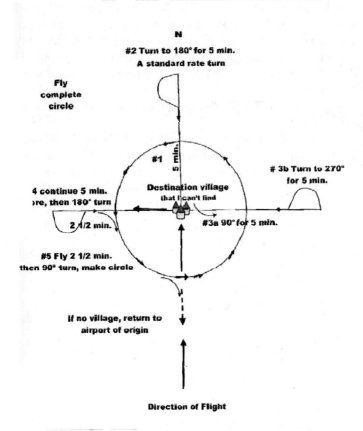

1. Continue on present heading for five minutes beyond the ETA (estimated time of arrival) to assume the presence of a head wind.

2. If the village is not in sight, turn 180 degrees and fly five minutes back to the starting point, in case of a cross wind.

3. Make a left 90 degree turn and fly for five minutes; if the destination is not in sight, return to the starting point.

4. Continue ahead for another ten minutes (passing starting point); if the destination is not in sight, then make an 180° turn in the direction of the starting point (which is the center of the circle). Turn 180° in the direction of 270° –past the starting point another 180° in the direction of 90° after a standard rate turn.

5. When 2 ½ minutes into last return leg, start a 15 degree bank and make a complete circle. This maneuver should have yielded the village under the left wing at some point. After a shallow turn for 360° plus another 90°, turn right to 180° heading back home.

The young lad, wearing just a loin cloth with particles of mud attached to various parts of his body and one of his leather-bottomed bare feet evidently chewed on by a rat while he was sleeping, was desperately ill. I knew from experience, his was probably a severe case of worms and pneumonia, but one never knows. With two yellow lines draining from his nose and his eyes rolling, the boy took his last breath with only 15 minutes remaining in our flight.

What happened next is hard to explain in rational terms. The mother began now pushing and pulling on her dead son, beating her chest, beating the back of my seat and the windows of the aircraft. A thousand things went through my mind at once-- should I just return since he is dead; should I let a doctor pronounce him dead, or should I in some way take a risk-- in some way try to right one thing for this bush woman and her son. I know the worms and pneumonia in his lungs are what doomed him.

Suddenly, I reached back and released the boy's seat belt and, against his mother's wishes, pulled him out of his second row seat as I laid down the backrest of the co-pilot's seat, bringing the boy's head face up beside me. Because of this maneuver, the plane was not in control and was heading for the trees only 250 feet below. I forgot the lad as I fought to regain control of the plane. Then I began mouth to mouth resuscitation, forcing air into his lungs while also thinking of my risk from both sickness and terrain.

My own demise was sure to come in a moment or less if this kind of flying continued! I made a hurried radio call to the Ghana Medical Center and informed them to meet me with a pickup and oxygen. The close encounter with the jungle and the wailing woman's attempts to stop this white man from "eating her son's tongue" continued all the way to the landing. I would have paid dearly for this bush woman's thoughts that day. One can only guess.

Her son did live, and they eventually reunited with their own. And I was reunited with my own, and as always, almost from reflex, received a nice kiss from my happy spouse. She asked me how my day had gone, and I told her of the lad. She yelled and wiped her mouth with the back of her hand, and I didn't get kissed for a month!

THE DAY I THANKED GOD FOR MY GLASSES -- *YEKEPA – 1979*

Not all days are the same flying days. Some are sunny-- delightful and uneventful. Most flights in Africa are eventful, marked by the unexpected. This day however was uneventful until I returned to home base in Yekepa to find everyone locked up in the house and afraid to go outside.

During the day, my wife Jane went out to the piazza, a large outdoor room similar to a porch, with our two little girls— Michelle and Carol. A half wall surrounded two sides of the piazza with two open doorways into the yard. It was to us what a covered deck would be in the States. A tiny laundry room formed one end, and Jane wanted to put some clothes in the washer there and the girls wanted to play. Also sitting there in the far corner by one doorway was an extra washing machine that was broken that I was planning to fix someday.

Before allowing them to play, Jane would always check for hostile wildlife since the piazza was at ground level and open to the yard on two ends. One time previously in another house at Tappi, she had pulled a lawn mower back and discovered a snake coiled underneath. She was not about to let two preschool girls play on the piazza without looking around first.

Jane saw a long black snake behind the old washer in the corner and determined to kill it. As she poked at it in the narrow space behind the washer with a broom and a machete, the snake stood up and extended two flaps of skin on the sides of its head. It was a deadly spitting cobra and it was provoked! Jane backed off in a hurry, and the snake slid around and climbed up the inside of the washer until it was hiding inside on top of the machine under the lid. The girls would not play out there that day.

When I -- Bwana, the Great White Hunter-- arrived home, I took up the challenge to "subdue the earth" and "take dominion" over that snake that had invaded my home. With machete in one hand and a tool in the other, I pried up the top of the washer. The snake zipped down inside that washer and out the back to the door, where it hid behind a piece of corrugated roofing leaning against the house.

As I pulled the piece of roofing away to expose him, the snake reared up and extended its hood. His previously plain white belly skin changed into an intricate mosaic pattern of red and white. Staring with his beady eyes right at my face, the cobra opened his mouth. On top of his tongue was something that looked like a short straw and it was aimed directly at my eyes! His toxic spittle sprayed over my entire face, and my lips began to burn almost immediately, but my glasses saved the day, protecting my eyes. I trapped the snake with the piece of roofing on his body and wielded the machete, and we could all breathe easier again.

On another occasion, a large spitting cobra emptied the church during the morning worship hour. All I had for a weapon was a four foot stick to kill a seven foot cobra, so I kept my distance until I could get outside, too. The wind was about 10-15 MPH, so with the wind at my back I went a after the snake. It would repeatedly spit at me and I could see the venom spraying toward my eyes, but the wind would blow it back at the snake. My stick was too short, and the snake kept sidling closer to the jungle until it finally escaped. It reminded me of the snake that deceived Eve and the Adam who wasn't there to cut his head off. I hate snakes!

POPEYE THE SAILOR MAN – 1979

Of the 28 tribes in Liberia, some tolerated and condoned stealing - others had zero tolerance and would cut off parts of the perpetrator's body, such as an ear, for stealing. One day a big black man, around 30 years, came to my house from a day's walk. His arms were larger than his thighs, protruding almost straight out, reminding me of Popeye the sailor man. His crime was stealing a cheap portable radio, but a status symbol in his village. For this he was caught and tied up to a tree with strips of old truck inner tube and beaten for 12 hours off and on. It wasn't the beating, but the lack of circulation in his arms that was really his punishment.

He went quietly to the plane, was helped in with all the seats removed and I flew him immediately on a clear day once again to the hospital in Ghanta. He lost both arms at the shoulder and his lifelong dignity. I would venture to say I could leave my watch on a stump for a year in their village, and no one would approach it. I took a look at the Ghanta wind sock, hanging apologetically like a flag of a domain so small that nobody could ever take it seriously. I knew I would remember him each time I turned on the plane's radio.

THE CIA IN MY PLANE –1979

A map in one's hands is a testimony of one man's faith in another; it is a symbol of true confidence and trust. They have always fascinated me with their myriad of lines beckoning me to more travel than time left in life. A map is not like the printed page bearing mere words, ambiguous, perhaps artful. A reader, including its author, must allow in his mind a recess for doubt. It won't be long and a better document will trump this printed page. But a map says, "Read me carefully, follow me, doubt me not. Without me you are alone and lost--doomed to wander aimlessly."

Within all those maps I have "trunks and shelves" containing continents. You feel at once by unfolding it that you are holding the earth in the palm of your hand. These lines mean something. And so I fondle its lines, feeling it. It is a cold thing, born of calipers, photographs and to scale.

I cherish my original map of Liberia given to me by Jim C. Smith (not his real name), retired military. Having flown several years in this rain forest of Western Africa without a map, I was finally able, in great secrecy, to procure this infrared map that had originated from the CIA of the USA. It showed all existing trails to villages under the jungle canopy, along with their names, many of which the government of Liberia didn't know existed. At once, I was able to figure true north and have a map more detailed than the best maps to date. Perhaps no more hopeful document, except the Bible, had ever been joined by ink and paper that could make the day of an African pilot. It was modest, yet so full of histories, of people and sagas of conquest and adventure. But maps couldn't tell you the weather.

TO THE IVORY THE IVORY COAST OR BUST - 1979

Most unread Americans don't know what "St. Elmo's Fire" is all about, especially in a small plane. St. Elmo's fire is static electricity built up in the clouds to the extent that a thunderbolt could happen at any time.

One of my regular long flights in West Africa was to transport several "MK's" (missionary kids) from several points in Liberia, to Bouake, Ivory Coast for schooling in an MK school. It was disturbing to see children in first through twelfth grades say a goodbye to their parents for three months. They would be reunited for six weeks and then back for three months again. It seems easy to write about it, but anything we might say can only trivialize the moment! Would the average family anywhere ever agree with this arrangement--to have someone else educate and moralize and codify your child for you, to say goodnight each night on your behalf?

The distance to Bouake, Ivory Coast, was always such that once beyond the half way point there was no return. I would have to leave on a day when the weather was good in my present location, look North and East and hope my destination was clear.

There are those flights that stress and tax man and machine to the limit. In a three hour flight, a compass error, the wind blowing the plane sideways, or inattention that accentuates an error in direction of only one degree, will put the plane quite some miles to right or left of the destination. All this, together with the fact that the inherent magnetic variation around the earth's waistline varied the closer you were to its top, coupled with weather the flight most likely would have to go through, made it essential for a pilot either to develop his intuitive sense to the highest degree or adopt a fatalistic philosophy of life. "If any man lacks wisdom, let him ask of God."

From the cockpit I could see clearly what appeared to be the nicest trip of all. The jungle lay beneath us, endless, unmarked, uninhabited, and un-welcoming, except from this bird's eye view. It was a large bowl of salad whose hot vapors rose upward in invisible waves and exerted physical pressure on the Cessna's wings, lifting and dropping her, as heat from a smoldering fire lifts a flake of ash.

In all of this, I as pilot must memorize and put descriptions away in my head forever, from a landscape which is nondescript, for if ever "temporarily disoriented," any memory of some landmark could lead me to a true course, to a friendly face somewhere. This was a land still more in possession of nature than of men. The drone of the plane, the endless horizon and steady sun had all combined to dull my senses; but blackness was on the horizon - this was indeed a "journey to the edge of the sky."

Behind me, all brightness, but the sun will be looking for the horizon in two hours. Ahead, lay the blackness of a tropical storm front which stretched from horizon to horizon, its thunderstorm heads topping 60,000 feet. I could no longer return to base; the gas gauges told the story, and it was true by watch as well. Only minutes away, our destination was being punished by thunderous tropical rain drops the size of small marbles. There was no choice now. We must plunge through! We were in God's hands.

Was it faith or fatalism? I was comforted by the fact that He says it "rains on the just and the unjust alike." I wonder which category was under my wing. I knew I'm one of the just ones, but even the just must be tested from time to time. The refiner's fire was then shown to me in the form of "St Elmo's Fire."

We then were engulfed in the darkness of midnight, violently being tossed about like a mouse that's being subjugated by a cat. We were more weightless than on the seats. Things were flying through the cabin against the downdraft, and I could not raise my hand to turn the radio knob against the g-forces on my body. The rain sounded like hail and was so heavy that now its torrent found its way all through the plane's air cleaner to the spark plugs. The plane shuddered and the engine sputtered and coughed toward a complete stop!

The air dome in Bouake had a weak beacon which, when close enough, my ADF (Automatic Direction Finder) needle would point to. The ADF needle was pointing straight ahead, chasing a lightning bolt and only jumped to the right or left as another lightning bolt blinded us in the darkness. But mostly, the ADF needle, which was supposed to point to the radio station in Bouake, only pointed straight ahead - to St. Elmo's fire. There was now so much static electricity in the thunderstorm that a blue arc of electricity had formed a circle around the tip of the propeller. As opposed to the perfect circle rainbow that often follows a pilot, this one held no promise.

The radio was all static, as I visualized our certain demise. In the same instant I thought of what a good pilot and mechanic would do. A good pilot would fly her to the last second, picking two trees finally to point the nose through so the trees could shear the wings off with some elasticity and slow our crash. A good mechanic would search his knowledge bank, his genius, to see if there was any way to save the whole ship. But he can't get out of the craft, remove the cowling and remove and dry the spark plugs. No inspections, only assumptions.

The thought occurred to me that I should pull that little black knob for carburetor ice that I had never needed to use in the tropics. The knob was located on my end of a thin control cable leading to an arm and a little door to direct dry hot air from the muffler into the carburetor, in place of cold wet air from outside. It just so happened that we never have carburetor ice in the tropics, so carburetor heat is unnecessary, isn't it?

There isn't a pilot school anywhere that teaches its students that someday you may have to be in such wet air that your engine will die and, when it does, pull the carburetor heat knob! But as a mechanic and pilot, I visualized a dead stick landing in zero visibility in driving rain in the jungle, with downdrafts tossing the plane 1,000 feet per minute up and down! I had to do something! It was worth a try.

I reached down and pulled on carburetor heat. I had never needed to use it for carburetor ice in Africa. In fact, it went against some instincts, such as lowering the nose of the craft to gain speed while losing altitude in order to keep warm dry air pumping through the cylinders--drying the spark plugs to get the engine running again. Prolonging a silent glide now would only mean a certain meeting with the jungle. Pushing the nose over only accelerated this meeting perhaps, but the alternative might be a running engine. She coughed at first like some poor soul having been revived from a drowning and receiving CPR. This never before and untried theory had worked. "If any man lacks wisdom ...."

Somehow we passed the storm and kissed the ground like a pope upon arrival at Bouake. The trip home the following day was bright and beautiful. Like a foal feeling his feet beneath him on a cool spring day, I headed for Tappi Town.

BUZZING THE DEVIL -- 1979

I was clicking my heels together as well, glad to be alive in a remarkably clean airplane from the previous flight. Having read my mail and blown off course, it must be Providence that brings my small plane over a clearing with a few huts and a palm tree branch fence around it. It is distinct in this way from all other villages; the fence means it's the "devil bush."

The devil bush is where the "country devil" performs the initiation rites for the youth into adulthood. It is where all the young people must go, not seeing their parents for as long as three years. There they must learn the tribal ways, where the boys and girls are circumcised, and all receive the tribal markings. They also learn how to become demon possessed.

One such young man, being a Christian, was forced into the devil bush and after some two years there and missing his parents, decided to sneak out of the fence around midnight and see his parents and come quietly back to the devil bush around 4 am. He would be "oh so quiet," and no one would see, but someone did. The next day the country devil assigned him the job of digging a trench. Then he tied the boy's hands and feet and placed him face down and crosswise of the trench. To teach all the young people a lesson by making an example of the boy and to control by instilling fear, the country devil then jumped on the boy's back, breaking his back. He pushed the broken boy down into the grave, and buried him alive. This account was told fearfully and privately to others by young people who had been present when it occurred.

This place had surely never seen my plane or any other, and I suddenly felt the urge to show the "devil" and his subjects not only the plane, but the rivets on her belly as well. By the third low pass, so low as to pass through their small fire's smoke, the naked black bodies were running in all directions. The jungle absorbed them, and, with a push of the throttle to the firewall, I left them to wonder, and I to repent . . . I think. My new application for "Resist the devil, and he will flee from you" became "Buzz the devil, and he will flee from you."

SEND OUT THE FIRE TRUCK, HONEY –1979

"So that's what I get for being so unkind to the devil," I thought. Of course, there weren't any fire trucks, but I thought I sure would need one. There was an airplane, a Cessna 337 that I was asked to fly for another man, "just to keep it in the air." This man didn't have a pilot's license, but he had a plane. Now the tropics do wonderful things to a white man's belongings. Your shoes can get moldy in a week and things rust and corrode. I decided this day to fly the 337 to the capital city, "just to keep it in the air."

Once in the air, I reached for the gear handle and put it in the up position. This was a twin engine plane with one engine in front and one directly behind—a push-pull configuration. As the landing gear began to retract, it only cycled half way and stopped. I put the handle down and nothing moved. The hydraulic pump on the engine had failed, I assumed, so I tried to use the emergency hand pump to pump it down. It too would not budge the landing gear. Now it's preferable to have the gear up or down, but in this configuration, I was sure to become a heap of scrap metal once I tried to land!

An airplane is so touchy at times, like a woman with nerves, or a person with no conscience, or even an imbecile! You treat her kindly, you nurse her engine, but the magnetos go bad, or the screen gets plugged.

"Why do we fly?" I once asked a friend. "We could do other things--like work in an office, have our own cubicle, or join the Army."

"Yeah, sure," He replied. "We could walk away from our planes and never feel a stick or touch a rudder pedal again."

"We could forget about weather and forced landings and passengers who get sick and spare parts we can't find," I told him. "And just forget about the new plane you have been reading and dreaming about, but know you will never afford. We could do all that and never look back and perhaps be happy men"

"I couldn't bear it--life would be so dull." he said. Happiness and dullness go quite well together for most people, I reminded him. But he and I were not most people.

And now I needed to deal with this crippled bird, which in the end would do its best to cripple me. With its legs half up and half down, I wrote a note to drop in front of my wife. I'm quite practiced at dropping the mail by now, as I drop it quite regularly from the plane's window whenever I pass by a point with too short a strip to land with my existing load. I told her to get every fire extinguisher and blanket she can muster and drive the eleven miles to the airport. Then I determined that I must fly all the fuel from the plane to lessen fire risk, all six hours of it.

I was dripping with perspiration from pumping 60 strokes on the emergency pump, so I decided to fly to at least 10,000 feet to cooler air. As I made this last ascent with this plane, I devised a plan conceived, once again, from pilot and mechanical experience and from "if any man lacks wisdom..."

I decided to do a very aggravated stall so as to have the nose of the plane as sharply skyward as possible until the wings quite flying. Then when the nose, the heaviest part of the aircraft, broke over after the wings quit flying, I could push the nose over very steeply without gaining too much immediate airspeed. At this critically low airspeed with no wind resistance and gravity working for me, I would again work the gear handle and watch to see if the gear would move at all.

On the first stall, I felt I had gained about one eighth of an inch. After about 50 stalls and only imperceptible movements of the landing gear, it finally went down and gave me two greens, meaning the main gear was down and locked. But the nose gear which I could not see out my window, gave no light. After burning out the fuel and gliding in with no engine power, I worked the front engine's starter to level the propeller, so as to minimize damage. As the plane accommodated me with the finest of touchdowns, the wheels held down and the nose wheel stayed down as well. It was time for a gallon of ice tea, a shower and a bed.

It wouldn't be long and I would be tested again, but from a different quarter. My Uncle Paul Zerbe in Montana who was then a dealer selling Massey Ferguson equipment, endowed me with a red cap advertising the brand with large red block letters— MF. It kept the early and late sun from blinding me and was the envy of every black man and his son in Yekepa, where we now lived, about 250 miles in the bush. Even the police chief, who was my friend, wanted it - begged for it. He thought the letters stood for "Mr. Frisky" and he teased me by calling me that name.

I managed to keep it till one Sunday morning when a thief, knowing we were in church, broke into our house and stole clothes, radio, shoes, food, and my hat. We arrived home from church to see the door open and partially eaten food, including a half melted popsicle, on the counter in the kitchen. It had only been minutes before that he had been in our house!

But the hat that could not be resisted became the clue. As he had left the house, the rogue had put that hat with the big red letters on his head and then had balanced a box with all the loot on top of the cap—carrying the load African style. He hadn't been down the road 100 yards, when the police chief just happened by in his car and saw the unassuming lad--a common box on a common head going down a common road, everything very common, except for the cap! He knew that if I, his friend, would not give my cap to him, why would I give it to this common lad?

Just minutes before I arrived home from church, all my things were at the police station, and the lad safely tucked away in the "crowbar hotel." But the cap was destined to belong to the police chief. He had earned it and the title "Mr. Frisky."

Not long after, the same rogue was out of the jail and back in our area, looking over our house again. This time our yard man noticed him and warned me. Not knowing quite what to do, I merely watched him for a while till he was about 150 yards down the dusty road.

Presently an old mangy dog, belonging to no one in particular, began wobbling down the road, slowly catching up to the rogue and passing to his left. I still had my rifle and ran for it now. If I did this right, the sacrifice of this dog would spare my next cap! With the dog a mere 15 feet from the rogue, the rifle roared, and the dog dropped where he stood.

The rogue first looked at the dog, then at my smoking rifle and decided that he would be much more comfortable if there could be found a hurried space between him and me. His headlong burst of energy carried him through the jungle with amazing speed until he disappeared, never to be seen again.

Another cap came in the mail.

BWANA—THE BIG WHITE HUNTER – 1955

You couldn't live in Africa and not hunt. Like the Eskimo of the North, young natives are taught to hunt early, and so I was taught by my friends at age seven, and thereafter, to view everything as "meat." Some animals such as a rat were called "small meat," a deer "big meat." My first weapon was a sling made from small rope woven from the palm tree leaf, similar to what David used on Goliath. When we graduated to rubber sling shots, we created our own sling works, and then graduated from bows and arrows and slings to purchasing gun powder from a Lebanese man and making our own weapons.

I found a 3 foot piece of 3/4 inch diameter copper pipe, used for house plumbing and made my first shotgun. To accomplish this, I took a hammer, bent one end of the pipe flat, crimped it over and drilled a small hole just in front of the crimp. Then using rattan and nails, I screwed it to a piece of wood that I had fashioned as crude stock. Then by gluing a matchbox striker to the stock, I could light a match and put it to the hole where the gun powder was exposed.

The resulting explosion would send the rocks and nails ahead of the powder out the muzzle with enough velocity to blow holes in tin roofing from 100 feet. I would increase the charge slightly each time until the soft copper tubing would begin to expand. I then made a measured charge so my African friends and I were "safe" each time. We then made pistols and, with a larger steel pipe, a cannon. Don't try this at home!

We were lords of the jungle then, and a fright to our parents. It's a wonder we weren't maimed, or scarred permanently, by our rabid foolishness. The specimens of "small meat" would show up in my mom's refrigerator, feathers and all, much to her "delight." The roasted termites, crocodile tail, and elephant meat we ate from time to time didn't seem to hurt me, as I never got sick with anything but malaria. Monkeys were quite tough, and snail soup rather slimy, but when you don't have a mind prejudiced about such things, mind over matter is rather easy!

Later on when I returned to Africa in my twenties, I took a visiting missionary on a monkey hunt. Moses Kpa would be our guide, a young ebony skinned man reported to be a very reliable guide in the jungle. There were men, it was said, and that had explored Africa and had written books about it. But I know the truth; they were mostly picture takers, exploiting Africa for some of her jewels. I knew that for myself, as much as I had learned as a lad and a hunter, that the continent had not yet been "found" or quite figured out by the white man. It was unknown. It had just barely been dreamed much less found out or conquered. With this in mind, Moses Kpa proceeded to get himself, and us, thoroughly and hopelessly lost.

On the way in to getting really lost, we had come upon a large sleeping chimpanzee in a tree about 30 feet up. We heard the terrifying scream first and then the blur of black fur as he jumped from the tree to our feet and screamed for quite some distance. The hunt was to be only a two-hour excursion, so we took no water, leaving our canteens in the car on the dirt road. It is the final indignity for a native guide to get lost, much more so, I think, it was perceived, if he had led a white man astray. The white man had pleaded incompetence from the outset, now our native guide must do the same.

He had led us on a long journey to the edge of a large swamp, to a small knoll at the base of a large 150-foot tall tree. Elephant tracks were all around us and we could hear their nervous trumpeting nearby. The Cape Buffalo had also left its mark here, and both he and the elephant that make their home here in the jungle are, for reasons only known to the Creator, of significantly meaner disposition than the East African counterpart. It was there that darkness prevailed and we had no light with us save the stars.

Our thirst for water became preeminent, so we dug a two-foot deep hole—a shallow well--which soon filled with swamp water, filtered through the soil, but too putrid to drink. We all lay at the base of the tree, close together, waiting for the promise of the sun.

All around us was some kind of plant that glowed white in the darkness. All night we could hear "visitors" creeping up to us, snorting and leaving in a hurry. Our weapons were quite useless when we could not see. We waited, listening, and sleep escaped us, as we contemplated waking up to a Gabon viper trying to warm his thick body near our legs.

My thought strayed to a pet of my childhood. It was from this forest somewhere that a captured pigmy hippopotamus was once brought to me for a pet. This is the only place on earth these creatures can be found, a hippo the size of a Great Dane.

Moses, our native tracker, having had six hours to think about how he got us into this situation, informed us at midnight that he now knows the way out! That he will leave us in the darkness, walk around for a while in the darkness, find us and lead us out! He insisted and silently crept away to save his embarrassment. After two hours, he somehow (we were sure through the providence of the Almighty) returned to us. He told us he'd get us out in the morning, but didn't tell us about the strange bird he had caught.

This bird the size of a parrot, with a long beak and two very long tail feathers, could only glide from limb to limb. Somehow capturing one of these in the darkness, Moses tucked the long bill between his short trousers and his rope belt. The bird hung there quietly for some time with this 180-degree bend in his neck.

Only now as our guide wedged his prone body next to ours, did the bird make another attempt to defy gravity. His desperate squalling and attempts to beat the air into submission with already inadequate wings, brushed the arm of one of the uninformed white members of our troop, Bob Smith, a very brave, but rather nervous man, a character who constantly had a whistle on his lips. His associated behavior closely paralleled a man about to float over Niagara Falls in an inner tube, or of a man being chased by a mad Mexican fighting bull! The bird was quickly dispatched as the 180 degree bend in his neck became more pronounced. And we stood guard, for what we knew not, for the rest of the night.

The wives meantime had awakened Dave Tappi--a descendant of the chief of Tappi Town and known to be the best hunter and tracker in the entire known world--and imposed upon him to come for us. At 4 am he walked to our tree holding a dead monkey he had shot on the way in. The carbide headlamp he wore signaled our ordeal was over. Soon, the family welcomed me as did my 50-cent African talking gray parrot.

FIFTY--THE BIRD THAT CALLED THE DOGS – 1979

Suddenly there he is, this bird of intellect, waddling to greet me like a duck, his wings having been clipped to ensure his continued residence with us. Twice a day, his kind that sold for $1500.00 a piece on the world market, would fly over head on their way to and from roosting and feeding grounds. Where else can you see fifty such parrots, wild and free, flying over head, making such a variety of sounds as to confuse even themselves?

We had purchased this African gray talking parrot from a young man for 50 cents so we named him "Fifty." Poor Fifty, one day he whistled for destruction, and it came. His doom had been building, as he mimicked mama's call to dinner, and we all came to find nothing on the table. His "car horn" would warn us of a stranger approaching when there was nothing but his insolent cocked head to see, his eyes mocking us as we answered the "bock-bock" –the African words spoken instead of a knock on the door.

But his were proud feathers, pretty feathers with a touch of red on his tail, long and all in place, stained with jungle color. He would proudly clasp his perch on the porch, looking with falsely philosophic eyes on all who entered. He could tell time too and always drew a laugh from the natives who would come twenty miles on occasion to see, not Fifty, but the trained bird the white man had, who lived in the top of a clock fashioned after a house. Fifty knew the cuckoo bird and just simply could not tell time as well. All these talents were the undoing of this noble feathered friend. Long life is usually theirs, but pride bringeth destruction.

He could whistle for a beautiful woman, notice or call a pack of dogs. A man would stand and make that sound, and the dogs would assemble at his feet. But who could make sounds if it were not Fifty? Was he to remain on a bird stick the whole of his long life? Was there to be nothing but seeds and water for a being as elegant as he? Who had such dignity, such feathers, and such a beak? Who could not walk around the house "pigeon toed" and not find some human to feed or pet him? Who could not call a dog? Fifty could. He did.

He practiced week upon week, but so much under his breath that we seldom heard him. He practiced though, this art, until he knew it as well as his favorite phrase, "my but you're stupid." And no self respecting dog that ever sought a flea could resist his summons. Fifty called, and they came. One day Fifty jumped down from his perch and called the dogs. It was the quick, urgent call I used when I wanted to call a dog quick. I saw Fifty, rocking his insolent head side to side, as empty as it was. "Come one, come all," his whistle said, "It is I, Fifty calling."

And so they came, a large dog and short one, coming with haste to their master's call. I could run fast in those days, but not fast enough to prevent the frustration of a dog--anticipating some scrap from the master's table--from turning to fury at the sight of this vain bird with gaudy feathers forging the master's voice-- insulting to all of dogdom, holding to ridicule the canine clan, promising perhaps a bone, yet giving nothing. That was the injury, the salt in the wound, the insult. He was the Judas of the kind only a called dog could know.

Fifty went down. He went under and over, he disappeared only to reappear again, feather by feather. His blaze of glory was short lived, a comet tail of scraps and floating feathers. Early on, I had owned a pet monkey that died one night. The next day I picked up my stiff friend and dragged him to my mother. I'm told I asked, "When Jesus comes, will he live again?" The question was now asked again of fearless Fifty. Fifty did live and mounted his perch once again, his eyes half closed, remembering his moment. He lived to call a dog another day, but from a safer and higher perch. So suffered an almost ageless parrot, blessed, I suspect, with a memory too short to be fatal.

As always in this country, there were things blessed and things cursed. The parrot and monkey had gone to bed, and so would I, as soon as I wound this Chinese alarm clock. The kerosene lamp no longer had competition from the sun. It seems everything was run by kerosene here--the lamp, stove and the refrigerator.

There was a very old lamp, Chinese too--cheap and chipped. Made from cheap metal, its wick could be trimmed and its sooty chimney cleaned. Watching it burn, I wondered how many men had read or written by it or eaten under it? Had it ever seen real success? I'm thinking it probably had, depending on how you grade success. It gave out a joyless glow, almost depressing in its flicker. A rhinoceros beetle with its steady drone arrived with a thud, his two large pincers trying to impale the globe, dumping him on his back with feet flailing the air. This lamp had drawn many victims with its dissolute eye. Its only use tonight was to illuminate another line in my logbook.

THE BIG BANG -- 1978

I had stripped all the old paint off EL-AHD down to bare aluminum in preparation for a new paint job. I would fly from Yekepa to Tappita where another missionary pilot-mechanic and I would work together to spray on a new coat. All of that masking and taping would go quicker with another pair of hands. I drove with the family to the airport, crossing the railroad tracks as usual, without slowing down—after all the train only passed here twice a day, and it wasn't time for it then. Besides, if a train should happen to be there, I had already worked out in my mind what evasive action I would take.

As we were pulling up beside the airstrip another plane landed, and five business men climbed out, looking around for a taxi. Now our airport at Yekepa was a remote strip in the jungle, miles from town, where planes rarely came and no taxis awaited. Jane and the girls, ages 3 and 6 months, watched as I took off, waving goodbye, as I would be gone for several days.

Jane continues this story:

The men, four who had come from England to conduct business with the management of the Liberia America Mining Company and a Liberian agent, asked me for a ride back to

Yekepa in our Peugeot station wagon. The five men piled in, seating the girls on their laps to make room.

It was a beautiful day and I was feeling full of energy and thinking about all the things I wanted to accomplish with Les out of town. Just past the airport, I did not slow down as I approached the railroad. In fact, I didn't even look down the track for the train, as I had never seen one there!

"Missy, train coming-o!" the Liberian riding on the far right exclaimed!

I slammed on the brakes, but was unable to stop on the gravel road.

"Oh, no!" I cried out to God in my head. "Not these men!" I meant that I did not want them to go out into eternity because of my carelessness.

A flash of yellow passed before the car and then the impact! Instead of the train hitting us, we had hit the train! The forward motion of the train turned the Peugeot around 180 degrees, so that it came to rest in the ditch facing back toward the airport. The impact broke the engine loose and tossed it 35 feet down the track! The front fenders were severed from the car and the brake's master cylinder was sheered right off the firewall separating the passengers from the engine! In fact, the leg room in the car seemed a trifle shorter after the impact.

That flash of yellow before the impact was a locomotive. The train combined three yellow locomotives, covered with armor down to the tracks, with dozens of iron ore carrying gondola cars. This story would have ended grievously had the train hit the Peugeot, or had I impacted in a different place. Between the gondola cars, there was just enough room for a car to become wedged and smashed. It was very close, a matter of a split second. I had collided with the side of the third locomotive near the back the armored panel!

With an accident of this magnitude, you would expect serious injuries, but by the time the car impacted the train it was going very slowly, almost stopped. Only one window in the station wagon broke—the rear hatch. None of the eight souls inside were killed or even seriously hurt! No broken bones! Only one person had cuts requiring stitches—Baby Carol! God had heard and answered my cry.

The British businessman who seemed to be in charge had seated himself in the middle of the front seat and was holding baby Carol on his lap. When he saw the train, he turned her sideways on his lap and held her securely against his body with both arms, supporting her head against his chest with his outstretched hand.

At impact, his head whipped forward and shattered the rear view mirror. The sharp flying pieces lacerated the side of the baby's face—in the temple area beside her eye, requiring only a few stitches. Thank God he had turned her body sideways; it would have cut her eyes otherwise! Thank God neither the windshield nor the side windows broke!

A LAMCO pickup truck happened by almost immediately and took us to the hospital. The men went on to the company office to report what had happened. They were so shaken by the close call that they did not stay to do their business as planned, but wanted to go home to England. Upon hearing the radio transmission on our mission network about the crash, Les immediately flew back to Yekepa.

The Liberian people have a custom of expressing sorrow or regret by saying, "Never mind," instead of saying "I'm sorry." That night one of the African believers came to the house to visit me saying, "Ne'r mind, Missy, ne'r mind" and offering to pray for me. This brother's prayer resounded in the room with thanks and praise for the safety of those in the accident. With eyes closed and head bowed, I felt lifted up to the gate of heaven and surrounded with the love of God ... and very humbled.

The next day the businessmen came to see me. Their leader, the man who had been holding Carol, said this: "We know the sort of lives we have lived. It is because of you--you are a missionary--that we are alive today." Then each man hugged me and left to return to England, sobered by their close call.

Another of our Liberian believers, a physical therapist at the hospital, visited me in the morning. Miss Sarah had heard at the hospital about our wreck and had been very upset. The last time there was a wreck at that crossing, the taxi had been hit by the train, and the rescue team had the gruesome job of cutting the car apart to get the bodies out!

"I could not sleep last night," Sarah said. "Finally I read my favorite passage and could sleep."

"Would you read it to me?" I asked. My Bible was on the table beside my seat on the couch, and I handed it to her. Sarah read Psalm 139, it was as if God Himself was whispering to me:

O LORD, thou hast searched me, and known me. Thou knowest my downsitting and mine uprising, thou understandest my thought afar off. Thou compassest my path and my lying down, and art acquainted with all my ways. For there is not a word in my tongue, but, lo, O LORD, thou knowest it altogether. Thou hast beset me behind and before, and laid thine hand upon me. Such knowledge is too wonderful for me; it is high, I cannot attain unto it. Whither shall I go from thy spirit? or whither shall I flee from thy presence? If I ascend up into heaven, thou art there: if I make my bed in hell, behold, thou art there. If I take the wings of the morning, and dwell in the uttermost parts of the sea; Even there shall thy hand lead me, and thy right hand shall hold me.... I shall not die, but live, and declare the works of the LORD. --Psalm 118:17

LETTING THE PILOT PILOT -- 1976

The flight next day was not about ecstasy in the sky. It was about sheer panic or something close to it. It was about letting the pilot, pilot. My passenger had only read of a pilot's duties, of his inputs to direct flight. All our jungle airstrips were short and narrow, a "postage stamp" in the jungle, surrounded by very large trees. Almost overnight, the grass would grow to a dangerous height, hiding obstructions like termite hills a foot high which would appear at random in one night. Goal posts on both ends marked the soccer ball field. Goats and cattle grazed and infrequent celebrations helped enliven village life. A pilot could not be too cautious on a take off or landing. Built by hand, each air strip had its own distinction: some very short or narrow, some up and down hill, some side hill, some one way in and one way out, some with rain washed ruts, with strange approaches and no go-arounds. Some you could land on with the grass wet, some you couldn't.

One day when on final approach, with a no-go-around, the final approach was just that. If not done right, it would be my life's final approach. I must approach this one with great care, the wind just right and the grass dry. Coming in 10 foot over the stumps at the end of the airstrip with the stall warning going off requires sincere effort--no down drafts or power surges or getting behind the power curve. There was a 10 foot square, the sweet spot, where my wheels should touch down. Beyond that point and the plane might not get stopped.

The old lady carrying 100 pounds of wood on her head was walking down the middle of the runway, and she wasn't hearing my approach. I had to firewall the throttle momentarily so she would notice me. She did and dropped her wood and began running straight ahead in the middle of the runway instead of running to the side.

I dipped my left wing and pushed left rudder momentarily moving the aircraft off to the side. The right wing just outboard of the strut passed within inches over her head. The other wing was getting green as it passed through the brush on the left side and the tail of the airplane barely missed her midsection.

After this flight, I installed a car horn on this plane that could be heard for quite some distance announcing my intention to land, but never matching the song of any bird capable of wild flight.

I soon left with another passenger, who had learned about flight only from a book and decided the pilot should have some help. I knew that airspeed was equal to altitude so the standard procedure for this take off followed a checklist:

•Push tail all the way to the tree line before taking off
•Nose straight
•Magnetos checked
•Runway clear of goal posts, people, and goats
•Set flaps 10 degrees to start the run
•Set brakes, full power, release brakes, roll 200'
•Pop flaps to 30 degrees
•Rotate airplane and fly 2 feet off the ground
•Maintain ground effect for 200 feet more while bleeding the flaps from 30 degrees to 10 degrees
•Bounce off the sweet spot where I should have touched down with 20 degrees of flap
•Go immediately to best angle of climb to clear the 150 foot trees
•Then to best rate
•Then to a cruise climb with flaps off
•Cowl doors open
•Prop governor and RPM set to 2300
•Set mixture control to 100 degrees on the rich side of its exhaust gas temperature gauge
•Set trim to cruise altitude
•Monitor oil pressure and other gauges
•Look at trees below to interpret wind direction on the surface
•Look at the cloud shape to determine direction of   wind at altitude
•Pick out object on horizon and time to the object, keeping direction of aircraft steady so as to determine rate of drift.
•It's simple!
•Oh yes, don't forget to check the time of departure or you may not find home.

The uncalculated factor was the passenger, whether man or chimpanzee. This man with rudimentary knowledge saw the short runway, the tall trees at the end and knew that when you pull the wheel back, the plane goes up, doesn't it?   True, but not without airspeed carefully built up in ground effect and a split-second use of flaps to overcome gravity. It's called pilot technique or "Letting the pilot pilot."

The passenger reached for the co-pilot wheel and pulled it back. The plane momentarily gained some altitude, but had I not firmly removed his hand from the wheel, we both would be helping trees grow in Africa. All he could see was the obstacle, the danger in the near vision.

In training a new pilot, like my instructor's teaching me the art of crop dusting and flying under the wires, concentrating on the obstacle will surely make you a prisoner of it. The obstacle is mesmerizing, almost hypnotic. Such is the case in all of life as well; concentrate enough on your problem, and it will find you and catch and consume you.

So I removed all the controls except mine on the left side of the cockpit. It's nice being in control, isn't it? But sometimes God lets you know that you are not in control. Try flying along, fat, dumb and happy and in control, with a cup of hot coffee in a thermos lid in your lap, while you open another letter. That's when God turns loose on you clear air turbulence. Who are you going to sue?

I am incapable of any word to the wise, of any profound remark on the workings of destiny or sovereignty. I just know that all of us are given life and a place in history; sovereignty knows what we are capable of and then leaves much of the decision to us as to the extent of what kind of a steward we will be. By the same token, can I stretch my worth to the Sovereign by reaching out, stretching my faith, looking for more for the right reasons? That is an easy conclusion to these speculations on the subject and certainly not the last word.

I had always believed that the important, the exciting changes that took place in one's life would happen at some crossroad where important people met and built empires and civilizations. But they don't. They happen when you understand that the Sovereign of the universe works with small things and sometimes small minds, in a dull setting, on a mound of dusty earth or over a cup of coffee.

How can one imagine where a word would fall except on the wind to be carried away, never to be heard or thought of again? Words mean things, as I would find out. You couldn't just sit on your piazza and watch Africa suffering or just watch the clouds go by. You couldn't in those days in 1979-80 in Liberia, West Africa.

THE ISRAELI CONNECTION – 1979

When I flew into Monrovia that day, I was summoned to the US ambassador's office for a chat.

"Are you the pilot that flies most of these missionaries around Liberia," he asked? I said that I was and how could I help? His questions were in regard to the culmination of events leading a relatively peaceable and democratic republic down the road to ruin and revolution.

A group of freed slaves from America in the 1822 had arrived on the shores of West Africa with American ships, cannons, and muskets to subdue the natives there and show them "a better way of life." They came with a Christian ethic and tried to force it down the throats of the local tribes through the use of ball and powder and by capturing all the political posts of any importance. These freed slaves were descendants, products of the slave trade carried on by the Africans themselves, capturing and selling each other to the white slave traders. The village of "Trade Town" still exists on Liberia's shores, its history of slave trade not that ancient. The twenty-eight tribes now confined in an area the size of the state of Ohio, had for years captured each other and carried each other by brute force to the auction blocks at Trade Town.

When the pilgrims, who considered themselves "slaves" to the British, had come to America, they were escapees from a dictator—freedom lovers to the core. It would almost seem that they did the same things that the freed American slaves did to the tribal people of West Africa. They arrived on America's shores, conquered the Indian with muskets and cannon, began the trek westward, and treated the Indian to a "better way of life."

It is indeed a challenge to find one, only one, good program that has originated from the American government that proceeded towards or came to completion that worked as intended or wasn't prostituted. Start with the Bureau of Indian Affairs; consider the prostitution of our money standard, the welfare state that started with Franklin Roosevelt and was promoted by Johnson; the United Nations and "New World Order" pushed by Bush, Sr., and even the granting of nation and diplomatic status to the Catholic Church by Reagan.

It gives one pause to think; to wonder, if "civilized" man, although able to read and write, to articulate the Declaration of Independence, the Bill of Rights and the Constitution, is any better than the African who may not have anything written down. We have been given so much and therefore much is required. Perhaps we are civilized barbarians at best. Perhaps we are approaching a quick decline as an evil nation.

It is clear that the forefathers did not believe in the "divine right of kings." Yet a recent excuse of a president declared his "divine right" to have "Monica." We deplored big government at first and now seem to embrace it. George Washington said, "Government is not reason, it is not eloquence; it is a force! Like fire it is a dangerous servant and a fearful master." So, we must turn our grand entrance into world affairs into mourning. Comparisons fade as we blend into the international landscape, camouflaged by the same failures as all men of the world.

The US ambassador had caused our missionaries great alarm by informing me that their best intelligence indicated a coming revolution in Liberia. All foreigners should flee the country as soon as possible, as President Jimmy Carter promised no help of any kind to the 5000 US citizens working in Liberia!

My Israeli friend Yechiel Ben Arzi appeared seemingly from nowhere, the memory of our introduction faded and pushed back by the importance of the subject matter at hand. Ben Arzi, having been a colonel in the Israeli army during the 1967 Six Day War and the Yom Kippur War in 1973-74 determined not to die in

a war not his own. He had become a civil engineer at LAMCO--
the Liberia American Mining Company, the second richest iron
ore mine in the world, nestled in the far corner of Liberia, between
Guinea and the Ivory Coast. We spent several evenings planning
our survival should a revolution occur.

If a man has any potential, any greatness in him, it will
come to light, not in one exuberant or flamboyant hour, but in the
log book of his daily work. We were aware of various political
and moral views emanating from the Liberians, the liberal
Swedish mine managers and the missionaries. The Lebanese
shopkeepers had their own thoughts of survival as well. Ben Arzi
and I thought hard and laid our plans. We figured that we and our
families had a right to live. In fact, if it didn't get too
overwhelming, we had a right to stay, having been invited there by
a "friendly" government. Soon, possibly, we would be asked to
leave by a rebel group seeking power with ill gotten gains of its
own. We planned to be alive, leaving in our path a terrible wake,
if necessary.

We first started by setting out a scenario and then asking
the Swedes and the missionaries one question: "the
revolution/coup is under way; the rebels are trying to oust the
present dictator. You have been asked to leave by the US and
Swedish ambassadors. You have a five shot pump shotgun in the
broom closet, when five drunken rebels come into your house,
demand to be fed, and take all your money. They will then rape
your wife and daughter and will cut your throats before they leave.
Will you pick up your shotgun and quickly kill all five rebels so
you can flee, or will you leave the shotgun in the closet?"

The Swedes, hopelessly passive and, for no reason they
could give, would not do the deed. The Lebanese would run from
the start. Some missionaries would not pick up the shotgun, nor
use it. Others said they believed the Scriptures taught self defense
as a "strong man of the house" principle. I looked around the
small coffee stand and saw no one worth trying to rescue from the
revolution--the native and Swede because they had liberty and
cared nothing for it, nor the soldier and the existing government
because they were trying for years to take all liberty away.

The president had killed hundreds who politically opposed him, stolen their wives and land, doubled the price of rice, bought his own personal Boeing 737 with the people's rice money and bragged that in a few short years, everyone in the country would be working for him. It appeared that only the rebels, which were all from the tribal people conquered by the slave descendants, had a just cause. But like a dog that catches a car, what would the illiterate rebel do with liberty once he had cornered it? We sat there for some time, drinking solemnly our coffee as if each of us were to be hanged at dawn.

We knew the plane I flew was the key to swift safety. One road went to the airport some eleven miles away where there was land enough for an airport, sky enough for the plane's wings and enough length for the plane's propellers to beat back the barriers of doubt. Ben Arzi set about to extend and straighten a mine road, known only to us as an airport, with gasoline buried nearby. Then a trail through the jungle to the real airport was made only for my cross country motorcycle. We assumed the main road would be blocked so I would be able to ride secretly, retrieve the plane and pick everyone up on the mine road.

In case something hindered that evacuation plan, we laid a contingency plan. Ben Arzi modified two huge dump trucks for ore from the mine with steel plows to protect the radiators and drivers from flying lead and to facilitate driving through any blockade. We planned to commandeer the railroad--the only train in the country--to take us to the sea, where we would commandeer an iron ore freighter and go out to sea. All the pieces were put together - the plan seemed sound and whole. It was our plan. A word grows to a thought--a thought to an idea--an idea to an act, if necessary.

Change in Africa is always slow, but when it comes, it roars and springs like the lion or the wounded leopard. The change was not yet, but soon.

1979 - Yekepa, Liberia, 5 pm. Having returned from the open market, I had bargained myself a delicious 50-cent-supper from locally grown fruits and vegetables and was now on my motorcycle, on the way home. Living outside Yekepa a short distance, I had a short stretch of relatively uninhabited road to pass over. It was here that a yellow taxi cab was parked and two gentlemen were struggling with a teenage girl. The young black girl broke free as I passed and ran for the jungle, one young man in hot pursuit.

I slid my motorcycle to a stop and ran to the driver who was still behind the wheel. To his complete surprise, I reached into the car in front of his nose and quickly shut off the car and took his keys. Seriously dumbfounded, he sat like a statute while I ran into the jungle after the girl and young man, soon catching them both. The police found out that the young men were attempting to capture her for human sacrifice as entry into a devil society. They had put a stolen license plate over their own to expedite their get away. All is well that ends well they say. The young lady, unaware of the "good Samaritan" principle, thanked me. I never saw her again.

The two young men were planning something that is a well known practice in Liberia, most of it happening around Christmas time. It was the ritualistic killing of a human being and doing unspeakable things with the corpse to join a secret society. Even senators and congressmen, some trained in the United States and wearing a white shirt and tie to work in the Liberian senate, did the same things. One day thirteen of these nationally elected cannibals were hung in public, due mostly to pressure exerted by the Western press when they were caught.

It would seem that all men everywhere have certain inalienable rights endowed by the Creator. These rights were recognized and fought for in the American Revolution. The pursuit of life, liberty and happiness seems to be a common goal of all humanity, regardless of the various means of attaining it, and the winds of Africa were changing subtly.

"Coffee drinkers make better thinkers," I had heard. So began this historic session of two buddies, Ben Arzi and myself, participating in food and verbose fellowship which dissolved time and space and dissected every government we had ever known. Ben and his wife had come to Liberia to be forgotten, to get away from Israel and her wars, and now we planned another one, just the two of us taking on the entire nation.

International problems were solved in words and the direction of fate was seen clearly through the facets of two crystal coffee mugs. It was a glorious adventure. It has been said, "Above average minds discuss ideas; average minds discuss events; below average minds discuss people. We mostly spoke of ideas, but the people and the events they created made it mandatory that someone with an idea must surface. It was a grand plan, but the only part I had in it came shortly after the new moon appeared.

My next trip to the capitol city of Monrovia, to Spriggs Payne Field, an airstrip that seemed to protrude from a swamp like a half submerged crocodile, would at the very least, seem to me to be a pebble that would send historical ripples throughout the country.

DON'T STEP ON THAT BANANA PEEL - 1979

As the plane taxied to the ramp, I was greeted by another aviator in a Cessna 180 which had just regurgitated a full stalk of bananas and a native woman who claimed them and had brought them there to sell on the street and the open air market. Also approaching were around six soldiers whose duty it was to guard the airport and keep the peace. Begging for money and the willingness to talk endlessly on any subject seemed also to be their duties. Monrovia in places was a mangrove of pinched and broken streets, dirty and infused with the odors of poverty. Everywhere were traps, catching the stagnant smells of stagnant life. Incessant blaring of taxi cab horns almost precluded conversation, but the soldiers were demanding to know, to have some answers.

This ragtag group of soldiers had not been paid in six months, their lives grinding to a despairing halt, living in the poorest of accommodations, their walls patrolled by cockroaches. They were more loyal to me than the president. I had at least purchased a Coca Cola for them on each of my arrivals in turn for their watchful eye on the plane while I secured my groceries and mail and medicine.

I didn't have time to talk with them then. I was in a hurry, but I could have some fun at their expense. As I hailed a taxi, all six soldiers begged me for "a small something"—a tip or donation. I noticed the stalk of bananas near by the plane. The bush woman was also gone to hail a taxi.

"Boss man," the soldier said, "I see you brought us some bananas."

"Yes," I replied. "I feel good today; you can have the whole bunch." Then I quickly disappeared into my taxi while a royal argument ensued over the bananas, like six dogs arguing over the last bone on earth.

When I completed my in city business and returned to the airfield two hours later, the six soldiers were up against the fence, the bush woman had them trapped like a dog with six cats and having a hard time choosing which one to eat first. She was speaking, but I understood nothing. Hers was a language befitting only this situation. For her speaking so blatantly, the soldiers were all but convicted and anything they said could and would be held against them. As I approached the fence and the plane, there were twelve outstretched hands, all pleading for redemption, for a double portion of mercy. Never had such betrayal befallen them except from their own government!

I approached them slowly, a slight smirk on my face, my hand on my wallet, their fate in my hands. Their beads of perspiration turned to tears of joy, but their eyes spoke of revenge. The bush woman was a great sport, accepting gladly a five dollar bill for a one dollar stalk of bananas. The soldiers broke into uncontrolled laughter. They were my best friends now, each clutching a tattered twenty dollar bill that had been in circulation longer than they. The bush woman became lost in the crowd, quickly hiding her jack pot earnings.

I beckoned to the soldiers and we returned to an old wooden table that had a culinary history inscribed on its surface in grease. And if this table could talk it would bring to remembrance to these neglected and desperate soldiers the answer to the question they all asked, "What made America great?" And white men did have the answers, for it was he who made the airplane, car, watch, cuckoo clock, many books, and the radio. And they had listened to my legal ramblings, to the descriptions of lasting foundations, to the principles that made America what it was. Perhaps out of real interest, or perhaps it was the Coca-Cola we shared that was important.

I had explained that an order of authority was important and that only one order would really work. And they agreed and seemed to understand. I told them and tested them like school children knowing that all they had was memory, since they couldn't read or write. The order began with God Almighty:

God Almighty
>   Creator of man
>   Source of all rights

The Bible
>   Supreme law of the universe
>   God's covenant with man

We the People
>   Creator and master of government by
>   constitution
>   Sovereign free men
>   Source of all government rights.

Peoples' Enforcement Controls
>   Electoral Vote
>   Grand Jury
>   Petit Jury.

Government
>   Servant of "we the people "
>   Sole purpose is protection of individual rights

Power and authority enumerated in and restricted
by the Constitution.
Restricted in arbitrary power by the
Separation of Powers doctrine
    The Executive (law enforcement)
    Legislative   (law making)
    Judicial   (law application),
A nation of laws and not of men

Corporations
    Government created entities --"persons"
    Free men who exchange their birth right for
    government privileges and become servants
        controlled by government rules and regulations.

I made it ever so clear that abuse of power was what they were experiencing lately, that the only solution was to "bind them down by the chains of the constitution." But "how to do this" was the question of six uneducated, unpaid soldiers. But wait I said, "We must review God's law to determine what ours must be."

I told them of Thomas Jefferson's pronouncement: "Rebellion to Tyrants is obedience to God." The review continued, because no clear answer was on their lips:

What kind of government do you want?
Do you think the people of the country have a right to
choose their form of government or do the presidents and
dictators decide?
Since God is the Supreme ruler of the universe, is there a
specified form of government preferred by the Sovereign
for His creation?
Do you understand God's three spheres of authority--
the Family is the ministry of Education, the Church the
ministry of Grace, the State the ministry of Justice?"

I asked and answered questions as I drilled them on principles of government:

Are you willing to say that governments have power and authority, but only exercise it as God allows? That God has instituted government to be His deacons, His servants, to be His exacters of righteousness? That if government is a servant, it must obey the people?

Whom must it obey? Is it the people who ordained it or someone else? Is government a theological issue? "Yes."

Is it possible to have a separation between government and religion? "No."

Can you have government controlling the church? Can you have separation between government and religion and have a God ordained government? "No."

Since government deals with right and wrong, good and evil, and moral values, is it religious in nature? "Yes." Whether a government is humanistic or Christian, is it religious by its very nature? "Yes." Do you see then that every law that is passed is really a religious law? Every law then should be Biblically oriented.

I also pointed out that whenever anthropologists studied an ancient culture, one of the first things they observe is the culture's law.

Why? Because whoever determines your law, whoever is the source of your law, is your god. If your law emanates from your mind, then you, yourself, are pretending to be god. If your law comes from nine black-robed justices, then they are your gods. If, however, your source of law is the one eternal and unchanging God, then God is your God and the God of your society.[45] *See it's either your reasoning, a dictator's reasoning, a supreme court, the witch doctor or God - right? Understand?*

Isn't it true that the one God who created you has ordained and put government in place to deal with righteousness and justice? "Yes." There- fore the subjection to human rulers demanded in Romans 13:1-2 is conditional. It is conditional upon the ruler or authorities being the ministers of God mentioned in vs. 3, 4 and 6.

Is President Tolbert a minister of God unto thee for good? "No," they answered.
Has the president violated his oath? Restricted the freedom of speech? The press?
"Yes," they affirmed. "Yes." "Yes."

Can you assemble and protest peaceably his dictatorial powers and edicts? "No."
Can you keep arms? "No - we don't even have ammunition."

Has the president killed many of the people in this country to stay in power? Hasn't the president said everyone would be working for him in the country within four years? Does the president make laws as he wishes? "Yes." "Yes." "Yes."

---

[4] Pastor John Weaver, *The Christian and Civil Government*, p. 89

*Does anyone get a fair trial? Does anyone have equal
protection of the laws? Can you vote your conscience
in any election? Does your president derive his powers
from the consent of the governed? "No." "No."
"No." "No."*

*Do you believe that whenever any form of govern-ment
becomes destructive of these ends, it is the right of the
people to alter or abolish it, and to institute new
government, laying its foundation on such principles and
organizing its powers in such forms, as to them shall
seem most likely to affect their safety and happiness?
"Yes."*

*Do you believe that "when a long train of abuses and
usurpations evinces a design to reduce you under
absolute despotism, it is your right, it is your duty, to
throw off such government and to provide new guards for
your future security?"*

I read directly from my own country's Declaration of
Independence and the writings of Abraham Lincoln.

*Does this government deserve to stay in power? "No!"
Why don't you do something about it?
"We're not sure how," was their reply.
Your people were here first before these freed slaves –
right? "Right!"*

*You mean you let a few hundred slaves come here and
take all this land from you, and make you slaves? "Yes,
that's what happened," they said.*

You know, if you don't care enough about your land or at least didn't really fight for it, you deserve to lose it - that's why you lost it.
"Yes, we agree, that's why we lost it."

You know guys, we in the United States did the same thing - we were few in numbers, we showed up on the East Coast of America, subdued the Indians and moved in. We did the same thing with Mexico. We moved into Texas, lived there a while and figured we could take on Santa Anna. We did, we won the war and Texas is ours. That simple. "For true, boss man?" they asked. For true, my man."

I had spent hours on the various days I flew to Monrovia trying to get them to understand our separation of powers doctrine, a system of checks and balances designed to hold in and check power. I tried to destroy the notion of the divine right of kings (chiefs), that the evil part of human nature whether embodied in the preacher, or dictator, or paramount chief, almost always tended toward an extension of their power to usually illegitimate ends. It is possible for an individual to be even kind, benevolent and have good intentions, yet if he has trodden on inalienable rights, he is a tyrant. Those who exceed their lawful authority in their home, church, or state, are tyrants in a real sense, endeavoring unlawfully and ruthlessly to impose their wills, prejudices and ambitions on others. An individual does not have to be cruel and oppressive in order to be classified as a tyrant, but that even "benevolent dictators" usually become real dictators when their wills are questioned.

To be free, you must be able to question your president without him always checking your motives, i.e. are you a traitor, questioning his authority for an insignificant reason, or you must want to see my downfall because

*you're questioning me? "We cannot talk to this
president," they assured me.*

*Since God is the only authority in the universe that is
sovereign, it is He that sets boundaries and defines
limits. So a tyrant is like your president, who rules
without God and is rebellious to Him. Whenever any
ruler tries to exercise his authority apart from God's
laws, no matter how kind or popular or benevolent, he
is still a tyrant.*

*Hosea 5:10-11 says, "the princes of Judah were like
them that remove the bound; therefore I will pour out
my wrath upon them like water. Ephraim is oppressed
and broken in judgment, because he willingly walked
after the commandment." So God judged Judah for
tyranny, for removing His boundaries, going over God's
authority. God judged Ephraim for willingly obeying
laws and statues that were given in rebellion to God.
That's why Thomas Jefferson said, "Rebellion to tyrants
is obedience to God."*
Do you understand what I am telling you?"
"Yes boss man," they assured me.

*Do you understand that God put in place, ordained civil
government - also that He ordained human instruments
to exercise delegated authority to set up and run the
government?*
"Yes, boss man."

*So God ordained government, but men set it up.
Whatever type of government you set up, its purpose is to
carry out the law of God. Why is this so? Because
government's purpose is to carry out the law of God. Because
God has said government should be His servant, His deacon,*

*His promoter of righteousness.   Did you know the Bible says
we must be obedient to biblical government for conscience
sake - Romans 13:5?*

*You know that government has the power to punish - that
God has ordained government to punish those who
violate God's law? Paul said in I Timothy 2:1-2, "I
exhort therefore, that first of all, supplications, prayers,
intercessions and giving of thanks, be made for all men;
for Kings and all in authority; that we may lead a quiet
and peaceable life in all godliness and honesty."*

*Did you know that in Bible covenants, when one party
violates or breaks the covenant, the other party is
loosed from obedience to the covenant? This is true in
covenants between men, God and men, and men and the
governments they create.*

*We had a man, a great man called Samuel Rutherford
who wrote Lex Rex. In this book, he was writing
against the "divine right of kings." He was saying that
rulers, presidents and the like were as subject to the law
as anyone. He said, "when the king (president)
defendeth not true religion, but presseth upon the
people a false and idolatrous religion (i.e. humanism),
in that they are not under the king, but are presumed to
have no king - and are presumed to have the power in
themselves, as if they had not appointed any king at
all." The power of government reverts back to the
governed; they must exercise a special form of
government with a right to defend themselves.*

"Do you know why?" I asked them.   "Because all
governmental power is derived from the consent of the governed,"
I told them. "If the people have given power to the government to

defend, and the government refused to use that power to defend the people, then the power to defend the people automatically reverts back to the people. In so doing, they are showing everyone that they can defend themselves, the best way they can."

"We understand boss man," they assured me, as we sipped on Coca Cola that I had purchased for them - a real treat in the 98 degree shade.

I continued now, as I had on many previous occasions to educate them with lofty American if not God ordained ideas. And I would not know if it was sinking in until the African acted. I assured them that as long as there are men who have made total commitments to the magnification of their own egos, there is no future for a stable government. Natural self interest and self love of man has to be checked. Communism removes the causes of factions by removing liberty and freedom of thought. The framers of the U.S. Constitution recognized the fallen nature of man in "which dwelleth no good thing." The people must write constitutions to anticipate the worst of man's behavior. When the worst happened, as was happening to them, then the constitution would cure the blockage or problem, rather than eliminate the entire system of government. I tried to get them to understand that ultimately, it was not the mind or the constitution, but the will that mattered--the willingness to put one's own will down for God's will. George Washington was right when he pronounced that "we ought to be no less persuaded that the propitious smiles of Heaven can never be expected on a nation that disregards the eternal rules of order and right, which Heaven itself has ordained."

Then I read them part of the American Declaration of Independence:

> *"We hold these truths to be self evident: that all men*
> *are created equal; that they are endowed by their*
> *creator with certain inalienable rights; and among*
> *these are life liberty and the pursuit of happiness; that*
> *to secure these rights, governments are instituted*
> *among men, deriving their just powers from the consent*

of the governed, that whenever any form of government becomes destructive of these ends, it is the right of the people to alter or to abolish it, and to institute new government, lacking it's foundation on such form, and to them shall seem most likely to effect their safety and happiness. Prudence indeed will dictate that governments long established should not be changed for light and transient causes; and accordingly all experience has shown, that man-kind is more disposed to suffer, while evils are sufferable, than to right themselves by abolishing the forms to which they are accustomed. But when a long train of abuses and usurpations, pursuing invariably the same object, evinces a design to reduce them under absolute despotism, it is their right, it is their duty to throw off such government, and to provide new guards for their future security. . . "

"Do you understand the American Declaration of Independence?" I asked them.

"We understand small, small."

"Then you might understand what Abraham Lincoln meant when he said:

"Any people anywhere, being inclined and having the power, have the right to rise up and shake off the existing government and form a new one. This is a most valuable and sacred right - a right which we hope and believe is to liberate the world."

"This country with its institutions belongs to the people who inhabit it. Whenever they shall grow weary of the existing government, they can exercise their constitutional right to amend it, or their revolutionary right to dismember or overthrow it." Abraham Lincoln, First Inaugural Address, March 4, 1861.

"Do you soldiers understand what President Lincoln said?"

"Yes, boss man, we hear, (understand) but we are small, we be too few to do anything. How can we change our government?" they replied.

One never knows what chapter in history one will write, or what ideas will take hold that he or others espouse. It was not my intention to make a mountain out of a mole hill, only to pass some time with small talk and redeem a friendship that had slid away on a bush woman's banana peel. It is not now my intention to enlarge a small story into a blood-curdling saga. The only disadvantage in telling of such an event lies in the fact that my story of it tends to be anticlimactic, and the world is full of skeptics, largely because they have never dreamed or worried about another's future on this earth besides their own.

These men, bush men from the country, would they care, understand, or look at the big picture? I wished for them the wisdom of the "soldier ant" and the single purpose and tenacity that was the ant's lot.

SOLDIER ANTS

There is only one ant like the "driver" or "soldier" ant. Study, honest, thrifty, determined, organized little fellow-- what has not been written about this ant? I would not wish upon a misguided politician, even a Democrat (or "Dumbocrat" as one of my aunts calls them), no matter what his misguided thoughts or sins might be, a single night in the company of the soldier and driver ants. He is a thief in the night, a man eater!

They are known as "soldier ants" since they march abreast in long columns, and as "driver ants" because they drive everything before them. This ant, part of Adam's curse, is sturdy and tenacious. At about ¾ inch long, he will march endlessly if there were a bit of live meat at the end of his labors. They will totally ignore a dead creature, even one freshly killed, to find one still breathing.

The ant's head is the largest part of his anatomy with larger than life pincers. An army of drivers is able to surprise and eat any prey on earth. Driver ants don't sting their prey; they actually bite chunks out of their living victims. Within a few hours a pet chimpanzee, if he is unable to escape his tether, or a baby left to sleep beneath a tree while its mother works the rice farm, can be reduced to mere bones, by even a reserve division of the "soldier" ant!

I have been in villages where other white men have not been, where the hut and the night belong to the ant. They come silently into the hut, cover the floor and walls; then make their way to the peak of the thatched roof to surround the snakes, rats, spiders, and tarantulas that make their home in the thatch. All at once, without a sound, the entire regiment attacks, biting chunks out of their living victims. The animals drop to the floor to escape, only to find a battalion of ants covering the floor. The only sounds made during the attack are the yells of the hapless hut owner fleeing for his life, the "whop" of the creatures hitting the hard mud floor, and the writhing of the creatures in the center of the floor. Once the hut is clean, the ants go elsewhere.

I have dreamed of many unpleasant things (as I suppose we all have)--bulls chasing and gaining on me, drowning, falling off a cliff, the leopard eating me alive, a wing falling off my plane in flight. But the dreams of the driver ants, climbing into my bed and clinging to my hair, relegate all other bad dreams to the category of sweet dreams. They are memories of the Curse--black, menacing pincers, numberless and inexorable, crawling all over me silently; then as if on command, chomp down on me in unison. I'll take rhino beetles, snakes and the like, but deliver me from the "black devils"-- the dreamed numberless clan.

And I wondered; would these human soldiers be anything as clever and devastating as the soldier ant? Would they be as brave? I knew Liberia was able to change - would it be for the better? It hardly ever does, it seems.

"You know," I said, as I took my last warm sip of Coca Cola, "You people have a saying, when two elephants fight, the grass gets hurt."

"For true, boss man? You know we can say that!?"

"We are ready to fight for our families," they assured me. "We haven't been paid in six months. But we are too few."

Almost in jest I said, "If I had five professional mercenaries. I could take this whole country in thirty minutes, but like a dog catching a car; what will he do with it once he had caught the thing?" I could only hope, knowing history was against me, that they could handle and form a better government. After all, I believed the right of the people expressed in the Declaration of Independence:

"It is the right of the people to alter or abolish - to institute new government - organizing its powers in such form, as to them shall seem most likely to effect their safety and happiness."

I knew happiness had eluded most of Africa, and perhaps would elude these men. But did they have a right now to try? In the time of man's history in Liberia, this steaming but waiting volcano had breathed little brimstone, barely a wisp of smoke. But in the annals of Liberian history which contain a history of tribal wars--of inter-tribe slave trade-- always moving like a sea of coral or a desert of sand dunes, the time of these men is too brief a period and so deep in the jungle to deserve more than a casual recording. Tomorrow, next day, maybe next year, Liberia may become again the country over which some passing deity, will for a small time or so, warm his omnipotent hands.

"But put all the pieces together," I assured them, "and the whole is yours." A word grows to a thought, a thought to an idea. And I could see an idea become a powerful thing as I explained how just six men--myself and five professional soldiers--could take the whole country. It would involve uniforms, darkness, approaching the presidential mansion, capturing for trial the president and then announcing the change of government on the radio; the mere announcement itself almost being sufficient to turn the tide.

The idea takes shape and the present is not the once sluggish stroller loafing in the path tomorrow wants to take. Theirs were jumbled thoughts--restless thoughts--absurd thoughts! It was not really a thought, of course, nor even one of those blinding realizations that come to these bush men of heroic fiction. Theirs was no more than a hunch or perhaps a goal set about in greed. But where is the man who is foolhardy enough not to play his hunches? I'm not one. It's difficult sometimes to tell where inspiration begins and impulse leaves off. I suppose that other than providential, if one's hunch proves a good one, he was inspired. If it proves bad, he is guilty of being the slave to thoughtless impulse.

Again, I reminded them that many nations had laid claim to parts of Africa, but none had wholly possessed her yet. And that without clear Christian purpose, they would fail as well. But they had smelled injustice; too much to bear, to now turn back. The die was cast. I explained to them that if it were my dictator, I would first get the consensus of the nation before I proceeded. I would then find the men and opportunity to capture the dictator to put on trial later. Then I would announce my victory on public radio, and become president or at least a benevolent dictator for some time until elections could be held. It was my time to fly, to return to the bush country, to leave the soldiers with their thoughts.

"What made America great?" they had asked. I had answered briefly, being incapable of any profound remark on the workings of destiny overall. God works in the affairs of men, but men clearly choose over them forms of government, there being many.

If God Himself had ordained each specific form of government, then He must be confused, since there are so may evil ones incongruent with His good character. He must not know which form works the best, since there are so many forms. And if Deity designed and put in place each government--setting up and putting down kings, then to vote in America would mean that even the Christian man would be trying to manipulate and damage the ordinance of God through his vote. If all these bush men could not recognize their right to a better government and implore God for His blessings in changing it, then I would have to condemn my forefathers. I would have to recommend that we give our country back to England.

Where would my words fall except on the wind? Their president had been a keystone in an arch where other stones were dependent on him. If the keystone trembles, the arch will carry the tremor along its entire curve; but if the keystone is crushed, the arch will fall, leaving its lesser stones in an inartistic pile, though for a while without design. This president's demise would leave some lives without design, but they could be rebuilt again as lives and stones are, into other more noble patterns.

Later the US ambassador called me into his office and informed me that intelligence revealed that a revolution could likely take place, and all US citizens should leave the country as soon as possible. So I climbed into EL-AHD, a Cessna 180, and headed home to pack. My mind was working overtime as I accelerated and defeated gravity, the weather low, and dark--the clouds totally eclipsing the sun. I was known to some as "Zig Zag Zerbe," because I was astute at hedgehopping. It's only natural to become proficient when flying two feet above the tree tops beneath miles of fog. Knowing my margin of safety was barely wider than my shoulders, enhanced my sense of self preservation. I managed to hang just under black clouds ready to rain and, on some occasions, fly between the limbs of two rain forest trees around 200 feet high. The trouble with this jungle is that "God forgot to erect any landmarks." When there is one, it's a mere hill on the earth's face, and one pimple looks like another.

I had to recognize limitations, while at the same time understand that only a handful of true bush pilots are ever born, much less philosophical ones, who sometimes believed the native saying: "A wise man is not more than a woman, unless he is also brave." I must find out just how brave all those white folks are that I must fly to safety. The ambassador's warning must go out, and so it did.

What would be our plan in case of civil war? Who should go out first? Which mission station would see rebel activity first? Which runway would be in danger first? If the airplane were seized, would not most of the missionaries be at the rebels' mercy? Absolutely! How could I, peering down from the Cessna's window, be able to tell if it were safe to land? Perhaps a red rag on the roof would mean "Don't land!" A white rag--"Land with caution; the rebels are close, but not here yet." Or a green rag would mean "All is clear; land and get us out."

A hard hypothetical scenario coursed through my mind. "If you are surprised by rebels, five drunken soldiers are in your house. You have not had time to change the green rag to red, and the pilot will be landing in around two hours. Should he land under these circumstances, he and the plane will be captured and all the other missionaries would be placed in serious jeopardy.

You have a shotgun with five rounds for five drunken soldiers who have already robbed you, eaten your food and are about to rape your women, before they cut all your throats. Will you take the shotgun and kill five rebels, so that the plane, pilot, you and others can be borne to safety?

"A wise man is not more than a woman, unless he is also brave." A person can't be brave if he has always lived in security and only had wonderful things happen to him. Big government is like junior high. School status depends upon the ability to persecute others.

Since all the decisions we make in life have some philosophical or religious background to them, here is the question I asked my fellow missionaries: "Would you shoot and kill rebels to protect the plane?

Some missionaries said, "I don't know for sure."

Another said, "God called me to these people. If I ever killed one, I would be ruined in several ways. I might get caught and executed later in this foreign country!"

"Remember, your wife and daughter are about to be raped and killed!" I reminded him.

"Oh, that's a hard question!" Another missionary replies.

"He that is double minded is unstable in all his ways," came to my mind.

Others said that they wouldn't hesitate. The rebels would be dead, and their women safe.

I soon realized that a common enemy does not a true friendship make. People are pretty much alike. It is only that our differences are more susceptible to definition than our similarities.

All this and I wonder why I am here. Why am I sitting here wishing this plane had the range to reach Montana and the farm? It could be because my soul is part of Africa, part of a providential plan. Still, I think as I turn the starter, and the propeller beats the air, that the African here is incorrigible on the whole in their politics. I hope for something new, something better for them. A life has to move or it stagnates; even this life.

It is no good telling myself that one day I will wish I had never made the change; it is of no profit anticipating regrets. Every tomorrow ought not to resemble totally every yesterday, or I might as well be in prison. Africa has always claimed the right to be Africa; the white man may enter, but not impose his will. Whatever is right for Africa, Africans alone will determine. It was Abraham Lincoln who said, "Any people any where, being inclined and having the power, have the right to rise up and shake off the existing government and form a new one. This is a most valuable and sacred right, a right which we hope and believe is to liberate the world."

So Liberia, West Africa, had her civil war, destructive and bloody, akin to many of the white man's including the one between America's North and South. I took the ambassador's advice and planned to leave for Montana and eventually Alaska, going from the frying pan into the freezer, never looking back, praying that Liberia would seek the face of God and find peace.

Some white people and missionaries would stay, ignoring the advice to leave, and would die in hails of bullets. Were they patron saints; martyrs or just plain stupid and bullheaded? Even history may keep this a secret. These tropics will keep this matter in confidence. But memory can be a drug - it can hold you against your strength and your will. Someday, I shall return, to see if all the school I put them through taught them anything.

But leaving Africa was not all that easy. I still had the rubber-stamping, petty officials to deal with. They had no reason and would give none for the exit papers being delayed. This has always caused some to say that "there is no hell like uncertainty, and no greater menace to society than a Liberian with three shelves-worth of authority." (Bureaucrats in the United States are none the better.) Their offices were dingy, the shelves and walls patrolled by cockroaches, dark places swept with odors of poverty. I would have to leave without papers and once again return to the interior.

There, it was announced, our pet elephant had died and negotiations were underway in regards to who would now benefit from its protein. Its mother had been killed and the three week old baby had followed the hunter to our doorstep. Its natural demise was seen by the natives as a godsend, something the stew pot hadn't seen in some time. To see this clearest representation of Africa being hauled off in a wheelbarrow to the stew pot was the direction I was sure Liberia was sure to go. And she did for almost twenty years.

Liberia is never the same to anyone who leaves her and returns again. It seems not to be a land of change, but it is a land of moods, and its moods are numberless. Africa is not fickle, because it has mothered men and races, cradled cities and civilizations, seen them die, and seen new ones come on the scene. Africa can be dispassionate, indifferent, cynical and revengeful, and too many eternally optimistic gold miners and diamond cutters.

Africa may seem to be that ever-promised land, almost achieved; but tomorrow it may be a dark land again, contemptuous and impotent with eager men who have futily scrambled over it since the experiment of Eden. Africa sits among the nations as the silent, brooding sister, a continent courted for centuries by eager empires, rejecting them one by one. It was the missionaries' hearts that I witnessed, whose presence in Liberia since 1936 was designed to change her not by mere human power, but they had to leave a people once again to themselves-- to their own ways of doing things.

I had received my exit papers and had one final job to do; one more gift to give. I was told of a rabies scare in the village. There were many dogs, some which belonged to no one--covered with mange and open sores-- were roaming the streets, frothing at the mouth and biting people everywhere. This had been going on long enough for the incubation period of rabies, and several people had died already.

The average yearly income being between $200 and $400 would not allow anyone in the village to buy the 25-cent 12-gauge shotgun shells to dispatch the dogs at a safe distance. So the villagers through their government representatives came to me for assistance, knowing that I was made of gold and silver and previous things. (All Americans are rich, they believe.) To stop the epidemic, I was asked to kill all the sick dogs in the village.

My weapon of choice was an old, well used Winchester single shot 12 gauge shotgun with a broken firing pin. This weapon had belonged to the chief's son and had killed elephant, cape buffalo, leopard and the like, and was now useless because of the broken firing pin. Because of the old shotgun's history and its previous owner, whom I knew well, I bought the weapon for $10.00 for its historical value. Then I cut the barrel down to 18 inches and removed the butt of the stock. It became a weapon I could hold in one hand and the throttle of a small Honda motorcycle in the other. It was the ultimate drive-by shooter's dream!

The only thing that could have distracted me would have been a population of cats. I feel the creator imposed them upon us to remind us of the curse--something akin to the mosquito. At least the dog would die and probably thank me, while the cat being totally lacking in any form of gratefulness in this life would surely scratch my eyes out in the next. Besides, even the most self respecting cat, however valued, would not be worth the 25 cent shotgun shell.

It must have been quite a scene: the motorcycle roaring after the dogs, the shotgun belching in the streets and alleys, and rabid dogs giving their sick lives for the cause of humanity. Some folks ran to shield or to hide their dogs, while others strongly encouraged owners to bring their sick friends out for execution. When the barrel was hot and my wrist sore, I myself had to leave to recuperate.

Dogs continued to manifest signs of rabies after the long incubation period, and the biting continued.

The parents of one bitten lad could not understand the process of incubation. "See his cut is healing," they said. To fly a child to the hospital for vaccine was costly, especially when it seemed he was healing well. Weeks later, the parents brought their sick boy to the mission station for me to fly to the hospital. They could see then that he was critically ill. I flew the lad, but he came too late and died of rabies the next day.

Then the soldiers were called in. They went house to house and killed all the remaining dogs. Because of the public outcry against their tactics, they took all the dead dogs in a loaded truck and threw them in the public water supply. The people would have to find water elsewhere until it could be cleaned out. Several of the sick dogs that fell to my drive by shooting, went to an old man who carried them off to be smoked and cooked for later fine dining experiences.

The experience of "going to the dogs" greatly pained me, but not so much as knowing I was soon to leave Liberia, possibly with no opportunity for parole, having been a willing prisoner of these people for some seventeen years.

Upon arriving at the capitol, Monrovia, with ocean-going freighter tickets in my pocket for New York, I was at once confronted by a black man who was on Main Street speaking to a crowd, expounding in a loud voice the virtues of communism to passersby who had never heard of the system. As I passed by he pointed me out as a white man, the cause of all capitalistic greed in the world. As I was pictured as a hater of black people, this graduate of ignorance from Cornell University in the USA was surprised when I joined him on his pedestal of prominence. He was so taken aback, that he was speechless while I told of all the evils of communism in every country it had touched. I asked the people if they knew that people from communist countries worldwide were seeking residence in the USA. The man left his perch in disgrace, fortunate to not have felt the flaming tire around the neck experience.

But let me not leave Africa's shores without protection from snakes offered by a sidewalk huckster. I could easily be persuaded by this snake charmer that I needed to purchase his copper ring as an insurance policy against snake bite. As is common policy among these people, I proceeded to "talk him down," from 25 cents to a dime, heading toward a nickel, when he informed me in his most persuasive voice, that a cheaper ring would lessen the insurance policy--that snakes would more aptly find me. So I paid him his 25 cents and then picked up a very dangerous nine-foot long King Cobra, which he had handled for hours. As I sauntered away leaving him in utter disbelief, the only thing that brought him back to reality was a throng of people demanding 25-cent copper rings! Having performed this "snake oil" magic, I figured I'd better board the ship soon before someone discovered that copper rings and snakes both tell lies.

Boarding the ship would not be easy. The shipping agent informed me that the Italian captain was refusing to take Americans to any port. Upon inquiry, I found out that his quarrel was with an American woman on his last voyage who, had insisted on sunbathing in the nude, thus taking ordinary sailors and painters to the brink of insanity. Not taking the shipping agent's word for this, I proceeded up the gang plank and wandered this quarter-mile-long ship till I found the captain on the bridge. Somewhat taken back by my intrusion and explanations that none of my tribe would be in the nude and that my time to leave Liberia had come, he graciously gave us the suite reserved for the owner, the most comfortable quarters on the ship. At once, we made friends, speaking often of world history of which he was a master scholar. We ate wonderful four-course meals at each sitting with him for the eleven days of the crossing.

Of course, revolution soon engulfed Liberia. The president, although deserving death for all the people he had inhumanely killed, was not even given a trial before he was slaughtered, as was his wife and eventually thousands of other Liberians as well. It would appear that all the civic lessons I taught over the table and Coca Cola at the airport had failed. Power corrupts and absolute power corrupts absolutely.

Samuel Doe was one of my listeners in those days, but the concept of the civil and spiritual being a cohesive power necessary to fuel a government to success seemed to bypass his presidency. All the alien people--Lebanese shopkeepers, relief agencies, peace corps and missionaries fled, leaving a vacuum of wandering tribes, all wishing for power. All the airplanes were eventually damaged beyond repair, perhaps melted to make aluminum pots. Flight after all is but a momentary escape from the eternal custody of the earth.

I sat on the deck and smelled the odors of the tug guiding our freighter to open sea and drank a hot tea to Africa, because I knew Liberia was gone. I hoped to see it again, but seeing it could not be living it; not in the same way. I may remember some of the paths and wander over them, and remind myself that while I remember this mountain or valley, they no longer remember me.

The sky has stars, the sea nothing except a few islands, like the trackless jungle. Create a quarter-mile long ship and put her in the mist of the sea, and you have achieved nothing. You can't build anything big enough to make any difference in the ocean. Likewise, Liberia, West Africa, is too small in the sea of nations to make a ripple that anyone would notice. Sooner or later, like a hyena running in defeat from a kill, his tail tucked between his legs in submission, I must leave these black friends to their own devices.

Sailing on this slow freighter reminded me of our parrot named Fifty when he was going through the indignity of having his wings clipped. At least we had left these people with something spiritually substantial, the belief that the God of heaven is the one and only God in the universe at whose feet all should confess and worship as the one "good" God of the universe. To try and appease a false god instead of pleasing the one and only true God is an effort in futility. To be sure, this concept comes easier to the appeaser than to the person who only seeks to please himself.

DIESEL GENERATORS THAT FLY – 1979

I must leave behind also the beloved, reliable Cessna 180, now sitting there with too many stories to tell. The green tipped propeller and the vines still clinging to the landing gear intrigued all passersby. "What happened there?" they would ask, and I would reply with this story.

A diesel generator had to be flown to the interior, into an 800-foot grass airstrip plagued by grazing cows, goats, termite hills and people. Since I had already experienced almost running over an old lady here previously with the plane, I had installed a loud automobile horn on the plane, which I now honked with enthusiasm. After buzzing the field to remove all obstacles, I made the landing. Wrong information had come to me as to the generator's destination, I learned, as I was shortly informed that I had delivered the heavy generator to the wrong station. Take it to another destination? My Cessna 180 could do a lot of things, but not this! I could not take off from such a short runway with this heavy load! I was, as they say in America, "ticked!"

I had the natives cut short the grass on the strip to reduce rolling friction. Then I pushed the tail of the plane all the way back into the jungle, with the wheels on the edge of the grass strip. I would have to take off and then climb over some 150-foot tall trees which the natives refused to cut down because they believed that spirits lived in the trees. The thought passed quickly. No time to dwell on it. Surely, just as surely as Adam had lived, "religion" as opposed to "pure religion" had once again prevailed and would now promote a dangerous situation. Sacred cows! Sacred trees! Why not hold common sense sacred?

I tried to fortify my courage with a cup of strong black coffee, but it only made me sweat more. I was about to prove that what would turn out to be only an incident, would also prove that

Africa is capable of a sardonic side. It would allow me this one attempt at cheating fate, but at the same time allowing no person or thing to escape its baptism.

I liked life too much to be patient with death. I would once again go in the direction of my fears. Those fears right now were personified in those looming trees whose branches, like grasping tentacles, would reach out and trap me like a bird in a net. My other concern was the 1500-pound generator behind me, covered in a coating of grease, waiting to come alive with inertia, waiting to form my body around the plane's engine should a tree stop me suddenly.

I sipped my coffee, stared into the cup as if it were a crystal ball, a fortune teller about to explain my fate on this take off. On many take offs, I would have the option of letting the plane try its best for the first half of the runway and could then change plans, apply the brakes upon cutting the power and stop in time to unload some of the load. But this time, any hard braking would turn that greasy object behind me into a deadly missile. Once throttled up and brakes released, it was do or die.

There is a technique among real bush pilots, as opposed to those who merely wear a belt buckle to proclaim their accomplishments, that's known as "milking the bird." Unlike getting all the milk from a milk cow, the reference here was for the pilot to get all he could out of his set of wings. The equator lies close to this part of the world. The belly of the earth here is as hot as live ash under my feet. There are fewer molecules of air for the propeller to grab, meaning less lift for the wings. The flaps are the aircrafts teats, and I must learn to milk them.

Black bodies gathered to watch. Birds left the sky unmarked, and there were no noble aspirants to fly this trip for me. I was alone and alone to my thoughts. Had I timed the magnetos perfectly last time around? I had to treat her kindly, nurse her engine along.

"Why do I fly?" I could do other things--work in an office, be a farmer, factory worker, or just work on planes. But I did both. I could give up flying tomorrow. I could, you know. I could walk away from this plane and never fly again, never put my feet on the rudder pedals again! I could forget about weather, spending the night on a river gravel bar waiting out a storm, and passengers who got airsick! I could forget all this and go off somewhere away from Africa and never look at an airport again! I might be a very happy man, so why don't I?"

An answer lay behind me, a greasy heavy piece of steel, designed to bring light and joy to some missionary in dark Africa; and knowing that only I, among all other pilots, knew this ship and this airstrip, with all its quirks. Only I could deliver. I remembered from the farm that a tractor runs better at night, the cooler air providing more horsepower. So I would wait in silence for a while, hoping for the slim margin I needed to clear those tall trees.

There are all kinds of silences and each of them means a different thing. There is a silence that is found in the morning in the forest, which is not the same silence found in a sleeping city. The silence before and after a rain storm are not the same. There is a silence of emptiness, the silence of fear, and the silence of doubt. There is a certain silence that now managed to emanate from this lifeless object with wings.

This kind of silence can speak, and she was trying to tell me something. But even with shadows now flooding the earth like slow moving water and the brush whispering under the half spent breath of the wind, there was no feeling of gloom and doom. The silence that was part of the craft at my side was, I thought, filled with malice--a silence holding the spirit of wanton mischief, like the quiet smile of a vain woman, happy over a petty triumph.

There is little twilight in equatorial Africa. Night comes quickly on the heels of day in humorless silence. Sounds of all the living things by day were quickly diminishing, soon to be replaced by the sounds of night. I would need to leave in this short interlude, as I watch small shadows creep from a nearby termite hill and saw birds in flocks homeward bound to who knows where. I began to consider my own home, a hot bath, the gates swinging open to welcome me, the glass of ice tea in my wife's hand.

Hope always persists beyond reason, so I took the seat, put on the seat belt, said a prayer asking for keen senses and a good "milking hand." Should I do this takeoff? I suppose the answer again is in the outcome. If my timing, experience, and hunch proved good, then I would be held as capable and inspired. If the outcome proved bad, I would be judged guilty of yielding to thoughtless impulse, hope persisting over reason.

With one turn of the engine, my craft yielded her doubting silence to a more promising song of "I think I can do it." She's warm now; her oil is circulating in all her veins as she trembles in place. One glance now to make sure all goats, cows, chickens and people are off the airstrip. One more look at those trees, fuel selector switch on both, magneto checked, propeller cycled, oil pressure okay, flaps 10 degrees, trim set just right, controls free-- it's show time!

Brakes locked, throttle to the firewall, forward pressure on the controls, release brakes. I had 800 feet to get her airborne and then the trees. After 200 feet the tail is up. At 300 feet, I jerk the flaps to 25 degrees. Slight back pressure on the control wheel now, and she barely clears ground, groping for better air, and settles back to earth. Now milk the flaps back to 10 degrees at around 600 feet, and then jerk them back to 20 degrees. She's more solidly in the air now, but not enough to clear the brush at the end. There are no choices left, no more lift available.

The propeller is now turning green, as it chops the vines that reach out to grab me! For a moment those vines entangled themselves around the landing gear and tail wheel, pulling me lower, slower! And then I was free, except for those "spirit-filled" trees! There was not enough of anything--speed, light, or distance--to clear those trees!

The only choice was to spirit my greasy partner between those trees. Fortunately, these rain forest trees have branches only at their tops, allowing me to put the craft on its side, slipping sideways through the tree trunks like a snake in an obstacle course! The trees thinned for a moment allowing a slight reprieve.

Time to level the wings and build speed before vaulting the next set of trees, which were quickly filling the windshield! Milking the flaps to 20 degrees, the engine roaring in protest, I was able to clear the obstacle, clearing the tops of those African giants by no more than 10 feet!

The stall warning buzzed loudly, singing its song of sure death if immediate action was not taken! That action could only be one thing--lower the nose of the craft and once again dive for the jungle! An old slash and burn farm lay to my right. Ah, a clearing! I dove to freedom, gaining airspeed. A growling farmer's stomach and the patient slashing of an African machete a year earlier, now saved my life.

Later at the correct destination, the landing was a "greaser." My dirty companion behind me, who, I was sure, had a life of its own, would once again generate electricity, but for now must patiently wait, as I remove 10 foot vines from all three wheels protruding from EL-AHD--Echo, Lima, Alpha, Hotel, Delta.

All my flying thereafter seemed mundane, simple. I could be casual to a degree, having received my honorary "doctorate" in jungle flying. Now I would teach lessons to others. This was a lesson on focus. Being angry can sometimes focus you in the right direction or a wrong one. Usually for pilots its the latter. We usually want to focus on the obstacle. To the crop duster, it's the wires. To the Republican, it's the Democrat. To a sister, it's her brother. To the bush pilot, it's the bush--the new termite hill grown overnight in the middle of the runway, the cow or goat.

As surely as you focus on the obstacle, you will somehow manage to collide with it. Just fly 3-5 feet above the crop and you will fly under the wires. Concentrate on your duty to country, not that low Democrat wanting a recount. Job said, "The thing that I greatly feared has come upon me." Peter focused on the water. Peter had gone in the direction of his fears, as we pilots must do daily; he is to be commended. But his focus got at least his knees wet! There is a way a man can master a craft, and a craft can master an element. I learned to focus, watch, to put my trust in other hands than mine.

My father, important enough to be crystallized into muted legend, had left Africa, and now so would I. A life has to move or sometimes it dies, or worse, it stagnates. It's no good telling yourself that one day you will regret making the move; it is no good anticipating regrets. Every tomorrow ought not to have to resemble every yesterday.

Still, I look at my yesterdays from months past and find them as good as a lot of yesterdays that anybody might want, for I too have found flight and no borders. I sit there in the flash of lightning bugs and see them all. The hours that made these memories were good, and so were the moments that made the hours. I have had work, flight, dangers, pleasures, good friends, good parents and a world without walls. These things I still have. They are part of me now, and I shall have them until I leave them, but I shall not leave them if I go to Alaska.

"Go in the direction of your fears," I say to myself. "A wise man is not more than a woman, unless he is also brave," Liberians say. All this and discontent too! Otherwise, why I am I sitting here dreaming of Alaska? Why am I gazing in contemplative thought like a lost soul, about to be expelled from Africa, seeking another place, when all that I love is at my wingtips?

The answer is simple; because I'm curious. I'm incorrigibly a wanderer in search of another land without borders, undiscovered--Alaska. And so I plan for the journey--one to the edge of the sky 10,000 miles away--realizing that this long journey, need not be fearsome, for it is mere short journeys all tied into one.

The maps I now held leading me to Alaska were more modern, more mundane, easily attained. That far coastline, that largest of mountains on the North American continent beckons me, to look in awe at her glaciers, to wonder about all the lives she has swallowed. How many bold and curious have been doomed to its fickle treachery - how many have barely escaped to tell their grandchildren? That brown, then white coloring marked "McKinley" at 20,320 feet which to the casual eye means nothing, though many men may have squandered life to climb it.

THE HARLEY DAVIDSON AND THE KKK--1981

A motorcycle has always been a part of my interest and history. At some point, I plan to ride one from Key West, Florida, to Prudhoe Bay, Alaska. It's hard to find a good deal on a Harley, as they attract respectable riders and a respectable price. But upon returning from Africa, I found a good one, priced right. Upon deciding to go to Alaska, I knew that I would need a 4-Wheel drive pick-up truck more than a Harley. I placed an advertisement in the paper, and received a call immediately. A man would trade his nice $19,000 Ford pick-up truck with camper shell for my Harley. He agreed on a straight trade, which surprised me since the Harley was worth maybe, $3,900.

We decided to make the trade early in the day. I drove my Harley to his yard and we drove for coffee near the license bureau. As we walked into the café, someone he knew hailed him over to a table for a friendly chat.

"Who is your friend?" I asked when he joined me.

"You don't know who that is? He is the Imperial Wizard for North Carolina, the top dog of the Ku Klux Klan," he stated proudly. I drank my coffee in silence, hoping the Klan would paralyze his mind to the point where he would not re-think the terrible deal he was about to make.

After the title swap, I drove my new pickup truck back to his yard, wondering all the way what this pickup had done in its young life. I was about to find out.

Upon entering his yard, three sheriff cars and six sheriffs pulled in around us. They ordered him out of the pickup and handcuffed him and never spoke to me. As they put him in their squad car, I asked the man what he had done–had he sold me a stolen pickup truck?

"Well," he said, head reared back with an arrogant smile. "I'm a Klansman, and I'm proud of it. They done caught me for gun running. I reckon I'll be in crow bar hotel for some time."

The sheriff informed me that I had beaten them to this man and his truck by twenty minutes, and that I had made a trade legally. The truck was mine, but the Harley Davidson was theirs. So they impounded the motorcycle and jailed the law breaker who had been hoping to escape unnoticed on the Harley. My Uncle Paul and Aunt Ferne would drive it fully loaded with our things to Alaska, while I flew the Cessna 185-- N1688R. To this day I wonder how many guns and wooden crosses had been carried by the truck I now possess.

GOING IN THE DIRECTION OF YOUR FEARS -- 1981

No matter how carefully I would undertake to travel the 10,000 miles to Alaska, or how casually I would view it as a trip to the north country, I was aware that it was, in fact, no trip at all, but a major voyage. I would have to plan, navigate, be weather wise. I would have to consider the geography, the handicaps, and the breakdowns in a remote place.

My wife and two small daughters climbed into the plane in Montana, in its northeast corner, joining me for the trip north. I left at a pilot's hour, but not on a pilot's day. Like the old saying, "every dog has his day." Fog had spilled over the plains and the morning found Lustre, Montana, cradled in mist. This town of nine souls (all family), the sunrise and the plane (a 1974 Cessna 185-F) were all isolated from each other by clouds that lay on the earth like sadness come to rest. The clouds clung to us like burial clothes, white and unwanted. A cup of coffee gave them time to consider the sun and to give way some 300 feet from the earth's surface.

I had done this before, I assured myself, as we climbed into the Cessna again and became airborne. I had become used to the flatness of the bleak prairie. Only a few silos to maneuver around, a few cows and buffalo to awaken, and I knew where the wires were. I had been crop dusting with this plane and knew well not to look for the wires, only the poles they were attached to. Poles meant wires, not the other way around.

True harmony and aviation finesse comes gradually to a pilot and his plane. The wing does not always fly true and seems to tug at the hands that guide it, like a child begging for correction. The craft would rather hunt the wing and turn into it, than lay her nose to the horizon far ahead. An airplane has a rebellious quality in its character; she toys with freedoms and hints at liberation, but yields her desires to do so gently, sometimes with only a thought transmitted to the pilot's hand, akin to a fine cutting horse.

It was not long before the prairie rose to meet the blanket of cloud, so I circled a farmhouse with intentions to land on the gravel road there, to taxi up and beg another coffee and wait for the sun. Any farmer in his lonely prairie existence would enjoy an out of place Cessna by his barn. I set up to land on the road beside his planted trees, designed to protect him from the persistent Northwest wind. And then the wire was in the windshield!

Crop dusting experience told me there was no time to duck under it, as it would have caught and ripped off my vertical stabilizer. No time to go over it, as it would have caught my wheels and landing gear, flipping me on my back. Fortunately for me, instinct prevailed as I fire-walled the throttle, bringing the engine roaring to life as I headed straight for the wire with the propeller!

I managed to hit that wire dead-center on the nose spinner, cutting the cable in two. It left a black mark there, a crack in the windshield and a dent on the front leading edge of both wings, barely perceptible as a testimony to me that sometimes wires are not where they are supposed to be. The pole that always has a wire attached was in his tree line, the only such arrangement I have ever witnessed on the prairie.

We taxied up to the farmhouse, the farmer happy to see us and informed us the power had just gone down: "that crazy REA working on the lines again!" I finally worked up the courage to point out the real culprit! The fog soon lifted, the farmer stopping traffic on the road for our take off. We invited him north, but I was convinced that he rarely ventured north of the pole hidden in his windbreak. He would call the REA; they would inspect his pole. The farmer would relive and retell his story to dozens who would be forced to listen, while I eventually paid $45 for the REA to splice the wire. It was a good experience, because I had survived it.

But now proceeding to the Canadian border, the prairie winds picked up to a speed uncomfortable for the Cessna 185. Tumbleweeds were making new homes in the fences, while cattle had their tails into the gale. We approached the border with a 25 degree correction, crabbing into the wind. She was like a piece of trash caught in a hurricane, and I experienced that sense of futility when natural forces of this planet reassert their sovereignty over puny man.

The plane was flying at an altitude of a hundred feet, and the prairie seemed to slip away faster than it was. The compass was swinging wildly, spurred on by turbulence. We were mechanical tumbleweed, nature letting me know that we were mere humans and subjects. And to think we have presumed this thing called flight in the last 100 years! It's as though the heavens were not used to this extravagance of man yet, and they were protesting.

We fly, but we have not really conquered gravity or the heavens. Nature continues to preside in all her dignity--permitting us only to study the hurricane, to try to predict, to flee from freezing rain. It is when one of her students presumes to know her secrets, when she has granted only tolerance, that her big stick smacks knuckles and reminds who is really calling the shots. A pilot must learn to respect "Mother Nature" as she is reverently, yet mostly nonchalantly called.

I used to work with a dear friend who worked with the off-scouring of humanity in Texas. He would help unwed mothers and young men in trouble with the law to find meaning in life through Christ in the pages of Scripture. He had a pilot's license, which is merely a license to learn, to study Nature's quirks, to respect her wishes. By nature, a sailor will sail and by his nature, a pilot will fly. As long as his legs can move the rudders and his hand grasp the stick, and as long as the sky was there, he should go on flying. There is nothing extraordinary in this at all. My friend had learned an art, but not well. He had made many foolish mistakes, as articles publicized. But to fly into a thunderstorm was fatal. Flying to him was a tool, but utter respect for the vocation itself evaded him. When a thunderstorm removes the wings and tail from an airplane, the result is predictable.

From all the lessons learned, I, myself, was learning the art of flying. My hands had been taught to search out the controls of a plane, to purchase another hour at the controls. I was at ease with the controls as a gunsmith is building a rifle or an ivory carver making something beautiful. But the pilot must learn to interpret his immediate universe and make valid decisions on what he learns. It was time to leave the wind and 100 foot ceilings and wait for Mother Nature to quit acting like a mother-in-law!

The Canadian customs agent never came out of his hut. The wind was too damp and cold for him to bother us with foolish questions around the plane, so he asked them in his hut: "Where are you going? Do you have any plants or fruits? Any weapons or handguns? How long will you be in Canada?" All his questions could have been answered untruthfully, and he would not have known the difference. All Canada would have been doomed, I suppose. The weather was so bad that I spent the night in a cheap motel, flagged by what I supposed to be a frozen cockroach on the bed. I was too tired to worry. I knew the weather would get better, the farther North I traveled.

My next stop was on the Alaska-Canada Highway at Muncho Lake. I flew low, checked the highway for pot holes, stop signs and other obstacles that could clip my wings--moose, cattle, dogs and, of course, cars and trucks. The drawing card here was a good cup of coffee and a famous cinnamon roll. By definition, a good cup of coffee is one that did not appear to be just river water, but indeed black enough so as not to be able to see the bottom of the cup. No dark brown cups allowed; they are only used by proprietors to camouflage the weakness of their brew.

The tourists there were stunned to see a plane pull into the parking lot at the restaurant. They all wanted to ask questions. I had one for them after coffee and the largest cinnamon roll I had ever seen. "Would you block the road so I can take off?" They still probably relate this story to anyone who will listen.

I then continued to Watson Lake, where some years later, tragedy struck on the same route. That time, when flying south, I had chanced to meet a pilot at Northway, Alaska. It is strange how soon two people going the same way, flying the same type aircraft, at the same speed, can find friendship. There is something about flying in the vast arctic in formation. You tell yourself you are not alone, that if your engine should fail, you would have some immediate attention. We decided to fly together. But it wasn't for long. Never had a friendship been struck so surely and ended so quickly.

We soon were encompassed on all sides by an arctic snow storm. We had discovered again that flight was but a momentary escape from the eternal custody of the earth. I had learned from the African rainy season the art of hedge hopping. Out of necessity you learn to be careful at what you do, when you are two feet above the tree tops beneath 500 miles of fog, or experiencing a white-out. You feel trapped, like trying to take a nap in a closed coffin. You can't allow for any altitude, or you will be absorbed in cloud, as are the mountains all around you. The trouble is God had forgotten to erect any signposts for us. There are no water towers or freeway signs to define our location for 1500 miles.

Suddenly, there was a light to the right. It was an opening to what appeared to be a valley, a break in the storm. The pressure was great in this poor visibility to perform the turns required to follow this winding highway. My new friend, weary of the struggle, bolted to the clearing to the passage promising clearer passage.

I made an instant decision to stay with the highway, knowing I could land if necessary. I was not willing to follow the light into an unknown mountain valley, merely hoping that its end would lead me somewhat closer to my destination. It was not until I landed in Fort Nelson that I heard the news and saw the search and rescue warming their planes. An emergency locator beacon

(ELT) had gone off in that hopeful valley. My friend had not closed his flight plan, and never would.

I left in a hurry, not willing to dwell on the thought of my new friend's flying into that valley. What awaited him there--a narrowing canyon, climbing beyond the ability of his machine into the clouds of snow?

I knew too little of Liberia, West Africa, and all her neighbors to leave the continent; and what little I knew, I loved too much to leave easily. There are many who have said they knew all about a continent, but I knew better.

Now my wings were carrying me to another place--Alaska, "the Great Land," a land of which much is yet unknown. It is a land full of dreamers, but it has barely been dreamed. My present trail in the sky ran northwest; at night it ran straight to the Northern Lights.

I learned that to leave a place where I had roots--where all my yesterdays and experiences ran deep—to leave it fast, with no looking back, else I might turn into a pillar of salt. I had to learn never to think that an hour I could remember was a better hour, because it was dead and gone to fond memory. I learned to go in the direction of my fears. Past years were safe years, all the hurdles conquered, while the future lives, formidable from a distance. It seemed to me that I was on a journey to the edge of the sky.

I arrived to take a man's place, a place he had left vacant. As a missionary pilot, Don Richter had to wrestle with an especially rotten weather system. To go through Lake Clark Pass is difficult at best, its glaciers creating their own weather. A cloud cover, initially unassuming, waited till Don and his passenger were well into the pass to spring the trap. The snow came suddenly, filling in behind them, blocking a return and saturating all forward vision with billions of snowflakes. The valley narrowed, and going anywhere was impossible, but they had to go somewhere in the white out. They circled a small green tree for some time, lost it as a reference point and crashed into a glacier, which threw them through the windshield onto the cold ice. When their plane failed to arrive on the flight plan's schedule, a search plane found them alive, but seriously injured. The glacier would eventually swallow the plane, Mother Nature's way of taking her medicine.

Why do bad things happen to good people? This question can only be answered by sovereign Providence, to be understood in the future. I am surely incapable of developing wisdom on the working of Destiny--to know how to work to a conclusion, or to know to what degree I can help create my own destiny as a free will agent. Several workings of Destiny, of Providence, came to mind as I moved to Fairbanks, Alaska.

I had sold a Ford van to a man in Winston-Salem, North Carolina, prior to leaving for Africa. Four years had elapsed since that event with a man I did not know, but Providence had an eye on this business transaction. Four years later after leaving Africa on an Italian iron ore ship, we landed on the USA Eastern seaboard. It had been eleven days of pure rest. We were the only passengers on this ship, eating all our meals with the captain and chief engineer.

As a pilot, I talked the language of the captain; as a mechanic, I talked the language of the chief engineer. Consequently, I had the run of the ship from the pilot house to the engine room. I decided that flying was far superior to the shipping lanes. As a pilot, I could watch the scenery change. I had time to reflect, to learn, to enjoy. The ship's captain simply had too much time on his hands to do these things.

I believe the ocean looks quite the same day after day to a quarter mile long ship. And I think there are no exceptions to the rule that familiarity breeds contempt. There are no boring moments in most missionaries' lives. Their moments are governed by sovereignty, by providence.

When we entered the river harbor, the freighter's engines had to be switched from a coarse fuel for steady power to a more refined fuel for maneuvering in tight quarters. A large pillar supporting a four lane highway bridge loomed just ahead as the ship's engine just quit to a deafening silence. If the engine could not be restarted, we would hit the pillar, most likely collapsing the bridge upon us. I've never seen men scramble to their posts with such intensity.

Orders were barked, hands and legs flew in all directions, and the engine coughed to life just in time. These men had not been negligent, so was it "Murphy's Law" or Providence? It is easier, requiring less faith, and more satisfying to believe that Providence always rules and is always trying to teach.

And so it was, when we left the ship and went back to Winston-Salem, where I had sold the van four years earlier, the first used car that caught my eye was a 1970 '98' Oldsmobile 4-door Luxury Sedan, advertised as a "cream puff," one owner, with 25,000 original miles on this 10-year-old "lead sled." I called and took directions to an apartment complex in a city of around 300,000 people. The man who answered the door was the stranger who four years earlier had purchased my van! I purchased the car for $850 and drove it 350,000 miles over the next twenty years. It still resides in my back yard, a reminder of a stranger I met and bought and sold with, and the incalculable odds of it ever happening just that way without "the hand of Providence" stepping in.

It was in Fairbanks, Alaska, where we settled and dreamed and built. It had a literary and almost unattainable quality, but we had arrived! What else but good and dreams could happen here in this elevated scrap of earth? I was about to find out.

A place to live, to share, to call home is what I needed; so I went to see about some logs to build a house I was assured by a bureaucrat in charge of forestry that, indeed, I could cut down house logs on state land, but he couldn't tell me where they were. His motives and refusal to help was a mystery to me. Perhaps he was trying to screen out folks who would waste the logs, not having the determination to complete their building.

I told him that since he had the job of head of forestry, I expected him to know all the trees by name--at least know where the house logs were. He refused to help until I asked him would he like to hear his name on "Problem Corner," a radio call-in show with the mayor, designed to publicly air citizens' problems.

His question to me was expected. "Are you really serious about building a log house?" he asked. I said that I thought I had made that clear, but there was an alternative. "What's that," he asked. "Well," I said, "my family could move in with your family, and we could live happily ever after!" He explained that there were indeed some house logs nearby with a new road right to them!

So I found and cut down those trees—fifty-seven of them, each one a hundred feet tall. One gave me a problem: it became caught in another tree, twisted, broke off and spit out at me, pinning my leg in the deep snow. The tree had slammed down against another log, saving my leg from being crushed, but there I was lying in the snow at ten degrees below zero! I was alone and would die if I stayed here. No one knew where I was working.

My chain saw had gone spinning through the air, but was nearby still running. Could I reach it? It was barely within reach. Now to cut the log, but wait! If I cut the log wrongly, the log would roll on me.

I wielded the saw to the left and again to the right on the tree. I was free! It had almost broken my leg. I gingerly stood on my bruised leg. "It could have killed me!" I thought. Providence was not through with me yet!

A man I had gone to school with years earlier read in my recent newsletter that I was building and contacted me and asked, "Do you need help?" So Jim Hodges brought up a team of men called "Hard Hats for Christ," one of them an experienced log builder. Peeling the bark off the trees by hand was the hardest part, as it was done all by hand with a draw knife. The mosquitoes took their share of blood each day and tortured the progress of our dream.

Many Americans dream of a log house to call their own, as did we, but few can imagine the labor involved. It seems that each man has his vanity or, perhaps, a better observation would be to say each man has some dream. Where does a dream and vanity blend? Can a Christian man have a dream, and it not always turn towards vanity?

The African bushman's dream is to walk a straight path on naked feet. If he can find one shoe to wear, he is on his way to his dream of wearing two, and the vanity in his heart strides with him. It is, perhaps, when we must have an audience for our dreams that our dreams become vanity, not recognized by duty.

Our dream for a log house became a solemn dream, and, in time, through the help of the Hard Hats, we made the dream live. People stop by and marvel at the dream accomplished and wonder why their dream of a log house never materialized. "I've always dreamed of a log house" they say, almost all of them.

In any project, however, any greatness will come to light, not in one flamboyant hour, but in a long ledger of a man's daily work. You have to just start and continue until the God of heaven puts handcuffs on you and changes the direction of your dream-- not the essence of it, but only its direction. Soon, if you start, all the pieces fit together, and the whole is yours.

Thus, I prevailed with the forestry man. He knew I would be unwelcome, unsettled company if my family moved in with his. He knew that I was a man who could smell injustice however softly it walks, and that he, a mere man, would not foil my dream of a log house. So I built this earthly structure, being reminded by Phil Smith, the Hard Hat log builder friend, that there is a "fine line between rustic and sloppy."

I built it near Gold Hill Road, the name a reminder at least of what drew so many to this country. It was a country lavished with streams, mountains, gold in the streams, bear and moose in the yard, where a garden could not survive because of the moose. A country where in the winter the sky and the earth meet like strangers, and the touch of the sun is as dispassionate as a kiss from your sister.

The logs went up, one round a day, the sun never setting on our efforts. When it was completed, it was so tight that a 55-gallon drum, converted into a wood stove and thirteen cord of wood kept us warm on even the coldest of days, one of which was -83 degrees F below zero.

GOING IN THE DIRECTION OF YOUR FEARS--2

Job, in the Old Testament said, "The thing that I greatly feared has come upon me." The wisest man in the world said in Ecclesiastes 11:4, "He that observeth the wind shall not sow; and he that regardeth the clouds shall not reap."

Job expresses a sort of death wish, a transparent fatalism. Solomon makes the point that if you wait for everything to be just right in life before venture, then you will do nothing significant. There is a line where a venture is viewed from afar, all the drawbacks weighed, and a person stays safely on the cautious side of the line, but the adventure begins when he says there is something to gain on the other side of the line. He analyzes briefly the wind and the clouds and then goes forward. In life there are those who go along with all that is happening; then those that aren't aware that anything is happening, and those that make things happen. I want to walk and fly with a man who can turn a venture into an adventure without the death wish. But to never venture with God's help is not really living at all.

THE SHOOTING IN BIRCH CREEK - DEC. 1983

The little Athabascan Indian village of Birch Creek lay northward, a stone's throw from the Arctic Circle, just north of the White Mountains and south of Fort Yukon on the Yukon River. Here lies a small sanctuary of around fifty Indians lost to the world, dwelling among the pines on Birch Creek.

There are no roads, nor neighbors. It is a wild place, and it carries with it the stamp of true wilderness and the freedom of a land still more a possession of nature than of man. The forests are unblemished by axe. When you see Birch Creek, you know then what you have been told--that the world once existed without roads or footprints and that it once existed for a time without adding machines or books or lighted streets and the tyranny of clocks. The tyranny of the clock is a slave master these people have not succumbed to. It was here that a white school teacher lived, determined to give these Indians the education they needed. But this was not her "day in the sun."

A bush pilot in the Arctic is expected to know many things. The main thing is being able to get to his destination. Get there you better, or you ain't no bush pilot. On a fair day, I may choose to fly at eight thousand feet and clear the White Mountains easily, making the flight look easy. Or I could fly with two thousand foot overcast, the clouds full of ice, snaking my way through Beaver Creek Pass. Or I could practice on a good day as though it were a cloud deck--only one hundred feet above the trees; yes, sometimes touching the trees.

So on our good weather days, I would practice for bad weather days, flying below the tree line along the river--my wheels almost in the water, with the cloud deck and trees just above my wings. I could travel like this all day were it not for the river, with its incessant turns; always following the path of least resistance, which tested severely the plane's resistance to these steep turns.

I must turn with one wing tip almost touching the water, with the other ticking the belly of the cloud layer. Turns must be made with 20 degrees of flaps, starting in the turn with low power and adding full power to keep the craft from stalling or descending. To go up in the clouds is to invite sure disaster either with ice or, more surely, an invisible mountain side. On a good day, I could do it, just barely. There comes a time when practice of necessity becomes the real thing.

The schoolteacher had been accidentally shot by her husband in her mid section (while he was playing with an "unloaded gun"--a 44-magnum pistol), and she was dying. In spite of her spirit, her voice had grown thin and uncertain. She was holding herself together by sheer willpower, believing as told that a helicopter was soon to take her to a hospital in Fairbanks. She could finally hear the 'whump, whump, whump' of the helicopter doing its best to beat the air into submission, but only picking up ice. The welcome sound, became a desperate tone as the helicopter and her hopes retreated to deafening silence.

The desperation in the voice at the other end of the line meant I must try it underneath. But this day, "underneath" meant below the tree line level; wheels of my Cessna 185 just above the frozen river; no room to turn around; to change my mind. I would be on an airborne rail, and it meant one way right through the Whites to Birch Creek.

Somehow I managed to fly the low altitude route that I had practiced on good days. I wondered to myself why I had not just played it dumb and safe. No one would have blamed me for saying it couldn't be done—no one except myself.

It was 54 degrees below zero when my wheels touched down! Immediately I jumped out of the cockpit and covered the engine with the thick quilted blanket designed to conserve its heat to restart. From nowhere came a Native Alaskan on a snow machine, offering me a quarter mile ride into the village. Upon arrival, I was informed that the teacher had not made it. I knew that I could be of no further help, except to the living. Her announcement in the paper would include these words, "Due to frozen ground, Mr.____ will be buried in the spring."

After several hours there were holes in the cloud cover, and I could see a few stars. I walked the quarter mile to the plane, only to find the engine and battery too cold to create life from this very dead aircraft. There were no lights, no help, no spare battery, no hope of any start unless I hand-propped the beast.

I locked the brakes on the icy surface of the runway and looked around for some kind of block or a chock for the wheels, but there were none. I could barely stay on my feet on the ice, as I walked to the front of the plane, reached up to the propeller and pulled it through. The engine fired and maintained a steady RPM OF 1100.

This was just enough thrust to slowly pull the craft forward, sliding her locked tires on the ice toward myself and the ten foot snow bank, where the snow had been pushed from the runway week after week. There was only enough time to step aside from the menacing propeller and to watch helplessly as the craft made its way to the hard-as-ice packed snow bank! There was just enough damage to the propeller to make it useless; the tips curled back in a snarl. I was done. The 54 degrees below zero would have its way now with the plane.

My trek to the village was hurried. How long would I have to stay with these people? They knew I had really tried to help them, but they could do nothing in return except give me a room to stay in and some smoked salmon. It would be tomorrow at least, but perhaps days or a week, before I could have a spare propeller flown in. Everything would be cold soaked. I picked up the phone to call home. I needed a miracle, because no one keeps spare propellers around.

The phone rang, and my wife Jane answered. I told her I needed a two-bladed 84" used, loaner prop for a 1974 Cessna 185F, 300 horse power and the tools to change it. This was more than a daunting order for a lady who is more accustomed to taking care of her family through the use of an egg beater and pancake turner. I had no clue as to tell her where to start looking for this prop. Furthermore, it was after 5 PM and the shops were closing for the day. Jane called several numbers and learned that the shop could order a prop and have it shipped next day air for a huge price beyond which we could pay.

While she was on the phone there was a knock on the door, and the kids let in a nicely dressed stranger. Many guys in Alaska wear rugged outdoor garb, but this man had on a really fine, expensive looking suit. Oh, yes, it was the man who had come to look at some old furniture that we had listed in the paper for sale. He had seen our ad and had made an appointment to come by earlier in the afternoon, but a crisis with one of the children had necessitated an emergency trip to the doctor at that time.

He stood just inside the door thawing out, overhearing Jane's phone conversation, while the children jumped and jabbered around him in delight --a visitor to break the boredom of their "cabin fever"—which overtakes us all in extremely cold dark weather. Jane showed him the furniture for sale, but it was not to his liking. As she walked him back to the door, she had an inexplicably strange sense of loss that he was leaving. She pointed to a picture on the entry way wall of the C-185, saying "That's my husband's plane."

"I am a pilot, too," he replied.

"My husband is stranded in the bush with a bent prop," she continued. "I'm trying to locate a prop to get him home, but there is none in town." It was as if a drill sergeant had commanded, "'ten-shun!" The stranger stood even taller and went from a genial visitor to "all business on alert"!

"Now I know why I was supposed to come by here! I know someone who has a prop on the wall in his basement." After making a phone call, the stranger had located a prop that we could use for a few days. The only fee was to follow the "law of the frontier" to pass on the favor when we found someone else in trouble.

"My husband will want to thank you himself when he gets back to Fairbanks. What is your name and how he can contact you?" Jane asked.

"I'm Doyle Ruff," he said, "the new manager of the Fairbanks International Airport."

The next day, a pilot friend flew the prop out to Beaver Creek in his small plane and quickly returned to Fairbanks in the short Alaskan daylight. Changing a propeller in the dark with bare fingers was a tedious chore. A Coleman lantern did double duty every thirty seconds as it warmed my hands and gave light.

When I finally reached my cozy log home, we recounted the amazing string of events. Two weeks earlier, Jane had mailed in the ad to the newspaper to get the best price. Then I banged the prop, forcing me to stay in the village with grieving people who needed my presence. Mr. Ruff made an appointment for 2 PM to see the furniture, but that was before the prop was bent. Our girl had a medical situation which caused Ruff to miss us, but he felt that he should come back and did so on the way to the airport Christmas party, at which he was to be the guest of honor (thus, the fine clothes). Jane felt that strange sense of loss, and Mr. Ruff felt a sense that he should come by again. We learned later that Doyle Ruff had previously been the base commander of Eielson

AFB and had done more than a little flying of military planes. The timing all lined up for the best for all involved.

There was one more act of providential timing, we discovered, when we received our statement of funds from the mission home office. We had received a large donation, totally unsolicited, that would cover the price of a new prop—but it had been sent to the home office a week before the prop was even bent! I knew that I had a Friend in "high places," "whose eye is on the sparrow, and I know He watches me."

THE MANLEY MASSACRE -- SPRING 1984

He came from Chicago, this wild-eyed dreamer. Keeping most thoughts to himself, he shed enough light on his dubious intentions to worry the people of Manley Hot Springs. His idea was to get to the" End of the Road"--as far as his old Chrysler would take him, to get away from humanity, to build a log cabin in no-man's land and to live happily ever after. Such dreams are sometimes the dreams of a madman. At about the same time as his arrival in the village, he ran out of money and ideas.

Now Manley Hot Springs, unsuspecting, is a remote village with, as the name implies, a hot spring, at the end of an "improved" mining trail. It lies in gold country and at the end of an "improved" mining trail. Bears and moose can be found wandering along its dirt roads, and yards full of chained sled dogs reverberate with barks and howls. The little dirt airstrip ends at the lodge and church where I preach.

Only one hundred people live there as an average, but that's because the public at large doesn't know that gold and hot, healing spring water can exist in one place. Manley's residents are gold miners, trappers, fish wheel operators and processors, school teachers, and a retired state trooper who owns a road house. A retired railroad engineer and store owners round out the population, but there are no policemen. These people were independent as any true Alaskan pioneers and quite a few like the study of the Bible.

We had a log church and some very good Bible studies. People came from afar, including Weedz and Liller Burke, a fine couple from 35 miles upriver. Sometimes they made it to services by boat, or snow machine, and sometimes by my plane on skis. This fine village also attracted some riff raff, unsavory characters who the villagers called "end-of-the-roaders." Some would come here with hopeless dreams, imagining a pioneer lifestyle in the wild, away from people and common sense. Who knows what happened in Michael Silka's head?

Spring had arrived, the days were growing longer and longer, and everyone liked to take a turn riding the three-mile journey on four wheelers to the river landing to see if the ice has gone out. In a village with few entertainments, nature provided what has been called "break up." When river ice "breaks up," it audibly grinds, groans, crunches, and cracks. The rushing water could throw huge slabs and chunks of ice one upon another. The river had long been the "highway" of the wilderness and their fishing grounds.

An eager fellow—an "ice inspector"--rode to the river and did not return. The young man from Chicago had shot him and thrown him into the river. The distance of the landing from the village had shielded the noise of the shots. Others would go to the landing and never return. A young family, who had settled in Manley from Minnesota, then went to the landing—dad, pregnant mom, and two year old child—all riding on one ATV together.

Within a few hours, eight people were dead, and soon a state trooper would be shot and killed trying to arrest him. Another trouper would end the massacre by shooting and killing the man resisting arrest. Five of the murdered were people from our church—the whole young Klein family and a fine young Athabascan Indian man—Weedz Burk.

The following excerpts are from Liller Burk's book, *On the River of Grace:*

May 1984-- Being married to a Christian is such a blessing. We would sit and talk about the things of God, talk about some good thing from the Bible or from a show on TV or from life around us. We kept learning from each other. We were growing together. We went through spiritual lows, getting caught up with the world, which would cause strife between us. Yet we always had that common ground, our center in God to bring us back in harmony, back to smiles. Praise God!

The devil really thought he had a victory, taking Weedz out of this life when God allowed it. But he underestimates the mind and power of God. Weedz may be gone from his earthly body, but his death is God's victory. Heaven's gain. The whole incident is going to affect many, many people. Weedz' love for God and for his family is so great. People from all over will be affected by this, because God is in control. God has a plan.

Weedz would go to the dances when we were in town and put up with the cigarette smoke, cussing, and beer, all in hopes of getting in touch with somebody for the Lord. He only wanted to talk about the Lord--quiet spoken, but bold and piercing. He was a vessel for the Lord, an instrument. He'd come home about four in the morning all tired and weary but smiling, so happy that the Lord had used him, that he had witnessed for the Lord and not given over to the flesh, not joining in the dancing or "having one" with someone. All these people had seen how weak he used to be, and they'd been watching the transformation. Everyone loved Weedz. His drinking buddies backed off and didn't know how to relate to the new Weedz. That kind of hurt him. Weedz was strong and determined. He'd come home drained from being in the devil's territory, but he would go back the next time. People had been watching Weedz those past two years. They looked to him for answers.

Sitting here alone now at home, the Lord is really talking to me. I feel closer to God since all this happened. I yearn for God and desire God. I want to live for God. My husband's testimony is something I can look at, something to put conviction in my heart. The edges of what he is suddenly clear, more defined. I am even awestruck. God is laying the truth on my heart, and I am laid bare. I cry out to God in repentance, sorry for all these things He is showing me now. Did I have to lose my husband for a season to come to the condition of an open heart? It is the Lord drawing me. I pray, 0 Lord that You would use me, cleanse me, and mold me! And keep the devil away. My Lord is faithful.

I don't want to be comfortable in this world. How can I be? I pray that the Lord will make me a strong witness, an aggressive Christian, seeking only the Kingdom. Weedz said once that if the Lord needed him to go through the Tribulation Period as a witness, he surely would. Weedz was willing. I want to be willing, even to be persecuted, for God's sake, for Jesus' sake.

Sitting out front last night, the heaviness settled in again. As I felt myself sinking again into grief, the Lord spoke to my heart, and with the words was also that wonderful peace. He made me see that Bill Burk went first (before us), and now it is Weedz' turn, and he is with Jesus and his dad. Soon enough it will be my turn to see Jesus and Weedz. He made me see just how temporary earth is, how transient all our lives are, and Weedz just got to go first. But the Lord is faithful. He shall let me abide under His shadow and shall cover me with His wings while I wait.

The day he left was Thursday, the 17th of May. We had planned to go to Manley on Friday, but on this Thursday, he was outside welding on some nicked up boat props. I was in the house and he came in all hyped up and happy and just Weedz ... He showed me a prop and said, "Look at that!" He had welded and ground and fixed up that prop so it looked really good. Then he said, "Let's go to Manley!" And I said "Today??" It takes me a while to gear up for boat rides. He said "Yes!" and sat down to eat. He was going to go to Manley and see if Dim was there and work on his truck, and maybe ask Dim to finish the job.

Inside me anxiety was creeping up, a real tug of war. Not wanting to go, but wanting to. He ate and went outside to get ready for the trip, and I wandered around the house trying to make a decision. I started to get gear together and then went outside to find Weedz. I went up to him and asked him if he really wanted to know how I felt about going, and he said yes. So, I said I really didn't want to go for the boat ride; I only wanted to be with him. "Do you mind if I don't go?" And he said, "No, I just didn't want you to feel left out." I told him I didn't feel left out, knowing I could go along anytime I wanted to. So the decision was made, but I felt very anxious about it. I had to ask him if he was sure he didn't need my help or want me with him, and he kept telling me it was okay if 1 didn't go.

He came into the house to grab a jacket, and I was following him hanging onto his arm, still asking, "Are you SURE?" (It was out of ordinary that I wasn't going for this first trip of the season, but something inside was tugging me to stay). He laughed and said, "What do you want me to say? That I really want you to go?" I said, "I don't know. I'm just not sure." Then I stopped him just as he was walking out, and said, "Weedz, I love you." And he smilingly said, "I love me too." He picked up the .22 rifle and some shells, and I told him he should wear his coveralls, but he said it was warm behind the windshield. He'd been wearing just at-shirt before. So he was off, expecting to be back by 7:00 p.m. It was 2:30 when he left. At 3:45 I was painting, the red gas cans white. Covering red with white...

MAINCAMP - FRIDAY, MAY 25, 1984

God has been trying to get the attention of both Manley and Nenana. Weedz has prayed for Manley, and when Les Zerbe started to come to Manley, we knew it was answered prayer. We wanted the people of Manley to turn to God. Weedz had a burden for their souls. And Nenana ... Weedz wanted Nenana to be revived and to seek God. He prayed for revival to sweep Nenana. His family and friends are in Nenana, and he sought them for God. And Weedz was willing, so maybe God used him in answer to his own prayers. A spark for revival. Help me, Lord, to keep his testimony alive, to never tire of witnessing with love and truth. pp. 4-7

MANLEY- WEDNESDAY, JUNE 20, 1984
(ACTUALLY THURS. MORNING 4:30 A.M.)

My God is so big. So perfect. Bergman prayed, "Lord, please release the body ..."And the whole family prayed the same. Today the Lord was in control and things happened according to His plan. And I had prayed that Dim and Pats and I would be together and find Weedz together. I had prayed also that the Lord would somehow prepare me. Yesterday the Lord answered that prayer.

Dim had gone up to Nenana for a couple of days. Pats and I were out on the river with the intention of meeting Dim as he headed our way on his way back to Manley. We went upriver a ways. He didn't show up so we drifted a while, heading back downriver. We were below the landing a mile or so when we spotted something in the water, floating and looking definitely out of place. We drew a bit closer and we both knew it was a body. We were very shaky and full of dread. Inside, though I was tired and still in somewhat of a state of shock, I knew that this was serious. Pats spoke and said that we should go get some help. When he said that, something came over me. I really believe it was God's hand and His power reaching out to me and sustaining me in this very scary situation. I stood up in the boat and said, "No! We have to do this ourselves. If we leave it, we may lose track of it." I told him to nose the boat over so I could reach it and tie it off and we could bring it over to the bank of the river and then go get help. He looked as white as a sheet, but he went ahead and eased the boat over.

As we drew nearer I could see clearer that it was indeed a body floating face down. It had dark hair up at one end. It was very bloated and very awful and because of the black hair, I knew it could be Weedz. We both knew it. It was a painful realization. I felt very fragile, yet at the same time I knew that there was indeed strength and purpose coursing through me.

And great love that was overcoming all human weakness. This could be our Weedz.

We drew along side and as I reached out to it I hesitated for a second as I saw my hand about to touch it, and in that brief second we both saw it was a bear! A dead, bloated bear that looked so human!--hairless except for some black hair at one end. We both sharply and groaned in relief and felt our legs almost give way. In our shock we even laughed. We both knew that we could handle Weedz. We knew more of what to expect. Then Pats said something very powerful: "Liller, the Lord is preparing us."

Dim arrived later in the evening and then today several of us went down to the Tanana River with the intention of taking the whole day and traveling 60 or more miles to Squaw Crossing, searching as we went. We brought food and three boats and walkie-talkie radios. We stopped along the way at drift piles and checked through them. I went through all the motions as did everyone else, getting a job done. It was an emotionally tough job, but I think we were in shock and on auto pilot. I was anyway. Mostly forgetting what we were really doing.

It was a beautiful day, sunny and warm. I was in the race boat with Pats. Dim and Joy were in their boat with Norman, Milo and Robert, and Barry had his boat. We had been traveling all day and it was evening when we found ourselves near Squaw Crossing, which is a place where the river is very wide and of drift piles. It's hard to see the main channel. There is shallow in many places. It is a place where things floating in the river are easily snagged and caught as they drift by.

We stopped the engines and drifted awhile and the guys made a plan. I was lying in the little race boat, with my hand over the side in the water, just watching the water flow and forgetting again why we were there. It was going on 8:00 p.m. and the sun was high in the sky. It was quiet except for the sound of the water and the guys talking softly. Suddenly I had a thought and then a prayer. In my mind I decided that I really wanted to find my husband's body. I even sat upright as this thought went through me, because I suddenly was positive about this. Before I had been praying for God's will concerning recovering his body, because I didn't know what God wanted. But this time I knew. Yes, Lord, let me find my Weedz. There was a sense of anticipation. Of readiness.

The guys had decided to split up and check Squaw Crossing as thoroughly as possible with the three boats. They would check in with the walkie-talkie radios so they knew they were staying in range of each other. So Pats and I went down one bank and we could see Barry working another section. We lost track of Dim pretty quickly and soon he was out of radio range so Barry left to go find him. Pats and I were drifting along looking at the different drift piles and logjams. Everything was the same silty gray color.

Suddenly I heard Pats say, "Is that someone's leg?" With his hunter's eyes he had spotted something in the silty gray foam. I looked at him and then followed with my eyes the direction he was looking. There were so many logjams and drift piles it was hard to see anything out of the ordinary. I asked him to get a little closer and as he began to, I suddenly knew I had spotted what he had seen.

We were still at least fifty feet away, but I could tell it was a pant leg, from the thigh to the ankle with the knee bent, as though someone was lying on their back with their leg bent. We slowly drew closer, and I saw a belt. Suddenly without a doubt, incredibly, I knew it was Weedz! In the same second, I could feel my breath forced from me with that startling realization, and then I felt God's strength and presence envelope me. His love was so powerful! I yelled to Pats, "It's Weedz! I know it's our Weedz! Get me over there!"

I looked at Pats and he again was as white as a sheet. He told me he thought we should get Dim on the radio. I was pleading with him to get me over there, and he was yelling in the walkie-talkie radio for his brother, Dim. For a few frustrating seconds, this went on until he slowly brought the boat over. I was up at the bow. He nosed the bow up to

Weedz and I reached out as though the Lord had me inside a bubble of love because all I could feel was pure joy and thankfulness. The horribleness of my whole situation was kept outside that bubble.

The first thing I did was pull up Weedz' pant leg and see what he was wearing! That was the only piece of clothing he had worn the day he left that I did not know the identity of, and it meant a lot to me to be able to know now. I took hold of one of his hands that I love so much. I said, "Weedz, I know you are not here, but I'm so glad I found you!"

How can I ever hope to describe what I was feeling? How can I find the words? There was not a doubt in my heart that this was a gift! I was praising God and I felt so thankful there, out in the middle of the Tanana River, that my God, the Creator of the heavens and the earth had done this for me, for us! I told Pats that we could do this, that the two of us could get him into the boat.

Weedz was on his back and the upper part of his body was under the gray water out of sight. He was tangled in a drift pile and needed to be pulled out. Pats was screaming into his radio and finally he called out to God for strength. I looked at him at that second saw a powerful transformation. His face, which had been full of pain and fear, was now radiating love and purpose. He jumped out of the boat, which at that spot was about thigh deep, and he made his way towards Weedz, pulling the drift pile apart as he came. I just stared at him, amazed at the transformation and basking in what I saw. Our hearts felt very tender towards Weedz. Tender with love and protectiveness. We were going to take care of him.

Pats was throwing pieces of drift out of his way and he was thanking and praising God. That bubble of love was surrounding him too. He reached Weedz and grabbed hold of him and pulled him loose. His head surfaced. I looked at Pats. He never even flinched. He also felt such joy. We laughed in relief, and when we saw that Weedz' watch was still ticking, we laughed some more.

There we were out in the middle of the river at about 8:30 p.m. The sun was high in the blue sky. We were over 60 miles down river from where Weedz had been thrown in five weeks earlier. We were at Squaw Crossing, a very unlikely place to find anything. And yet we had found him! The Lord left no room for coincidence. I believe, in the Lord's mercy, He had held Weedz' body under the water so he wouldn't look so very bad-like the bear.

Within a short time the other two boats arrived and they too were in awe of the bigness of this. We put him in Barry's boat and I rode with him for the eight miles on down to the village of Tanana. There was a trooper there and we gave Weedz to him. While we were in Tanana taking care of that business, the Lord continued to sustain us. It was a hard business, but we were able to do it. We came back up to Manley after that and got here about 4:30 a.m. My mind is just spinning right now.

Lord, You let me find my Weedz. And Pats and Dim and I were all there to take care of things, just like I asked. Lord, You are so good. Pats kept praising You. How wonderful to hear that! I was filled with strength from You through the whole thing and everyone could see Your hand in it.

MANLEY - THURSDAY, JUNE 28, 1984

And now, Weedz, your body is buried up on the hill. Four days ago. Still there's no relief. I need to go to Maincamp and sit alone with the Lord and cry my aching heart out. I miss you, sweetheart. It has been 6 weeks since you left and I am so spaced out. I need to come to terms with this. You are not here for me anymore, and it's so hard to grasp. Out of reach, unattainable. And yet the Lord is faithful. He's there for me. I find it hard to write tonight. So much has happened and I need to write it all down, but I don't have the energy. Maybe when I go to Maincamp in a few days I'll feel like it. I love you, sweetheart. You've got the best of my love after the Lord. I'm your wife and I want to finish the race as your wife.

I pray the Lord will give me the grace to make it without the heavy burden of loneliness. pp. 21-27.

MAINCAMP--WEDNESDAY, APRIL 24, 1985

I was thinking about the day that Les Zerbe flew in here, November 29th, and asked me if I wanted to go to Wasilla for that workshop. After he had left I had run around my trap line and men settled in for the evening. I thought about what I should do and I was overwhelmed with crying. I lay there on the bed and really cried hard, and it kind of surprised me. Why all these deep-seated tears? Weedz used to say that when this heaviness came upon me that the Lord was really going to use me. I was in such turmoil. I longed for Weedz to be here to help me make a decision. To pick up and leave Maincamp and go to Wasilla of all places, was a monumental task for me at that point. I didn't have the energy or the desire. Yet part of me wanted to go, because just maybe God wanted me to, but I didn't know for sure. So, I just lay there on the bed in tears. I realize now that I was going through another breaking, another breaking of my will, which had begun to take form again, and making room for God's will. My will was poured out with my tears and I remember saying, "Lord, If You want me to go, then I will trust You to open doors for me. I am willing either way, Father." That was Thursday night and all doors did open and pointed me towards Wasilla. I let do and let God, not knowing what was ahead of me. I was so blessed at that workshop. *On The River Of Grace*, p. 124.

What I did not yet know was that at the landing in Manley there were vehicles sitting there, Joe McVey's pick up truck and the Klein's four wheelers. Dale and Joe had arrived first together, getting ready to go down river, Mike Silka had shot them. Next was Albert Hagen. Then the Klein family. Lyman, Joyce who was pregnant, and two year-old Marshall. He shot all of them and threw their bodies in the river. Six people from Manley, with a population of about 40, were suddenly missing in one afternoon. Nobody yet realized that Weedz was missing too.

Knowing nothing, I was frantic for information and communication to somewhere when the helicopter first appeared and just hovered. Eventually they touched down and asked lots of questions, about Weedz and how long he'd been gone and what he looked like and about the boat. They told me very little, and took off. When they returned, about 3 or 4 hours later at 7:30 p.m., they landed right away. I was shaky, walking toward the trooper. It felt like I was walking into a dream.

As we got closer to each other I saw he couldn't meet my eye. He told me I had to go to Manley with them. I said, "WHY?!" Then there was one long run together sentence: "We found your husband's boat on the Zitzianna River and the fellow who had it killed a trooper and we had to shoot him and we have to presume your husband is dead as well." But I thought, or maybe said out loud, "No, Weedz is a survivor." He asked me to come with them to Manley, and I said, "What for?"

The unrealness of the situation was frightening and making me a bit obstinate. There was denial and shock and real life was beginning to waver. I agreed to go with them on the condition that we fly low along the river to look for Weedz. So I packed up some overnight stuff.

Trooper McDonald saw my Bible sitting on my nightstand and asked, "Don't you want to bring your Bible?" I said, "Thank you, yes." We called Weedz' brother Mickey from the helicopter to meet me in Manley. Only when I got to Manley and saw Dorothy crying so deeply, did I hear that there were six dead from Manley. *On The River Of Grace*, pp. 125-127

MAINCAMP - FRIDAY, MAY 17, 1985

Evening. It's been an eventful day, full with blessings from the Lord. I had gone for a walk and arrived back at the house about 3:30. I sat out in the yard for a little while just thinking and remembering. And then right before 3:45 I got up and went into the house. Inside in the kitchen as the clock was approaching 3:45, I heard an airplane approaching and I stepped back outside. There was Les Zerbe flying low over Maincamp and he waved his wings. I was so blessed, because I knew that my Father God had done that.

At the moment, when I thought that Weedz had been shot a year earlier at 3:45, God had brought Les Zerbe to share the anniversary of the moment with me. God is so thoughtful! Then at 8:30 tonight, the river ice started breaking up big time. It took my mind off everything but that really big show out there. And then at "trapline chatter" time I got 5 messages from special people and again I was blessed. Right after that I talked to Dim and Joy on the CB radio, and for the first time of the season they came in loud and clear! God's perfect timing! Lord, You are so good to me!

MAINCAMP - MONDAY, MAY 20, 1985
Remembering a year ago today. I was in Manley, had been up all night and the troopers brought the boat in from the Zitzianna River, which is as far as Mike Silka got with it. When my eyes saw boat, the reality of the situation came down on me pretty hard. I remember walking up to the boat as it was tied up on the beach the landing, and it had all the gory details in it. Its contents were a confusing mixture of Silka's and our belongings and there were people standing around. I just stared into the boat and couldn't see any of that right then. All I could see was the harsh cruel reality that here was Weedz' boat and he wasn't in it! His life jacket was laying there and I picked it up and held it to me, and looked up and caught Dim's gaze and I said, "He didn't have his life jacket on." And then I turned and walked away. What an intense heaviness came upon me when I saw the boat! That's when complete acceptance came upon me and it was so sad. pp.135-137

Lord,
You walk each step of the way
Within me,
And around me.
You know my pain
Before it pierces me,
And You know my joy
Before You let it wash over me.
Dear Father, You count each tear,
For they are Your tears
Offered to You
Upon the altar of my heart.
You know me well in my weakened state.
You lift me when I fall.
You hold me when I cry.
All of this, all of this from the Almighty Father.
It is because You know my heart.

--Liller Burk, *On The River Of Grace*, p. 139

"My father was the best in this earth of preachers and pilots, preaching the Word with clarity and pioneering the idea of flight in a Piper Cub to the heart of West Africa."

Wm. zerbe on his motorcycle

Grandpa William Zerbe, seated on his 1913 Harley Davidson--the only picture of him smiling, my journey began with his.

Above: Little Les. Right: Jane and Michelle with elephant orphan. Below: Carol, Michelle, Les and Jane on the way to church in Yekepa, Liberia, in 1979.

Top: All our jungle airstrips were short and narrow, surrounded by very large trees. Goats and cattle grazed there. Built by hand, each airstrip had its own distinction: up and down hill, on side of hill, one way in and one way out, rain washed ruts, strange approaches, and no go-arounds. Below: Les with EL-HD met by many villagers in Liberia, West Africa

Les flies to the village of Manley Hot Springs to preach on Sundays in an old log building which was a bar.

"Weedz has prayed for Manley, and when Les Zerbe started to come to Manley, we knew it was answered prayer. We wanted the people of Manley to turn to God....Weedz had a burden for their souls....He only wanted to talk about the Lord—quiet...but bold...."

We found your husband's boat....We have to presume your husband is dead as well." "...shoot him and throw him into the river." Liller Burk, On the River of Grace

"Many Americans dream of a log house to call their own, as did we...

but few can imagine the labor involved." Jim Hodges, Hard Hats for Christ Founder, notching a corner

The mosquitoes took their share of blood each day and tortured the progress of our dream.

"There's a fine line between rustic and sloppy." Motto of Phil Smith, Hard Hat log builder

Flying missionaries and native peoples in the interior of Alaska in the Cessna T-206, the ¾ ton "pick-up truck"

Above: C-185 take off Below: An FAA licensed Airframe & Powerplant mechanic for over thirty years, Les prefers to do his own maintenance and repair, and believes that every bush pilot needs to be an A&P mechanic.

Daughter Carol

Daughter Michelle

Son Nathan

Below:
Our kids "adopted"
Athabascan Grandma"
Agnes

Son Jarrod
(with caribou antlers)

Les and Jane
Zerbe

Carol began flying
at age seventeen
and won her private
license in six
weeks. She was
hired by a regional
airline at age
nineteen.

Top: Nine and a half foot bear Les took with his 44 Magnum. Below: It was the last day of the hunt--the last five minutes, when one of the largest bears ever taken in Alaska walked into the clearing 50 yards away. His 30" skull would soon grace Billy Bloom's office.

Hunting and
Fishing the
Last Frontier

King salmon

Moose

Over the years because of an airplane and a bush pilot, hundreds of young people from remote villages have attended summer youth camps.

These pictures were taken the same day, just a block apart on the same street. Any takers?

N-1688R--The Cessna 185 that I took to Alaska was given to me by my Uncle Paul and Aunt Ferne. I used this airplane for crop dusting, personal transportation, missionary flights in St. Thomas and the Bahamas, Mexico, Canada, the continental US and all Alaska. Also used for medical emergency patients; flights around Mt. McKinley; and to transport moose, caribou, dall sheep, bears, salmon and halibut to the freezer.

**Above: Les with "Dog Musher's Version" of Bible portion--John and Romans at the Iditarod.
Below: Les is "going to the dogs."**

THE DAY I WAS GIVEN A GOLDMINE - 1983

It was on one of these cold days that found me in downtown Fairbanks with an elderly friend, a real sourdough (properly defined as "one sour on the country and not having enough dough to get out!") We were hailed by one of his friends, Bill, who urged us to step inside for a cup of hot coffee, where he related to us his dilemma.

An old prospector had just given him seventeen forty-acre gold claims, and he didn't know what to do with them. He was asking our assistance to sell, lease or work the claims. I told him that maybe we could help, but could we see his legal claim to the land? The papers he produced looked real, notarized, signed, sealed, and delivered, but I smelled a proverbial "rat."

I told him we'd need to look at this paperwork overnight, to locate it on a topographical map, and my friend and I departed with his legal claim to the gold bearing parcels of land. I told my friend that I thought his friend was a crook. Who would give anyone that kind of opportunity, that kind of potential wealth?

We spent the following day searching for the old prospector who was drinking himself to oblivion on "Two Street," the local slang for Second Street, which was home to many bars. I took him outside and explained to him that I wished he had been my friend. Maybe he would have been so kind to me. Then I showed him the Quit Claim Deed, his gift to Bill. He seemed to sober quickly, seeing with blurred vision his twelve hard years of prospecting slipping away.

"Is that your signature?" I asked.

"Yes, it is," he muttered.

"Clyde," I asked, "what have you been doing the last two days?"

"Right here drinking," he explained.

"And who has been buying you drinks, Clyde?"

"Well, Bill has!" he exclaimed.

An attorney quickly verified that any such document, fraudulent at best, would not be a legal one.

I called Bill to come to a restaurant for breakfast to discuss his future. I wore my Ruger, stainless, 357 magnum pistol under my jacket, just in case a point of fact needed to be more clearly emphasized. Bill and I sat face to face, measuring the sunrise, rays of hope written all over his fraudulent smile.

"Bill," I said, "this sure is a bright sunrise, and I've never had the privilege of sitting across the table from such a con-artist as you!"

What do you mean?" he asked.

"You bought Clyde drinks, got him stone drunk, and then got him to sign away his life. What kind of a man would do that?" I asked.

"You give me back my paper work!" he ordered.

I slowly but deliberately zipped down my jacket, put my hand over my heart, and grasped the stubby, but potent 357 magnum. Bill didn't know if I was going for a gun, a pen, or his paperwork.

"Bill," I said firmly. "I've got your paperwork, but it's not yours, you know. It's Clyde's, and when I leave here I'm going to Clyde's and burn this bogus claim. The best you can do," I said, "is to apologize to Clyde for this and hope he doesn't shoot you; then apologize to me for wasting a whole day on you, and hope I don't shoot you!" With my hand still concealed, his eyes transfixed on my chest, not knowing what my hand might come out with, Bill bolted for the door. "Don't forget to pay for your breakfast coffee, Bill," I called, but he was gone. So I gave Bill's name and telephone number to the management, who called the police on Bill for an outstanding coffee bill.

I found Clyde very sober, and my ensuing lecture on the evils of drinking only sobered him some more. I then told him of Christ, His power to save and deliver Clyde from sin, hell, the power of the grave and drinking. Clyde prayed to receive Christ and His forgiveness, and he never drank again.

Two weeks later Clyde called me, and we met. "I've never had someone look out for me the way you did!" he exclaimed. "Now I'm going to give you something for getting my claims back."

"Clyde," I said, "I'm glad to help you out, and I'd hope you would help me out the same way if I was in the same trouble."

"No," he said, "all I've got is these claims, and I'm going to give you three of my best." And so he did. We flew in my Cessna 185 to the mountains, the Alaska Range, twenty-five miles east of Healy where Iron Creek meets the Totatlanika River. Saving a gold prospector now made me one, but never having even held a gold pan in my hand, I was certainly not a miner. I have sewn buttons on my shirt, but I'm not a seamstress. I can boil water, but I'm no chef.

Even though the earth gave up a few flakes of yellow, she did not yield her wealth. But we did build "Wilderness Skills Bible Camp," a camp for teenage young men to develop outdoor skills. With no road access, every camper and worker and all supplies had to be flown in. The boys lived in their own tents and received a complete survival course--as do the Army Special Forces—including fire building, knife sharpening, mountain climbing, and hunter-shooter safety. Morning and evening for at least two hours daily, they had Bible study. All meals were homemade, and all participated in KP.

At the end of the week, we had an "Iron man" Contest, in which the young men demonstrated the skills or lessons learned—such as rappelling, compass use, hiking, physical training, Bible memory verses, key Bible concepts, etc. Just before the trip back to town, I flew them to McKinley Park for an exciting commercially run four-hour white water rafting trip. The real gold, I had discovered, was to be mined here--in the minds and hearts of young men.

I still wonder at the part Providence has played many times in my life, but I achieve little progress in explaining it. God's miracles for me may not be appreciated by you, simply because my miracles are not your miracles, but I've had a few.

SANTA FLIES A CESSNA –1984

All that happens in the Arctic regions is not tragic in its ending. Christmas is, of course, one of these times, especially for the pioneer people who live in such a remote area of the bush that their existence is known only to God and few of us pilots. On occasion the banks in Fairbanks would give food care boxes including turkeys and milk and all manner of fresh fruits to these people, many of them living some two hundred and fifty miles from the nearest human. The banks would put all the gas in the plane to deliver these gifts, and I was a missionary Santa at the expense of the banks!

Now people who live so far away from others have their reasons, some of them unspoken, but most readily verbalized. High on the list was to get away from people with the "herd instinct," whose houses row after row about touch each other, whose lawns are all manicured and white picket fences all painted based primarily on what the neighbors would say if they didn't. It was to make a statement against white shirts and ties and eight hours of the same repetitive work.

To live in the true wilderness requires more work, they admit, but to trek through another shopping mall or to be condemned to shop K-Mart for a day would be sheer torture. The idea to them is to see how little it takes to live and be happy as opposed to seeing how much you can consume to be seen in the right light, trying to keep up with the Jones. Wilderness to them becomes their civilization, and they have the right to define what civilization is, they point out.

"Don't fence me in…"

"I'll shoot out my back door, if I please, Thank You."

Many of these people are revered and remembered as people who faced hard tasks with irresistible will…and accomplished them all. Some practice their solitude with less will than patience, less aptitude than loyalty to their ideas or spouses ambitions.

One such man recently came to Manley Hot Springs with a wife and a young daughter. His ideas of tranquility included building a tree house somewhere in the wilds of Alaska. His would have been the first tree house in this great land, a monument to stupidity! Many mosquito bites later, they all left for the East Coast; All those who knew of their plans, agreed that the East Coast and they deserved each other. There are many more who in my experience, are great and good people, whose characters have many facets as a cut stone, each facet shining with individual brightness.

Albert Yrjana comes to mind. As a Finish immigrant, he came to the USA. Penniless, he hitchhiked to Alaska and settled in Ruby, on the Yukon River. Living on homestead land and a dream, he became a legendary trapper, gold-miner, fish-wheel operator and hunter. When I wanted to learn the art of arctic survival, it was to him I went. He could tell when he would catch the beaver and which one. He was rarely wrong. His ability to call moose and make them walk right up to boat or plane was uncanny.

He would buy equipment for mining and a new snow machine, but not shoe laces. He often looked the part of a vagabond. One day he flew with me to Fairbanks with a bag full of gold to buy a new Caterpillar earthmover. All salesmen bypassed this vagabond, until he finally asked, "Does anybody around here know anything about these here Caterpillars?" One lucky salesman addressed old Albert as "Sir" and sold him a new machine for gold! Albert was as close to Santa Clause as you could find, with a year-round heart of gold.

N1688R THROUGH THE ICE – 1985

The day began bright, the sun high, glistening on the April snows. I awakened to greet the day with a short trip through the pages of scripture while nursing some Louisiana Chicory coffee.

At the urging of another friendly pilot, I was convinced that I should help him out by flying about 20 men to a "frozen" lake near Mt. McKinley for a men's retreat at a lodge there. I had objected quite strenuously, stating my concerns that the ice should be melting on the lakes this late in the year. But this bush pilot was a big game guide, a trapper who landed with skis on his plane many times a week on various lakes. He should know! He said he had been there the day before in his Piper Cub, had drilled the ice and it was three feet thick, the lake was shaded by the mountain and was the last to thaw. "You can drive a D-9 Caterpillar across it!" he answered me.

My coffee and his words had given me false comfort, but I would do him this favor. He had placed two five gallon cans on the ice, one indicating the touchdown zone, the other where I would stop. His radiant smile was catching and engaging, and he knew the day was his. But, ah, yes, the best laid plans of mice and men!

We loaded six in the plane, but we were no where near the weight of a D-9 Cat! He jumped in the co-pilot's seat, and we were off to the lake. The landing was flawless, and we rolled to an easy stop at the second can. That's when it became very interesting! My pilot friend had not distinguished between three feet of good ice and three feet of "rotten" ice!

We were sitting in the plane like six proud peacocks when a sickening, cracking sound accompanied the ice breaking up beneath our weight. In a moment, the wheels, landing gear and fuselage were in the ice cold water, the water beginning to seep into the airplane through every crack and crevice. It occurred to me that an airplane was never designed to be a submarine.

Our first predicament was to be able to overcome the water pressure and all the large chunks of ice that were exerting great pressure on the outside doors, keeping us from opening them. Of course, after opening the doors, ice cold water would gush in, and we would be wet, but we would get wet anyway!

When flying, I always carry certain items of survival gear within easy reach. I always carry a cigarette lighter in my pocket, because if down in the wilderness, I can start a fire for cooking, for warmth and a forest fire, if necessary, for rescue. A razor sharp hatchet is in easy reach also, to be used for cutting my way out of a wrecked plane, possibly so bent up that the doors won't open. I can also beat out the windshield and escape a burning plane. A razor sharp pocket knife is always on my belt to cut my seat belt should I be upside down and or in some fashion unable to unsnap the seat and shoulder harness. A 44-magnum revolver rests beside my leg in the plane's map pocket, to provide that much needed partridge or moose on the long walk out if no one finds me. A hand held ELT (emergency locator transmitter) also goes with me out the door.

An ELT, which is mandatory equipment on all planes, sends out a repeating signal to at least three satellites, establishing its location so that search and rescue can find the plane. They don't work underwater, if the aircraft is upside down with the antenna broken off, or if the aircraft burns. I now view the FAA, which makes the rule that these ELT's are to be installed in all aircraft for its speedy recovery and the safety of its occupants, with mixed emotions. Almost all aircraft have these ELT's mounted in the aft fuselage, behind the baggage compartment, usually requiring tools to get to it.

The ELT is meant to send its signal upon heavy impact or by manually turning it on by someone in the plane. If the pilot should not survive or if the aircraft burns, the passengers are usually helpless to turn on the signaling device. The ELT should in every case be mounted in a panel or within easy reach of the pilot as he and his passengers exit the plane before it burns. Thus it seems to me that the FAA is really only interested in finding a crash site, not concerned about the survivors.

So after a struggle, I managed to open the C-185's door just enough to squeeze out and try walking on water. I managed, as did all my passengers, to get on top of the wing and walk down the main spar (so as not to crush the wing) to the end of the wing. Then we had to roll our bodies to shore for weight distribution, else the ice would break under our weight. You should try rolling on your side in the snow and ice for 300 hundred yards! This added a new dimension to the definition of what a "holy roller" really is!

Our next problems now were what to do to be able to walk to the plane and then how to rescue the plane so we could get out. I would do it in logical, methodical, frantic steps.

Step 1--Use my trusty ax to beat down storage shed near to the lodge for its plywood.

Step 2--Put the sheets of plywood on the rotten ice so we could walk to the plane.

Step 3--Cut two pine trees down and lift each wing slightly, putting the trees under the wing for more weight distribution on the rotten ice.

Step 4--Go back to the lodge and get two 55 gallon gas drums and two mattresses from the beds to put under the wings.

Step 5--All six of us lift on wing at a time and get a drum and mattress under each wing.

Step 6--Wait for some water to drain out of fuselage.

Step 7--Get six-5 gallon cans from the lodge and, one by one, add three cans on top of each drum, one can at a time.

Step 8--Note the plane is now high enough in the water that just the tires are submerged.

So now we have most of the water drained from the fuselage, and a stationary plane propped up on rotten ice that is groaning and cracking and slowly sinking beneath all the combined weight. In fact, the ice has sunken so far that where once the ice was flat, now the real lake level is about three feet above us. So now I go to shore, cut one more pine tree and take two more 55-gallon drums to the plane. By lifting the plane, one wing at a time, using the tree under the fuselage in front of the landing gear and resting the tree on the two drums, we were able to push the opposite wing down to remove all the drums and cans propped under the wings.

Step 9--Now we could roll the plane on the tree under the fuselage and do so without much effort. But so what?

Step 10--Go to shore and use the ax to cut the chain locking up the canoes, then take two canoes to the plane.

Step 11--By rolling the plane on its side till one wing tip touched the ice, we were able to get one canoe under one tire.

Step 12--Not being able to lift the other tire out of the water, we had to put the canoe under the water, under the wheel and then scoop the water out of the canoe. Now we removed the drums and tree and we had a "float plane."

Step 13--Get some garden hose from the lodge and siphon most of the gas from the wings except just heavy enough to fly 15 minutes to the road between Fairbanks and Anchorage, where I would land and then hitch-hike for gas.

Step 14--All six of us pushed the "float plane" backwards getting the canoes to jump from the water onto the "good" ice.

Step 15--Push our wings up one at a time and remove the canoes and replace them with one sheet of plywood under each tire. The tail of the plane had always stayed above the ice and did not need plywood under it. With each tire in the middle of one sheet of plywood, 8' long, I had four foot of runway! Now some of us bush pilots are pretty fair at the controls, but we're still subject to gravity and rotten ice. I was sure that as soon as the wheels left the plywood, I would fall through the ice again!

Step 16--Convince the passengers, these "brave" men, that it's now time to fly out of here. I would need them to put at least three more sheets of plywood in front of each wheel, and then lay their bodies on the outside edge of the plywood while I attempted to takeoff between them, so that the propeller blast would not blow the plywood into the tail of the plane. This was not met with much enthusiasm and summarily dismissed as a bad idea by all except two of the men. I had no choice in the end but to take off on twelve feet of "runway," the four feet under the tires and eight foot of plywood in front of it, with the propeller only inches from the men's heads lying on the plywood. I told the men they had several choices: they could walk out (with no snow shoes, they knew better), or starve and freeze to death slowly, or die quickly with a propeller turning at 2,850 RPM, or I might just get airborne straight ahead.

Step 17--Get in the plane and start it. Of course nothing happened. The engine had been partially submerged in the water, and the electric priming pump used to start the fuel-injected engine was shorted out with water. There was no other way to start the engine.

Step 18--Get the few tools I had on board and remove the cowling, top and bottom and then remove the fuel pump. This was just barely accomplished with the tools I had.

Step 19--Take the pump to the lodge and take it all apart.

Step 20--Build a wood fire to warm up and dry out the pump motor all the while watching the plane slowly sink in the melting ice.

Step 21--Reinstalled the pump and try it--it worked! Reinstalled the cowling--Reinstalled the bodies on the plywood-- Get in the plane and make sure bodies are still on the plywood, holding it down so the propellers blast would not pick them up, remove my "runway" and crunch the tail of plane on the way back.

By now, 24 hours had passed of constant work, and hunger and fatigue were taking their toll, but the plane would soon fall through the ice again and disappear in 60' of water. We had to proceed. To my amazement, the craft started easily and after some warm up time and a serious prayer for God's wisdom and guidance out of this place, I was ready to fly. By now the plane had sunk down so far in the rotten ice, I would have to go uphill for about 30' once I was off the plywood and on the ice. I thought it would be a problem and it was.

As I fire-walled the engine, 300 fire breathing horsepower came to life, swinging an 86" sea plane prop. With the flaps at 20 degrees, I could feel the plane defy gravity, but not enough. As the wheels rolled past the 12' mark, the left tire broke through the top layer of ice, went down about 4" and created so much drag, it turned the plane 90 degrees to the left, and the plane was now heading right for the lodge, trees and the mountain. But at that moment, both tires started to roll freely on top of the ice. There was no choice--go straight ahead toward the lodge on the bank of the lake. But the power of the Cessna 185 overcame gravity, the airframe very light, the wing did its time honored thing, and I was airborne, just in time to turn away from the lodge, the inside wing tip almost touching the ice in the turn.

Step 22--Go back for the men with a Piper Super Cub on skis and take them home from the "Men's Retreat" one by one.

Step 23--Weld the steps that had broken off when the fuselage hit the ice.

Step 24--Analyze the situation--debrief--learn--reflect--make commitments to yourself and talk to yourself.

The "Men's Retreat" was just that--a retreat from the battle with the ice. But the sky was never quite so clear, the mountains and the landscape never quite as vivid as the flight off the ice to the safety of the road. As I landed and taxied up to a road house, the coffee and dinner was delicious, the atmosphere warm, the pressure was off. Let the avgas take its time getting here. Let the "holy-rollers" wait too, still at the lodge, putting all the plywood, drums and cans back in their proper places. They would have time to think of personal things and analyze themselves.

A person can learn some things in the comfort of a lodge as one nice guy to another or one can learn how resourceful and persistent he could be in retrieving a plane from rotten ice. Useful things they could do before attempting this flight were:

1. Be a nice guy.
2. Understand computer and read email.
3. Make a bed.
4. Mow the lawn.
5. Paint the fence.
6. Sing bass.
7. Drive a station wagon.

Some of the useful things some of them learned after this adventure were:

1. Learn to think under pressure.
2. Chop down trees for something other than fire wood.
3. To use all materials at hand to make sure of a positive outcome.
4. To trust each other and their lives to the pilot on a plywood runway.
5. There is more to life than just talking about the   weather.

HUNTING THE LAST FRONTIER – 1983

It is a well-known fact that in all recorded history, one species will always be hunting another or that one is trying to survive another. It would seem that God Himself was a hunter as He clothed Adam and Eve, and He probably had what some would call an unfair advantage. "No fair chase," they would say. The wisest man, Solomon, was a hunter and makes the observation that "the slothful man roasteth not that which he took in hunting, but the substance of a diligent man is precious."

As noted before, one cannot be part of the true Alaska landscape and her people without being a serious hunter. The sooner you become a hunter, the sooner you become one of them. Give me five days on a hunt with a new chap, and I'll tell you all about him and his character. I'll know if he knows the discipline of getting up early, of listening to instructions, of pitching in on regular house chores, of getting his hands dirty, of maintaining happiness with weariness in his bones, or of showing initiative at inconvenient times. I will know of his skill and tenacity and endurance. I will know if he is prone to truth or fiction. I will soon know what kind of man he is through and through.

It is over the campfire that all the political questions of the world are discussed. All of the hunt is necessary and makes sense--the life outside in the elements, the hunt, the fun, and the danger. What if my plane should fail me? The bears get me? What if I would cut myself to the bone, but the weather is too bad to fly?

Well, that is the chance, and that is the job. I'm really not safer in "civilization," I conclude.

I find it amusing to watch "civilized" men, who would be hunters, adjust to their new surroundings. They are like potted plants in a green house that must be pruned and tended daily. First the watches come off, and there are no telephones. One soon realizes how quickly men deteriorate without razors and clean shirts and underwear. A single day's growth of beard, and a man looks careless; two days, a derelict; four days, polluted. After ten days, I'll tell you what this man is really made of! And at least once a year, it is good to go to the limit myself, to see myself in nature's mirror.

I hope that, for these and other reasons, my prodigy will take up hunting. Yet, today there are those who think hunting is barbaric, brutal or boring at best. As to the brutality of hunting or trapping, I could use this logic: hunting cannot be more brutal or barbaric than ninety-five percent of all other human activities. I'm sure there is nothing more tragic about the death of a Kodiak bear or a moose than the death of an Angus steer; certainly not in the eyes of the steer. Think of the poor steer, made that way with human premeditation, a portion of his male anatomy and dignity removed with a knife. Then feed him some corn to prepare him for slaughter to become the steak on your plate. The only difference is that the steer has neither the ability nor the chance to outwit the executioner, while the moose and bear have both of these to outwit the hunter.

Now bear hunters may be unconscionable brutes, but it would be a great error to rank the bear as pacifistic animal. The popular belief that only certain bears are dangerous is quite wrong; so wrong that a considerable number of men who believed this tale have become one with the dust without gradual disintegration! A polar bear aroused by human scent will stalk and attack quickly, his speed-- greater than a race horse for a short distance--is as unbelievable as his mobility. His teeth and claws are his weapons in the distasteful business of killing a mere human.

Who is to determine who should kill whom and how? Does the poor mouse have a chance against the trap, the poison, or the cat? Should he be afforded legal protection? Why not? How do we make choices to domesticate and raise reindeer for sausage and protect their close cousins—caribou--from domestication? I think the point is quite obvious. Animals will do to each other what comes by God-given instincts, but to man, He has given the right to manage and take dominion. Whoever comes to other conclusions, I believe, has some Ostrich blood flowing in his veins. Often times the bear has the last laugh, as you shall see.

DOES GOD WANT YOU TO PLAN FOR SURVIVAL?

There is a small church on Kodiak Island, Monaska Bay Baptist Church, which invited me over to speak from time to time. To get there, I had to fly between Homer and Kodiak over the frigid water. A person lucky enough to be immersed in this icy water would only last about three minutes at most. Concerned about my survival should I have a forced ditching, the church purchased an expensive insulated survival suit. Colored bright orange in contrast to the grey sea, the suit would enable me to float and to endure the cold for several days. Invariably there was someone that wanted to ride with me who was perfectly content with life, until I put the suit on before crossing that treacherous water.

"What's that?" my passenger would always ask.

"It's my survival suit in case we go down in the water," I replied.

"Where's mine?" he would ask, with a hint of fatalism in his voice.

"You don't have one. You'll just have to pray," I told him. I reminded him that perhaps praying is the best recourse, as opposed to the survival suit, but it does little more than silence him. To answer to the contrary would be failing to take the moral high ground, and most of us would not do that (although we keep all our insurance policies safely tucked away in a safe somewhere).

"Let us be practical and diligent," I told him. "Let us fly." And we did, hoping that this flight would not become a habit. Upon landing, we made our way to a restaurant, where I ordered oyster stew and black coffee. My passenger could not stomach the thought of coffee being poured upon oysters, so he went outside and sat on the curb, believing that eating with me was a greater risk than flying with me!

How quickly perceptions changed, as we watched the lovely ocean bay a hundred yards in front of us erupt in froth, as three killer whales attacked a large blue whale. Each time the large whale surfaced, he was missing another part of his anatomy. Then my passenger was glad we had made it safely over the water and delighted to see coffee being poured over oysters! But, then again, maybe it would be safer to stay in Iowa or Ohio and just watch the corn grow.

THE MAN WHO DROWNED IN HIS OWN TEE-PEE – 1986

There is a story of an Indian of old who drank so much ice tea one day that he drowned in his own "Tea-Pee!" This is not as farfetched as this next "great" hunt will bring to light.

A well known evangelist, who shall remain unnamed, came to hunt moose with me on the North Slope of Alaska, north of the Brooks Range on the Chandler River, which runs into the Colville River. To reach this place on the planet that is home to many moose, caribou and grizzly bear; the hunters would first drive to Coldfoot Truck Stop at the south side of the Brooks Range, then fly through the mountains to the river valley beyond. Fog had our hunting party of four socked-in on the ground at Coldfoot Truck Stop for about two days.

Both the coffee and stories were getting stronger, the anticipation mounting. The evangelist, however, had three cases of Pepsi Cola with him as he drank nothing else. He drank Pepsi Cola as though he owned stock in the company. Now, in Alaska we tend to suspect the true gender of the male species if he does not drink coffee at least once a day.

When fog had lifted slightly, just a few hundred feet, I announced that I would try the Anatuvik Pass through the Brooks Range. The evangelist immediately volunteered to chance this trial flight, understanding that I would fly and leave him there while returning for the others. Then I would come back and hunt with him. I warned him that if the fog settled back in, he could be alone for several days.

"I am an experienced hunter," the evangelist claimed. I've hunted elk in Colorado, mule deer in Montana and many other species." His experience had kept him through blizzards in the wild and a multitude of nature's other surprises. Besides, he was a champion in karate and judo. He was not afraid.

On the way in, we flew tree tops, the tops of the mountains hidden in cloud, but made it through the broad mountain pass. Once on the Chandler River, we spotted a grizzly bear chasing a cow moose and calf, which ran into the river for refuge. The persistent bear charged into the river after them and was gaining with massive butterfly strokes. I thought it quite unfair that such a large bear was about to catch and eat such a small moose. I wanted that small moose to grow up and, perhaps, become part of my table fare someday! (After all, I'm part of the food chain, too.)

Banking the Cessna 185 left and reducing power, I entered into a spiral dive, recovering just in time to almost roll one wheel on the bear's head under full power. Quickly turning around, I found the bear just getting up on the river bank and running the other way, as though he had forgotten something very important. The evangelist was just as frightened as the bear, having seen his first bear in pursuit of other flesh and experiencing his first unannounced aerobatic plane ride.

Another ten miles downriver, found a herd of moose nearby and an adequate gravel bar in the river to land on. Just as we touched down, a good sized grizzly bear, weighing around eight-hundred pounds, ran just about one-hundred feet in front of the plane. I told the evangelist that bears can cover great distances in a short while and joked that this one was here to get revenge. The evangelist's expression told me he probably believed me.

As we walked to the gravel bar, we could see the bear had made it his home for quite awhile, leaving his tracks everywhere. I explained to the evangelist that the bear probably had a "kill" nearby that he was guarding, but that the bear wouldn't bother him if he didn't bother the bear. I helped him unload his gear (including those three cases of Pepsi) and helped him set up his three man tent. Then I loaned him my 458 Winchester Magnum for "insurance" reasons and left him to his thoughts as I flew back to Coldfoot, AK. When the fog moved in again, my prophecy about three more days of isolation for him came true.

Now to some men, being alone in the Alaskan wilderness would not be torture, but a blessing; to this evangelist, it was torture. When I finally returned to his gravel bar three days later, he emerged from his tent like a slow turtle--neck first, looking around as though some creature had frightened him thoroughly. He thought that perhaps my plane had gone down, or the fog had swallowed me, only to fly into the face of a mountain, an avalanche covering me forever from any search party.

"Boy, am I sure glad to see you," he exclaimed. "But, man, am I sick."

"Where is your moose?" I questioned.

"Well, I've been scared of that bear, so I've been in my tent mostly. But, I did have to use nature's restroom, and I heard this grunt and looked up, and, there--right over there--fifty feet away stood a nice bull moose! But, by the time I got my britches up, he ran off! Been in my tent...haven't seen any more. But, I'm sick. I've got to get out of here."

"What precisely is your sickness?" I probed.

"Well, I've been drinking this Pepsi, you see, and since I was scared to get out of this tent on account of the bear, I just put my empty Pepsi cans around the perimeter inside my tent. Then, when I'd have to water the grass myself, I would just go in the

Pepsi cans. Well, this morning I got up and had to have a drink. I reached out and grabbed a can and took a big gulp, but I got the wrong can!" He had drunk recycled Pepsi!

"Did you even see that bear? I asked.

"No, brother, no, I never saw him, but his tracks were everywhere!"

I thought I had the last laugh, but it wasn't I; it was the bear! So he was known to me as the man who drowned in his own tee-pee!

THE MOOSE WHO WOKE ME UP – 1986

The fog was finally gone, the day crisp, the visibility two hundred miles. I know this is so, because I can see that mountain clearly two hundred miles away. I dropped another party up the river that were so noisy that I decided to hunt by myself down the river two miles. As I stepped out of the plane, my boot stepped on something--something from the past. Upon closer examination, it became clear it was a rear molar, a very large tooth from a prehistoric wooly mammoth. Close by I found some of its ivory tusks.

By now, it was only forty-five minutes till dark. So I decided to just take the seats out of the plane and sleep on an air mattress on its floor. In such a situation one had to sleep with the windows open so that condensation from breathing could escape the cockpit, preserving the instruments, and to keep ice from forming on the inside of the fuselage. Moose were all around me no more than a half a mile away, and I knew they had marked well my arrival. Moose have an uncanny ability to locate a sound source from great distances to within a few feet.

It was around 4:15AM, when I heard the first grunt, just loud enough to nudge me awake. Slowly I came to my early senses. The sun was just attempting to negotiate the skyline, but had not yet made it to the horizon. It was just 15 degrees outside;

so when I put my glasses on to see outside, they just fogged up. After spending some time inside my arctic sleeping bag, my glasses cleared up and so did my thinking.

I would grunt a reply to the animal outside the plane. I reasoned that, if it was a bear, it would not grunt back when I grunted a challenge, but a moose would. My first grunt brought an immediate response and movement just ten feet behind the tail of the plane.

I slowly sat up and held my 375 H&H magnum out the window with one hand pointing the miniature cannon at the ill defined object and pulled the trigger. The muzzle blast and noise blinded me and deafened me to the degree that determining the outcome was impossible without my flashlight.

One flip of the switch revealed a large bull moose lying just behind the Cessna 185's tail section. The Coleman lantern provided the light I needed to clean the magnificent beast, and the sun came into being as I put my knife away. Still tired, I crawled back into the sleeping bag for more shut eye.

Thirty minutes later the clacking of many hooves awakened me again, and I did not have to guess. I simply leaned out the window of the plane and shot two big bull caribou, which fell a half stone's throw from the moose. It had all been too easy. But, it took me all the rest of the day to bone out all three animals, hardly leaving even a scrap of meat for the foxes and ravens.

Around 8:00 PM, the other gentlemen came floating around the bend in the raft I had loaned them. They had scraped bottom too often,, and torn the bottom. The raft was full of water and their things, including their sleeping bags, were all wet. Had I not been there with a dry bag to share with them, hypothermia could have had its way that night. Bragging rights are bragging rights, and that day they were mine! My friends had talked their moose into leaving for a quieter location, while I had shot three prime animals from my sleeping bag!

MOOSE MOUNTAIN – 1987

There are as many areas to hunt in Alaska as there are acres and lakes. Once when flying back from Kako Bible Camp in heavy weather, my route to circumvent a series of large storms took me over a very remote and unused area of Alaska--the Northern Seward Peninsula. The distances here seem never to shrink and could seem mundane except for the weather challenge. I had been flying so long, I now had an urge to sleep, but not from being physically exhausted. There were simply no marks left anywhere by humans to catch my eye, for they had never been here.

Looking down was a pleasure though, the colored leaves of the fall season bringing to life the landscape. Several large bright objects caught my attention, as I diverted somewhat from course and then circled. Could it be a downed aircraft with scattered debris? No, it could only be one thing, so I did a spiral dive to see this large moose herd. The astonishing thing was the size of the herd and some of the great bulls—antlers like huge paddles! Closer inspection revealed several large bull moose and a herd of thirty-six cows. I knew I had found a gold mine of protein and fine table fare.

The country here, except for the river in the valley, was an undulating wasteland of tundra, few trees, and stark ridges of granite. The moose stood out against the landscape like the chalk artist's drawing when the lights are turned on. To have my very own moose pasture made it necessary for me to find a place to land, to visit the moose that had never seen man before. I swung low and knew for certain I could land right next to the moose, but what if anything went wrong?

Could I find a place to land on one of the mountains nearby? There was such a place, I thought, on the very mountainside where I had seen the moose. It was approachable for inspection by a low pass going down the mountain. The open grassy area appeared to be 1200 feet long and had two small trees that I must pass between with my wheels.

Trying to land uphill could be disastrous, as the airplane could not out-climb the grade, if I had to go around. Take off would only be accomplished going downhill. Landing up hill was a no-brainer--the only way it could be done. When a mile out and approaching the little grassy strip half way up the mountain, the pilot's mind must be made up, requiring him to have assessed the wind, any animals in the landing area and the sun.

I would have to land to the west, but not between four to six PM--a two hour window of direct sun in my eyes--which would make me land blind into a blind canyon. Perhaps that was why these moose were so plentiful here; either no one had seen them before, or no one was willing to try this kind of off-airport landing. I would need to decide a mile out at precise altitude, lined up precisely with the landing area, precisely ten knots over stall speed whether I would try the landing. I would then fly directly toward the touchdown zone, the mountain rising sharply to meet me.

All preconceptions and lessons learned from all former experience had not prepared me for what awaited in this kind of landing. The mountain was steep enough that, if good power were not maintained when I touched down, I would not be able to taxi forward to the top of the hill to the take-off zone. Land with too much speed, and I would float too long up the hill before touchdown, making it hard to stop before I ran out of "runway." Or, if heavily loaded (as I always was when going hunting) an accelerated stall at the flare just before touchdown would bounce the airplane out of control.

It was not like any airport I had seen; it surely wasn't O'Hare, Oshkosh, or Sugar Valley, NC. But I had dreams for this place, and I have now lived that dream for over ten years. The dream was my own moose "pasture" and caribou "corral" and musk ox and bear "farm." And the "airport" required such precise technique that no other intruder had dared venture there.

The other part of the dream is to hunt, to camp, to drink from the creek where no one has been before, where watches and telephones mean nothing. If this part of Alaska lacked roads to unite it with "civilization"-- like threads in a net, then at least there was this one mountainside for the wheels of my plane, the sky enough for its wings, and skill and time enough to beat back the barriers of doubt we fly against.

I decided not to try the landing that day for safety's sake, until I could tell my wife its location, in case she needed to alert those who could find and rescue me. I was so far off course, I would never be found should I manage to misjudge the landing. I must continue home, marking this place and swearing myself to secrecy as to its location. There was wind enough on my tail, and the sun was going fast, and the lusty song of the plane spirited me home. In a little while I was seeing trees again, the Yukon River-- as murky as a glacier can make it, and after that, Fairbanks.

I had found a place that God had made for me. This place would provide me with continuing adventure and wilderness. The masculine heart needs this. He needs a place un-sanitized where nothing is prefabricated, modular, non-fat, and on-line—where no hairspray is allowed. The soul needs room.

It seemed that everywhere else in the world, at least villages and highways had come first and then landing fields. Only not here, for Alaska's future was already the part of other places. It was like a new thing shining with the ingenuity of modern times and trying to superimpose itself on an old order. And the old order could be obstinate, resenting something new. But my Cessna 185, in bondage to this obstinate and ancient mountain host, has already performed hundreds of landings here, waiting at any time to become a vessel of death.

Many a moose and caribou, if asked, would have said that life would have been more peaceful had we not arrived. They at first welcomed me with curiosity, and then disappeared over yet another horizon. Most times the animals, it would seem, are the winners.

WHEN "MOTHER EARTH" CLAIMS A PLANE – 1987

I have had others try and follow me, to try to hunt "my" area without experience. But you can't drop into pleasure, without paying your dues. I once dropped a pastor and his son on a gravel bar which was one of my favorite areas. In one day they had one moose, five caribou and one grizzly bear, all taken less than five hundred yards from their tent. This gravel bar had become their Garden of Eden, but later was to become their purgatory.

That game taken so quickly, so close to camp, had become a compelling hook in memory; they must go back! It had also made an impression on many of his friends, who were desirous to follow. Thus the pastor purchased a Cessna 182, so they could return.

He asked me to help him fly his new purchase from California to Alaska, as he did not feel competent to do it by himself. I agreed, and all the way up he kept asking me if I thought he could land his plane at the same place? My answer was unequivocally "NO! There are too many variables! Not unless you could once again find that one nameless gravel bar on the Colville River, and only if you had experience and time in the airplane, and only if the gravel bar was good that year, and your load not too heavy, and only if your technique was perfect." But the pressure was on from his friends, and he tried it and failed.

I was hunting the same river, not aware he was in the area. My flight path providentially led me right over the same spot. I thought I recognized the color of the craft, but not its twisted shape. He had landed too fast, too high. The gravel bar, covered by the river water most of the spring and summer, had changed, and he had not noticed. Several hundred feet down the fifteen-hundred-foot bar was a washout, just deep enough to catch a landing gear and rip it off, but camouflaged from the untrained eye. The plane had found the washout: the nose wheel of the Cessna 182 folded back, cowling and muffler smashed flat, and propeller gone-- reengineered by the earth and prehistoric rocks.

One wing was bent 90 degrees skyward, and the rudder and brake pedals had broken from their mounting on the firewall.

How long would these men have stayed here had I not flown over? How would they have made their way to wife and children 600 miles away? The bears had already stolen most of their moose meat. What next?

The main question of the Arctic and all its flying ventures is "What next?" If that question cannot be answered all the way back to the moose on the plate back with mom and the kids, the venture should not commence. Sometimes the Lord God of heaven and 'Murphy's Law' have nothing to do with the outcome, but only a pilot's God-given common sense and all the skills he can draw upon from the day he smelled airplane gas for the first time, not forgetting to answer the question to its final consequence -- "What next?"

The "What next?" could have meant that the bear, which are numerous here, would become braver, expecting another free moose supper which these men could not provide. Would the bears then starve them out? Would it mean a sudden confrontation in the night, shattering the kindly belief that the similarity of the grizzly bear and the Teddy bear goes much beyond their claws? And since men still live by the sword and smoking barrel of the rifle, isn't it a little optimistic to expect the bear to withdraw its teeth and claws from this opportunistic scene?

"What if?" some of them had broken bones or the plane had caught fire? "What if?" they escaped the wreck, but all their warm sleeping bags and the emergency locator transmitters burned along with the plane? This land is home to 600,000 caribou and wild. It carries with it the stamp of true wilderness, and the freedom of a land still more possessed by nature than of men. "What if?" we had plied some other trade and never tried our wings and the sport of hunting? To this pilot, it was worth the risk, and I am no different. Others are content with their books, the steady temperature of the office, and the mundane.

So I landed with due caution, the main part of the gravel bar being blocked by the wrecked plane. After removing some rocks and brush, I was able to fly them all out to find aluminum, rivets, hammers and tools and cables and turnbuckles and a new propeller. Getting the wrecked plane ready for flight was no small task: the bent wing had to be folded flat, cables and turnbuckles running from the wing tip under the fuselage to the opposite landing gear, new aluminum skin riveted to the bent wing tips, baling wire holding the brake and rudder pedals in place, and the nose wheel bolted with angle iron to the firewall with no turning capability. Once the propeller was installed and all the cowling and muffler beaten somewhat straight, she was flown out, never to fly again, destined for the scrap heap of parts and memory.

CHEATING MOTHER NATURE

"Cheating Mother Nature" and "close calls" are subjective terms and concepts. You must understand "Mother Nature's" terms if you intend to trespass.

We landed successfully on one remote hill in caribou country, north of the Brooks Range, just Ken and Joy Dale, he our song leader in our church. Caribou were everywhere, and we had landed on their migration trail. They would run around us, close by, going southwest.

We each selected and shot trophy caribou. We stuffed the meat in game bags and then put them in plastic garbage bags to keep the blood from soiling the plane. After loading it with meat, I taxied the plane to the take off point on the caribou trail. Then I turned the plane and shut the engine down to load Ken and Joy.

At that moment, the right wheel and tire broke through a thin dry crust of top soil and sank out of sight in thick brown ooze--the consistency of chocolate pudding, until the wing tip touched the ground on the other side! The situation was incredulous and desperate and not hastily solved!

We lifted the wing with our backs, and propped it up with four, five-gallon cans of av-gas which we had brought along. Once the plane was somewhat level, with the tire still half in the mud, we forced rocks under the tire in endless numbers. Upon removing the five gallon cans, the plane just sank out of sight once more. We had to repeat this process three times, finally digging a graded trench in front of the tire. When we removed the cans, the propeller was only 6" from the ground! Under full power, I was able to free the stricken plane.

OTHER CLOSE CALLS

The only way I know how to put this in context is to adopt the assumption that most peoples' lives are so boring on the average that there is a singular refrain that they mouth over and over again. "Tell me about your close calls." Tell me about your closest call." It must be the thrill, the danger involved that gives their life some excitement. We all watch the Indy 500 in part to see the close calls and wrecks. We watch a bull fight to see if the bullfighter pr the bull survives. But I consider my "close calls" no different than theirs which they experience several times each day.

Just going down the highway, one passes other autos and trucks and buses by a mere 2-3 feet of space, separated only by three feet of air and a white or yellow line. Some of those drivers are speeding, drunk, or sleepy or speaking on a cell phone. And yet they think that when a plane flies past me at the same altitude and a mile or more way from me, there has been a close call! I have traveled to Alaska from North Carolina several times and have never seen another plane. But that's not to say that time and providence are not realities to be faced by the most optimistic of us.

One day in about 1994, I was flying cross country at midnight going home after a meeting where I had made a report to a church. The flight would be about two hours in the plane—5 ½ hours by auto. I looked forward to my own bed. Some beds I sleep on while on furlough are more like an Africa hammock, or the fold out couch has a metal bar down the middle which leads to an enormous back and headache. You can say Jacob and Christ had no place to lay their heads, but that might have been better than some couches I been on.

Have you ever wondered what it would be like to have a special chamber built for you, like the man of God in the Bible who passed by and found a great bed put there by a great couple, who also gave him a lamp and homemade bread to go with it. Let's see, which one would you choose? This night I want to make sure of a good night's sleep—I'm on the way to our temporary furlough home.

Only the stars are shining and the city lights below me in Georgia twinkle with more exuberance than the stars. Once in a while the sky supports a weightless cloud which envelopes me in a cocoon of sightless wonder. How long will this last? How high, how low, how far reaching are these clouds? I'm clear of clouds now and the twinkling lights below give promise once again of an over-civilized civilization. Even a green and white rotating beacon persisted here and there, hopeful of staring down the night and at the same time giving me the comfort of a nearby runway.

I was invading the stronghold of the stars and the heavens at night. I would usually fly high at night, taking advantage of a greater gliding distance if I ever needed it, trying to reach the stars, my plane filling the dark and silent sky with a throaty, boastful song. It was supposed to be just me, my plane, and my God, alone together, and going home. At 6,500 feet, those skies were supposed to be barren of towers and mountains and such. And I was at home as much in the skies at night as I was in the day.

Suddenly there was a very loud bang! It was enough to bring an English guard even stiffer to attention than he already was. The bang also shook the Cessna 185 with a small seismic tremor. One always suspects an engine coming apart in rapid fashion, but the engine was running smoothly. I proceeded to the next green and white beacon of hope, keyed the microphone switch seven times on 122.8 to turn on the runway lights and landed.

I taxied to the nearest ramp to inspect my "close call." A large bird—duck, eagle, pelican, goose or some other fowl at odds with nature, was flying at 6500 feet at midnight on a moonless night and just had to hit my propeller. Then it put a serious dent in the engine cowling, leaving blood, guts and feathers from the front of the plane to the tail. How big was the bird? What kind was it? Why was it in the sky at this altitude and hour? If it had been four feet higher and hit my Plexiglas windshield, what would have happened? What am I supposed to learn from this? I wish I could positively know.

I thought it was only humans, trying to act like birds, with their make-believe flying apparatuses that could get in trouble. But in November of 2006, a ruffled grouse flew right through a triple pane window in our log house and was instantly killed as a result of his folly. His body came to rest right in the middle of the living room floor—leaving a seven foot trail of shattered glass--on the carpet, furniture and inside the open piano. I pealed his skin and feathers back, cooked, and ate him for supper all right, but this crazy bird was the most expensive grouse I ever eaten!

I hit birds in the strangest places and birds get in my stewpot in the strangest ways. My work day is finished, dead as the calendar page that bore its number and my schedule. But this furlough year is thick with other pages, full with other work and travel. I determine still to take the road less traveled and then answer the questions again of my much bored friends, "Had any close calls lately?"

There was a relatively close call in that fine Piper Navajo twin that carries eight people. It was a complex airplane for a single pilot to fly, but I enjoyed the challenge. One December day, I was preparing to make a night flight (because of our short winter daylight, the day was dark) transporting some Native Alaskan Christian people to their village.

The conditions at Fairbanks International Airport were darkness, heavy snow, and "three runway lights at a time" in Runway Visual Range or simply the RVR of the runway. The run-up and checklist accomplished, we were on our way. The runway was two miles long, and I started my takeoff roll on the end of 1-Left. I had just reached an altitude of 300 feet, the gear was up, and I'm accelerating skyward at 1000 feet per minute. The runway lights were just a dim glow in the heavy snow. At this precise moment, one engine started sputtering and obviously losing power!

I was compelled now to immediate action, an instantaneous decision based upon previous pilot training. Possibly I could fly on one engine in this snow storm, but could I climb high enough, soon enough to miss the taller buildings and towers in the Fairbanks area? How much runway has passed beneath my wings? Is there enough runway ahead for me to put the gear and flaps down and still maintain control on one engine under unequal thrust conditions? Should I land straight ahead on the remaining portion of the runway? If I did go for the landing on the remaining portion of the runway, would I get it stopped in time before I reached the end of the pavement? This whole scenario was a recipe for indecision, which would lead more certainly to our demise!

I decided in one instant to land straight ahead. I pushed the nose down with my left hand and closed the throttle and put the flaps down with my right hand. About two seconds later, the faint glow of the runway lights were in view. My directional gyro and localizer needle said that I was in the middle of the runway. I landed with a "greaser" and, with heavy braking, got stopped at the end of the two mile runway, right at the last taxiway turn off.

My passengers were merely disappointed as to their having to spend one more night with me, never realizing what a dreadfully close call they had experienced that snowy evening. I put my hands straight out to see if my fingers were trembling. They weren't. I cleaned the fog off my glasses to double check my nervous condition. They were still not shaking.

Now I believe there is a reason for every process we go through, whether it's trying to find God's perfect will or the reason philosophically why my hands are not shaking. We had prayed for God's keeping and wisdom before the flight. I can only assume that God's wisdom which was given to me liberally this night has saved us.

Maybe I believe this so much, I don't now shake. Maybe I'm a confident and good and well trained pilot. Maybe that's why my hands are still. Maybe I'm too stupid to be afraid and that's why my hands don't move. I sometimes think it's all three reasons that compel me to go to the same runway the next day after a failed fuel injector o-ring has been replaced. The run-up was fine at full rpm that day. After another prayer for wisdom, my village friends must go home.

HONEYMOON MUD – 1982

The Alaskan mud and silt becomes in many places a serious form of quicksand, ready to snare and swallow all trespassers who do not understand or discern the signs.

One fine honeymoon day on the mudflats near Anchorage, a honeymoon bride was riding a Honda three-wheeler when it tipped over, spilling her onto the mud's surface. Her mistake was to try to stand up. Trying desperately to free one leg and then the other only made her go deeper. Soon all her strength could not raise one leg free. And the tide was coming in, and coming in very fast.

Friends rushed to her aid, trying to stand on plywood to pull her out. They used their shovels to dig her out, and then water pumps to hopefully release the mud, all to no avail. Finally a helicopter was considered to pull her free, but it was decided it would tear her in pieces.

It would seem that everything had failed her, her own common sense, her cautiousness, her friends, and all of civilization's modern helps. The bride was trying to breathe through a tube, when finally the cold, muddy waters of Turnagain Arm swiftly covered her, never to be seen again.

A simple thing as old as Noah's flood had prevailed--a simple thing called 'glacial silt'. It is easy to pass blame in these situations, but duty simply shows our foolishness. I can step out in front of a fast moving freight train and say, "I have faith in God to stop the train," but He won't. The case of the honeymoon bride was a tragedy with too petty a plot to encourage much speculation and too little irony to invite much reflection.

BEAR HUNTING MUD –1983

A man who had attended our church had much the same experience. He and a friend had left that morning in a small skiff to hunt bear on the shoreline in Southeastern Alaska. All was well until he discovered that he had forgotten the elixir of life back on the shore in his thermos.

That black liquid that flows in the veins of most Alaskans, that liquid monster blamed for ill and good health, the liquid that coined the phrase "Coffee drinkers make better thinkers," had been left behind. Such an oversight could not be tolerated, so one of the men went back to the camp on the shore to get the precious commodity.

What happened can only be speculation. Upon arrival, did the brave hunter find that the tide had gone out, leaving two hundred yards of mud between him and the coffee? Did he attempt to walk to shore on that tricky mud flat? As he stepped out on the mud and took his first steps, did he find his boots sinking into sticky brown quicksand? As he struggled to pull one foot out, was he horrified to find that the other would sink deeper? Perhaps he could get the other free! But, no, the mud only provided his loved ones with a cheaper funeral. The mud had left no trace--not a single clue.

FORGIVEN

Alaska's weather is legendary, and foolish intrusions within her whims by the unskilled usually led to unhappy endings. A pilot sometimes trespassed where he should not have ventured because the weather had closed in around his plane. But just on the other side of the storm, the sun would shine again, as if to remind the pilot that on this occasion he had been forgiven the trespass.

My hangar for twenty years in winter had been a WWII parachute draped over the plane, weighted down on the corners with stones and heated inside with a space heater. The extreme cold carried many liabilities, the least of which was discomfort. I would have to wear 'Bunny Boots' rated to 70 degrees below zero, each weighing about five pounds. In this cold, the landing gear becomes so brittle, it could break on a hard landing.   Or a crankcase ventilation tube could freeze over from condensation and cause serious crankcase pressure, blowing a seal somewhere.

On a Sunday when I was flying to Manley Hot Springs for church services, the crankcase ventilation tube froze shut.   Just after takeoff at about 40 degrees below zero, the engine blew a seal and five quarts of oil departed the engine in two minutes, covering the hot exhaust and starting a fire. Smoke instantly filled the cockpit. Immediately, I opened the windows of the plane and closed the heater to "off" to stop the influx of smoke from the engine.   The engine compartment was on fire!   I made an immediate sharp turn back to the runway and landed.

For mandatory survival gear, I always carry an ax to chop my way out of a wrecked plane, a few tools, a tarp, bug dope, flares, and snow shoes. A screw driver was in my hand as I exited the cabin. In thirty seconds the top cowling was off, and a small fire extinguisher and some snow put the fire out. It was so cold, the wires in the engine compartment, although engulfed in flame, did not even get damaged in the least! This would be enough to scare some pilots enough to never fly again. But the plane is just another type of a horse--one must just get up and get on and ride again.

"I KNOW THE RIVER LIKE THE BACK OF MY HAND" -- WINTER 1985

A young Athabascan Indian man came to church in Manley Hot Springs Alaska to be in our worship service, riding his snow mobile around eighty miles one way down the Tanana River. Several of us advised him not to travel the river. As a pilot, I had observed the thin ice, the overflow, and the cracks and had concluded it was a bad year to travel the river. But he went against the advice and met with open water across from the village he called home, and only his snow machine was recovered.

To this young man, a trip need not be undertaken unless it was manifestly important and nearly impossible. Coming to church in this manner and at his time of year had to have been important. Had the need in his heart been filled? I would like to believe that it had.

And so I fly on Sunday, and church in Manley
Is good with all the faithful and visitors.
Little do I know of his soul and, typically Indian,
He shares little of it with anyone.
I preach clear salvation, have conversation
And send him on his way,
By the snow machine trail to Nenana,
Some eighty miles away.

It seems right that I warn him,
That I tell him all's not well.
For this year is so different;
The river seems under a spell.
As I fly the mighty Yukon,
I see the open leads, .
And thin ice that glares up at me,
Waiting to swallow your steed.
"So be careful" I tell him;
But he gives me that look;
"Don't worry 'bout that river;
I can read it like a book."

So now I stand at forty below
On the river that swallowed him whole.
And peer into the depths
And ponder the place of his soul.
And the arctic lights and the pale moon bright,
Mark the spot on that dreadful ice.
Where the man so wise, with a gleam in his eye;
Met his doom in the deep and the night.
He clung to the edge of the ice for a time
Screaming for life, some say;

But no one came to ease his pain,
And the river had its way.

Robert Service puts it this way:

There's a land where the mountains are aimless,
And the rivers all run God knows where.
There are lives that are erring and aimless.
And deaths that just hang by a hair.
There are hardships that nobody reckons.
There are valley's un-peopled and still;
There's a land...Oh! It beckons,
And I want to go back and I will.
This is the law of the Yukon,
And ever she makes it plain;
Send not your foolish, your feeble;
Send me your strong and your sane.
One by one I dismayed them.
Frightening them sore with my gloom:
One by one I betrayed them
Unto many manifold dooms
Drowned them like rats in my rivers,
Starved them like curs on my plains...
This is the will of the Yukon...
Lo, how she makes it plain!

HUNTING ESKIMO STYLE -- THE TRICKY TUNDRA

It can be said of our Eskimo friends that they are some of the hardiest people in the world. Their land is endless and empty-- a repository of loneliness--where there are no trees, but there is wind enough. Theirs is a land of herds of caribou--750,000 strong, of whales and walrus and shellfish; with months of daylight or months of darkness. In the winter, one cannot tell where the land ends and the ocean begins. There is nothing as far as the eye can see except a caribou to break up the horizon and, as far as one can walk or ride, the view is the same.

The Eskimo are hunters at heart, one and all, who use the entire animal which they have taken for some purpose. When a walrus is killed, his stomach contents of fresh swallowed clams and oysters are washed off in sea water and then swallowed whole. The ivory tusks are used for tools of various kinds and the hide is used to make "skin boats" from which they row and sail after whales. This "art form" of hunting is fast disappearing from the landscaper of the far north. In its place are power boats and explosive harpoons for killing the whales.

The whole village participates in whaling in one way or another. The old men—too old to hunt actually have a very important role in the hunt because you can't hunt what you cannot see. These old men sit or lie on their stomachs on rooftops or on a knoll and scan with binoculars all day to spot a whale at sea. The call goes out when a whale is spotted, and the hunt begins in a frenzy of hurried activity.

For some reason, no one wears a life preserver, and few Eskimos know how to swim, because their waters are too cold to learn this life saving skill. But then, everything comes down to practicality. A person may last 15 seconds to a few minutes at best, so what's the point of a life preserver? To bury oneself at sea is far cheaper than an expensive funeral on the land. The Eskimo is an avid and expert hunter who prides himself on never getting himself wet anywhere. To get wet simply means you will be cold.

These hardy hunters in Point Hope have killed enough whales over the years that they constructed their older homes – walls and ceilings—from whale rib bones, which were then covered with dirt and sod. It has often puzzled me as to why these people continue to live in such an inhospitable place, but it also puzzles me to see a modern white man with a college education rebuild his house on the same flood plain or hurricane coast that claimed his first home.

Once a whale is beached after a long, slow tow to shore, the whole village meets at the water's edge to devote whatever time is necessary to winch the whole creature onto the shore. The whaling captain oversees the butchering and distribution of the whale blubber to the whole village. As they work, the villagers chew chunks of raw blubber, known as "muck-tuck" for nourishment. The strong fishy flavor stays with you for about 24 hours! Contrast this delicacy with that of an educated white man who eats SPAM and even creates a Spam Museum in Austin, Minnesota, as a tribute to his skill in creating something tasty from "small pieces of animal meat!"

In this setting, we worked with Eskimo teenagers, flying them from several villages to Kako Bible Camp. It was the highlight of the year for them, and the campers always wished camp would last longer. Over the years with Missionary John Sleppy heading up the camp and Earl Malpass and myself flying for the camp, many young lives were changed for the better.

Their land is the host of all my darkest fears, a mystery never solved, always intriguing as to why they would live in such a place. Their land is more ruthless than any sea, more uncompromising than any desert. It is without temperance in its harshness and gives few favors. It yields nothing. Its soul, its integrity, the slow inexorable pulse of its life, is its own, and there is nothing to compare. It is a land of such singular rhythm that no outsider, unless born and bred from childhood in its endless even beat, can ever hope to really experience it, except only as a tourist might experience their dance--nothing of its music, nor meaning of its steps. For an outsider to survive a plane crash here would be hopeful at best. There are no landmarks and no trees for fire and shelter.

If you can visualize a million square miles perhaps of frozen flat treeless landscape, which in the summer encompasses thousands of lakes that seethe and crawl with millions of mosquitoes, you have some understanding of northern Alaska and its land. It is a sinister land, eerie and treacherous, an example of all the less attractive byproducts of all the rest of Alaska. Try to walk on it, but you cannot. Walking upon the tundra you would be heaving slowly on a mat of decomposed and living things, affected by permafrost; under which flows a sluice of black water.

The surface of the tundra is inviting from the air, brown and flat, it seems. If you should ever be forced to land upon it, you would find grassy clumps as tall as a man's head, with water between them. At once, your landing gear would be ripped off, and your plane would be on its back. Your wings would sustain your plane's weight in all probability from sinking right away.

Assuming you were safe--no broken bones, seat belt loosened so you could turn yourself right side up, gasoline dripping from the wings, but no fire--and, assuming you still had a radio antenna unbroken on the top of the fuselage (which is now upside down), and the battery is still somehow attached to its cables, and assuming that some airline overhead flying close enough would hear your "mayday" with position and other details, you might, if you are naïve, expect a rescue to happen. But nothing would, because nothing could, except by Providence, you were found and rescued by helicopter.

There are no roads; boats cannot move on the tundra; planes cannot land on it, and men cannot walk in it. It is more likely that those little by-products of the fall of man, those messengers of misery--the mosquitoes, would take your blood much quicker than the Red Cross.

In any case, the anticipation of such doleful prospects must become part of the bush pilot's repertoire, a constant nagging thought that he must plan for. My many thousands of flying hours over it have to this point contributed no new footnotes about flying safely over it. I have noted that most conversation ceases, as my passengers realize their vulnerability to the land. It is as though we are hanging for several hours under a flat blue sky and above a flat piece of utter desolation. You can only think and pray to your Maker and hope He has plans for you tomorrow.

Try flying over this devilish panorama in the night, and none of the shapes, if you can see them, are real or permanent. If you could just see some flicker of a light, but the darkness is boundless, comfortless, and infinite. When you finally see the light of the village, you experience the desperation of a sleepless man waiting for the dawn which only comes when the importance of its coming has lost its importance.

It seems you have flown forever over a landscape of which God used little imagination. You become weary with the invariable scene, and when at last you are released from its monotony, you remember nothing except your safe passage, because nothing was there to remember.

ADVENTURES ON THE ALEUTIAN CHAIN – 1993

Pavlov Volcano overlooks Canoe Bay and Trader Mountain. In recent times, it has breathed brimstone and frequently hisses steam. Who knows really how long this has been going on, but in the time of man the recording of Pavlov's beginnings does not exist.

We were chilled to the bone on a bear-hunting day and took the Cessna 185 to eight-thousand feet to get warm. It was a clear day…we could see for two hundred miles. The wind at eight-thousand feet was blowing about fifty knots, and we hovered just above Pavlov's spewing lip, not moving over the ground, getting a steam bath and staring at death. I then landed at the four-thousand foot level in its ashes and volcanic rock, black as night. The bears were everywhere on the volcano, maybe enjoying its warmth as well. Some would slide all the way down from eight-thousand feet to five-thousand feet on their bellies on the snow, and then climb back up and do the slide all over again.

Under the shadow of such sovereign furnishings, we made our bear camp. Our crab pots were set in the bay and eventually, the supper table hosted a heavenly feast the Queen of Sheba or England could not surpass! Deity has surely passed this way and warmed His hands here. But as we hovered near the steamy craters, we knew simply that we are not Deity, but that we were playing in His playground and breaking the rules.

This is the lavish background against which I cooked a supper of giant crab legs, mussels and butter clams from the beach. A tarp for the cook-shack and a tent for a castle could not be surpassed by any building in any country. Most people who build a castle spend their lives staring at its walls and hoping others will come stare too. My castle was set up in less than an hour, in a different location each day if I wished. The necessity of my human spirit to experience stability and refinement was not limited by my necessity to create, but to simply enjoy all each day and know that He created it. I was released from the pressures of having to make an impression, for I was the one being impressed, and glad to be so chained.

Instead of one coming to admire my home, I was here to admire His footstool. As I explored a little, just beyond the plane's tire tracks that mark the volcano's belly, I stepped with both feet into the track of the king of the mountain--the immense 10½ foot, 1500 pound Kodiak bear! We had come together to spar; to see who really deserved the title--king. I saw his prodigy everywhere, their smaller footprints crisscrossing the volcano. When I finally spotted him, I knew he was old--too old to live another year--but not too old to kill bear cubs. Perhaps he will die of starvation or in a fight with another dominant bear. So I listened to his last request and confession. He had survived thirty years, fought and killed a lot, and defended his fishing hole against all others. He had claimed this fishing hole year after year and his footprints indelibly put on the tundra led to his same bed year after year. Now he is worn out and doesn't mind really being made a rug for my wall, where he will be remembered year after year, and generation after generation. The earth-- the volcano-- has been his to rule. Others will take his place. It is the warrior's last day. I will always respect his domain, and I tried everything to get the bears to respect ours. Yes, everything from a very clean camp to mothballs, to bright lights and rock salt in a 12-gauge.

THE WEE LINE WINS THE DAY –1992

All bears are opportunists and can soon develop a welfare mentality; developing the attitude that "what's yours is mine, and I'll take it if I can." The bears had their territory, and we had to work hard to preserve ours. Understanding bear culture helps.

To keep our food supply intact or our raft or airplane in one piece, we would have to establish a "Wee" line. Almost all four legged creatures that claim the title "carnivores" know what a "Wee" line is. It's a line more smelled than seen and is much more practical to a creature than to one who can read or post no trespassing signs. So all in camp would have to faithfully "Mark their Spot" around the perimeter of the camp. Quite often a bear would walk right to the line and retreat on a dead run, not quite sure what to make of Pepsi, Orange Juice or coffee "Wee." Some bears would almost turn themselves inside out trying to get away so fast. But there is always one bear that has no respect for such time-honored, unvoiced agreements. In the end, none of us are the winners, but the Pavlov Volcano will once again mark her spot and the entire world will know that all of us who play on her flanks are there by permission only.

But I must stop this senseless hovering in the Volcano's steam, trying to get a glimpse of the earth's inward parts. I could say to myself, "You needn't do it, of course; knowing at the same time that nothing is as inexorable as a promise to your pride." There was nothing extraordinary about this flight, but to my passengers it should have been entered into some book of records.

The real records are set by Mother Nature, the coldest I've seen in Alaska was 83 degrees below zero; actual temperature without wind chill. When it's too cold to fly, it's time to maintain the craft. My "regal" hanger consisted for twenty years of a WWII parachute draped over the plane, weighted on the corners with some weight and blown up like a balloon with a space heater. Warm at the top and cool at the bottom was the rule, and I hoped I didn't drop a screw or a tool in the snow. The Alaska weather rule of thumb was and is that at 30 degrees below zero with wind at 30 MPH exposed skin freezes in 30 seconds.

But, whoever said it would be easy? It seems that all humanity wants to make all things happen more easily. If we could invent (grow money on a tree, make things warmer or colder, more convenient), we would. Even God's callings are not easy, though it would seem that man has made many foolish attempts to make it so. When Christ had conversation with the rich young ruler, He refused to be influenced by his wealth or dogmatic assertions of virtuousness, but made it hard on him. Rank and privilege have nothing to do with entrance to heaven, Christ said. When He asked the fishermen to drop their nets and follow Him, it was not easy. The lesson here surely is that all of life is not easy and perhaps the best things in life, though free, really are not free, but cost somebody something to make it free for others.

Nothing of flying is free, but when I learned that the propeller of the 90 horsepower Super Cub could beat the sunrise silence of the Texas plains to shreds and scraps, I was hooked. The plane cost me $6.00 per hour dry; $9.00 per hour wet and $12.00 per hour with an instructor. Now the wind can blow in Texas, and each aircraft has its own crosswind component capabilities, beyond which any aircraft rudder can overcome a crosswind. The ineffectiveness of the rudder usually takes place near the stall, which has to happen just above the runway for a successful landing to take place. But T. D. Brown taught me to "fly the airplane on," to touch one main gear down first, the wings into the wind at 10 to 20 above stall, then level the wings and get both wheels on the ground, where I would then have individual brakes to help the rudder out. All the manuals in the country were devoid of this wisdom and of no use when the chips were down.

Such practice is good for those rainy and windy days. One day in Alaska near Canoe Bay, near the Pavlov Volcano, we camped in a wall tent and counted twenty-one bears from the tent in two days. But we didn't count on the wind. It blew for twenty-four hours with peak gusts recorded at 125 MPH. We had buried two large logs in the sand four feet deep, to which we attached rope from the tie down rings on the wings.

When we returned from our wind blown tent among the trees, we found a plane that required emergency surgery before we could fly. The wind had pulled one of the logs right out of the sand, allowing the free wing to lift high in the air, smashing the tied wing's wingtip into the sand.

Only a certified airframe and power-plant mechanic would appreciate the details, so I won't bore you with them, except to say a damaged airplane <u>can</u> be flown with one wingtip missing and crunched aluminum, if you have some rubber bands and bungee cord to put constant pressure to one side of the controls. About all this, I don't consider myself a test pilot, only a fortunate one.

Rubber bands also worked in the Piper Super Cub when it was a little too heavy in the back. A few rubber bands connecting the control stick to the instrument panel makes the pilot's job easier as long as he remembers to land with extra speed to keep the tail feathers active, and his runway is long enough. Some of our "runways" were three-hundred feet long, a test of skill for any pilot. But the highest risk factor is often with your "passengers." I never guaranteed the life any animal that I flew in Africa or Alaska. Whether it was a goat, snake, chimpanzee or common house cat, all can cause great moments in the cockpit. A chimp is much stronger than a man and his flying skills would be less than honed. Humans are not much better at times.

One fine cold day in Alaska, the battery in the Cessna 185 was too cold to turn the engine over even one time. It was hand propping time, and I would need my passenger to help to hold the brakes and pull the throttle back once the engine was brought to life. I gave thorough instructions to the passenger--"pull this black knob BACK once it starts. It was rehearsed time and again..."pull the throttle BACK once it starts!" And so the engine came to life and the frightened passengers PUSHED the throttle all the way forward and froze! I was barely able to get out the way, let alone open the door in the prop blast and grab his hand to PULL the throttle back. There were several expensive airplanes nearby that I had envisioned being shredded to mere scraps of aluminum foil!

There are many people who find it difficult to work with the controls properly or to keep their hands off the controls. And in their lives, the accidents and crashes continue. We can to some degree sympathize with the frightened passenger, for we have a way of doing the same things in our spiritual journey. Thinking, God has lost control or His instructions inadequate; we panic and lose it.

The controller's voice from Anchorage center was calm and direct: "Turn right," he said, "heading 90 degrees; descend to 4,000 feet." For the past two hours I had been enjoying the bright Alaska sunshine; the 200 miles of visibility, but we were above an overcast with rain and fog. I told the passengers that we would soon be on the ground, not to worry. But who was around to comfort me?

I reached for the microphone once again and soon the reassuring voice of the center controller filled the cabin: "Turn left to 060 degrees. Descend to 3,000 feet." I followed his directions to the letter all the while keeping the plane trimmed and level at the same time. At 3,000 feet we entered the clouds, flying blind through the rain and clouds.

"Descend to 2,500 feet and turn right five degrees," the steady voice instructed. "Descend to 1,500 feet and turn right thirty degrees." The ground and unknown terrain was coming up to meet us, but I couldn't see anything. But I knew the controller was there, and he knew who I was and where. I had never seen his face, but I knew I could trust him. I had no other choice really, unless I wanted to do this on my own.

Suddenly we broke out of the clouds just 300 feet above the ground, and there it was--a mile of wet asphalt glistening in the rain. We, as pilots, tend to miss this truth because it's so common, but asphalt is beautiful, you know! I had been more than willing to trust my life to this faceless voice speaking difficult directions through the fog and rain.

Touching down, I thought of another "Controller's Voice"--patient, calm, always present in the storms of life. It was His voice. Did I really trust that voice as much as I trusted the faceless voice in some air controller's tower?

"Whom having not seen, ye love, in whom though now ye see Him not, yet believing…"

PETRIFIED FOREST--FROZEN DINOSAURS – 2000

Just take the path less traveled, go in the direction of your fears and see what happens. How terribly dull it must be to be a cow, destined to follow the same trail to the watering hole each day! Should a man be like that? He may choose so to be, but not destined, I believe. It is his choice, but as the old Alaskan sled dog saying goes, "Unless you're the lead dog, the scenery never changes!" All men die, but few know how to live.

One day while "chasing" large brown bears on the Aleutian Chain, I landed on a small island's beach when the tide was out, which exposed enough sandy beach to land on. The rocks on this beach were white and blue from the air, unlike all the other rocks. As I taxied to a stop on the sand, I found myself amidst trees, but they were not trees, only a facsimile thereof. Upon further research, I discovered that this was a forest of petrified sequoia trees--wild, prehistoric and unique. Unique, because on the entire Aleutian Chain, there are NO trees in existence, at least none of this magnitude any way.

Here are large trees, logs, root systems; all petrified. And some logs are in the cliff above me, stacked upon each other and covered with hundreds of tons of earth. Since there are no such trees native here or anywhere in Alaska and put here in such a unique fashion, one would have to believe that a world wide flood--the same one that put sea shells on the tops of mountains--had done this. To sit here, airplane tires rolling over prehistoric bits and pieces of God's dealings with man in the past, was persuasive, awe-inspiring and too much to take in all at once. But I took samples as proof, and later brought both my father and a team of scientists from the ministry Answers in Genesis to document this valuable find. The island's exact location will be my secret, and I hope few humans find her treasures.

When you work with humanity day in and day out, attending to so many needs, one can despair of men. But fly away to the Aleutian Chain, find a petrified forest, the result of Noah's flood, and I could find poetry in a field of rock. Don't try to convince me that I'm "off my rocker!"

On another expedition still to be scheduled, I shall fly a team from Answers in Genesis once again to a rare find, a frozen dinosaur on the North Slope of Alaska, on a river that used to be my moose pasture. The number of grizzly bears on this river is legendary. It was one of the few areas in the wilds of Alaska where the hunting regulation book specified that in this area only, "one must remove game meat from the field immediately." The reason was simple--within two hours or less, a grizzly bear would challenge the hunter for his moose or caribou meat in some fashion, sometimes with disastrous results for the bear or the hunter.

In the fall of the year, a plane can land, avoiding the quicksand, on the exposed bed of the river (called a "gravel bar"), if it's long enough, straight enough, no washouts or driftwood in the way, and no caribou or moose hiding nearby (waiting to run in front of the plane at touchdown). This area is a bone yard full of animal remains. The frozen dinosaur's jawbone indicates he was forty-foot long and ate plants. My father and I both had landed on this river and upon disembarking from the Cessna 185, our feet had stepped on the rear molars--very large teeth--of the great wooly Mammoth and Mastodon. We have found broken ivory tusks on this river's banks and more intrigue and wonder than any man could drink in-- in one day!

If a pilot makes any mistakes here with the plane on takeoff or landing, his fate could be no better than that of the dinosaur he is bringing again to the world. And bring him frozen to the world we will! All packed in dry ice, he will be flown to a scientists lab, his DNA to prove that he lived at the time of man and not billions of years ago.

The carvings of dinosaurs and people on the same prehistoric rocks in Siberia will prove the same things, as we take that less-traveled path in the future. I'm determined not to be like this river whose borders I have trespassed, following in all of its turns, the path of least resistance. So on another day, I shall fly a fortunate few to Northern Siberia, to a remote prehistoric site, to show that someone with "Design" and "Purpose" created all this. As a pilot, not to believe in a "Master Designer" is like believing a great tornado blew through an aluminum scrap-yard for at least a million years and the result was a Boeing 747! It takes a man with a larger faith than I to believe the tornado theory.

But now my attention must be fully given to this landing and takeoff. Is the tide fully out; is the sand too soft; are there any washouts; sharp obstacles to puncture tires way out here; can I miss all the rocks and petrified wood on landing now and the takeoff later when the tide comes in? This is the bush pilot's checklist, as opposed to a standard airman checklist, which presupposes a paved airport with all the trimmings. The bush pilot's check list assumes that at some point, should he forget anything, the ground will come up and smite him.

FORGET THE BEARS—THE SHEEP WILL KILL YOU –
2000

Being alone with bear in very close quarters in a vast wilderness, even for a very short time, with nothing to depend on but your own hands, your reflexes, and your rifle, may leave you with nothing to contemplate but your survival, the bear's demise, and the size of your small courage. Such an experience can be as startling as the first awareness of a stranger walking by your side at night—and you are the stranger.

But consider a dall sheep. What is he anyway but just about the best eating meat in Alaska? Is he inherently dangerous? Would he ever stalk an individual or charge a man that was after him? No, he is shy, reclusive, has seven-power-vision and runs from all potential enemies. But his domain makes him dangerous indeed--his domain and his courage to live there in that lonely place at the top of the world. It draws man as well, with strength and pull as strong as the darkness pulled below the horizon by the sun. There are men who will hunt nothing else in Alaska, bearing the cost and not blinking.

The dall sheep or mountain goat live in the high places, often at the seven to eight thousand foot level, the earth his footstool, the rocks and boulders his playground and bed. His white coat blends with the snow and he seems to be comfortable in sleet, snow, rain, high wind, or sunshine of summer and darkness of winter. His speed and agility in the crags and steep places is legendary. In a moment he can disappear like white lightening and usually chooses to show himself only when he is "seven powers" away, requiring a seven-power binocular to spot him among the rocks which are more difficult for anyone to ascend but him.

A hunter or photographer can never go there and return on the same day but must take his tent, sleeping bag, ground mat, rifle, ammo, food, water, stove, knife, rain gear, warm clothes, binocular, matches, spotting scope, back pack and more. With all his gear, he then begins to climb the steeps to usually 7,500 feet. It's for a man in shape, a man with grit, a man willing to die should he fall and break a leg or ankle, or get caught in some terrible blizzard. The whole time spent with sheep is a calculated risk, and you begin to reflect with every ponderous step forward, your sanity and your reason for doing this. One slip and broken bones or sprained ankle can cost you your life in the cold snows and rain and fog.

The majesty, the mountains, the challenge of getting close to a sheep is irresistible. Yet, a refrain echoes through the valleys, the driving snow, the incessant wind; all your senses tell you this is no land for the timid. If you are fortunate enough to have the wind in your favor and remain hidden from the ram and all the other sheep sentinels, you still have to pack about a hundred pounds of sheep meat on your back down the mountain. This descent from the clouds is usually harder than the ascent to them.

About 75 miles south of Fairbanks lies the Alaska Range of mountains. They are very high, very wild, mostly uninhabited, and perfect sheep country. It is also the home of grizzly and black

208 *JOURNEY TO THE EDGE OF THE SKY*

bear, caribou and moose. The eagle soars effortlessly in the sky, watching for the arctic squirrels and the arctic hare. When it's clear in these parts, the F.A.A. weather service gives the visibility as 200 miles. When it's not clear it can be measured in feet.

To be at the top of this world on a clear day at 7,500 feet, following a well worn sheep trail, is to say the least, intoxicating and breathtaking at the same time. The rivers below are silver ribbons of silk. There are no noises except those made by nature. Unlike the bear who may hunt you, you are here to hunt the sheep, but the terrain can swallow you whole as a glacial crevasse waits silently to swallow you when you trespass her frozen secrets. And when you disappear in the glacier, the world will probably never know; and it all happened with much more speed than the bear attack.

It is here, near Wilderness Skills Bible Camp, that I have hunted the dall sheep, not once but twice. You would have thought I would have learned the first time, but sheep tranquilize you, inhibit your ability to think straight. So it was that I took one Mr. Greenfield, an army serviceman, and flew to the airstrip at the camp. We rode a Honda 3-wheeler four miles to the base of Sheep Mountain. My parents, Ludwig and Lorraine Zerbe were spending the summer out at camp in a cabin he had built, and they wished us well. It wasn't long and we discovered two good rams resting below us. The 3 wheeler took us through the Totatlanika River on several crossings with water three feet deep at times and put us at the base of the mountain in about two hours.

By late afternoon we were looking at our sheep. We were fortunate to have found them resting below us, because they are always looking for danger below, rarely above them. After all they are the king of the mountain. But so it is that all creatures are created with their weak spots.

These two sheep were looking down with seven power vision, but not up. These two hunters of sheep have poor eyesight most of the time except when corrected by seven power binoculars, and certainly poor feet and footing and muscles that ached with each punishing stride. The sheep with his "one hide does it all" surely smiles at our tortuous ascent with our 40 lb.

packs, complete with warm jackets, long underwear, rain gear, socks, moleskin for blisters, medicines, small stove and fuel, matches, knife, small tent, sleeping bag, spotting scope, and more—miss one necessary item and you can be in trouble. But with all this, the sheep were below us now, unaware that they soon would be fare for the table.

Pulling the trigger was easy, but it was almost impossible to get down the rocks to them. Once down we knew in an instant we would never go back up that rock face with 140 lbs. of sheep and gear on our backs. Our only choice was to go down a new part of the mountain. And all was going well for a long time on our one day hunt, until we reached the bottom of the mountain. We were in a canyon with rock walls and only a narrow strip of sand. We had approximately a half mile to go against the current in raging whitewater, sheer rock cliffs on both sides, and darkness was approaching. To make matters worse, it had begun to snow.

There was one solution to our problem and that was to get "buck naked" in the snow. Then with our meat and packs on our backs, rifle and clothes above our heads in hands, enter the ice cold water. We would zigzag among the boulders for about a mile against the current, which was waist to chest deep.

My companion in this foolishness, Neil Greenfield, made it across on the first try, making 20 yards of progress. My try was at first unsuccessful, as the sand washed away in front of a boulder I was using as a lever against the current. I immediately went under the current, and everything was wet. Another boulder got me, and then I finally inhaled a big gulp of air. Making it to the other side, I had to gain the ground I had lost just to make it back to my partner. I finally made it with him all the way back to the 3-wheelers, but we had very serious hypothermia--shivering uncontrollably.

My wet clothes were colder on then off, so it was back to "buck naked for me!" I knew that there would be no one out here to witness the spectacle, except perhaps the God of heaven, and I hoped He would laugh only once and give us the wisdom to make it home. But the book of Hebrews describes "a great cloud of witnesses"—it was these I wondered about! I hope it is above these heavenly bodies to ever bring this up to me in the future as some sort of blackmail.

At any rate, we had only made it two of the four miles on the 3-wheelers when we knew we were dead if we didn't get a fire going immediately! About that time, we stumbled upon an old abandoned prospector's camp and found the remnants of some old blankets he had left, which the bears, rats and porcupines had ravaged. We grabbed those pieces anyway and covered ourselves somewhat for two hours in front of a small fire.

After that, although we didn't feel warm yet, we thought we could continue to the cabin. The remaining two mile ride to the cabin was cold, but uneventful. We arrived at 4 AM to a sleepy Mom and Dad. There I stood, wrapped in ragged pieces of torn-up blanket decorated with rat and porcupine dung! The gorgeous sheep now hangs on my wall in Fairbanks, Alaska as a reminder of these noble creatures and of a hunt I barely walked away from. But I was soon to forget the lessons of recent history.

I have a good friend, older than I by a few years, whose grandchildren had made a most solemn but challenging observation. "You're too old to ever get a sheep, Grandpa," they said. If life isn't about friends and helping them, then of what value are you? A word grows to a thought—a thought to an idea—an idea to an act. But put all the pieces together, and the whole is yours!

Our restless thoughts turned to absurd ones, and we knew the grandkids challenge must be answered. We made our plans, putting together each part, to hunt the same band of sheep on the same mountain out by the camp. At least I now knew the mountain and its pitfalls, or so I thought. After assuring Ed Jones that youth and speed were not the criteria for successful sheep hunting, but that experience and wisdom would prevail, we set out, on the same three-wheeler, crisscrossing the Totatlanika River on the way to where California Creek joined. From there our slow progress brought us almost within shooting range, but some sheep saw Ed, and the whole bunch headed for higher territory. It was either retreat or sleep on the mountain in just a plastic tarp and meet the grandkid's challenge the next day.

We made it through the night—no rain or snow, and the morning light revealed about fifteen sheep above us, not too far away, all lying down and facing different directions. They were being very careful sentinels and any movement from behind the tree we had slept under would have sent them to even higher ground. At just before dark they began all at once to feed. We knew it was now or never so we tried to remain hidden and ran toward the feeding sheep. At about 400 yards we let age and cunning take over and soon we were 30 yards from a very nice full curl ram.

At the shot from Ed's rifle, the ram fell where he stood, and the rest of the sheep ran to a place on the mountain I remembered--a rocky ledge 200 yards from Ed's sheep. Below the rocky ledge was an almost 2000 foot drop straight down to the Totatlanika River, which I knew would be a real challenge, even for a sheep. The rocky ledge was just 25 feet below the top of the mountain, so the sheep couldn't see me as I stopped to catch my breath in the approaching twilight. Then with a shell in the chamber of my 375 H&H, I crept, then I crawled to the peak of the mountain and looked over to the rocky ledge.

There, 25 feet away, were at least ten rams, all looking straight at me. They began to dance around on the ledge, all sheep bodies touching each other in their dance with destiny. I picked out a good one and the 1.5x5 Leopold scope told me when to pull the trigger. At the shot, all the sheep left the rocky ledge, and my heart sank. I had seen where wolves killed a dozen good rams just for the fun of it and left most of them to rot, and I worried that I could be so irresponsible. The sheep just went into space, it appeared to me, and I just knew they would all be at the bottom of the 2000 foot chasm! But to my pleasant surprise, they had landed on about a one-foot-wide ledge on the mountain and had disappeared somewhere.

The sheep I had shot was down the mountain about 25 feet, hanging by one of his massive horns to a single small pine tree. As quickly as possible, I let myself down to the sheep on a rope. The tree was almost coming out of the mountain by it's roots, so I had to keep most of my weight on the rope while I sat on the sheep's nose and head. The sheep's body was hanging straight down as I hung onto the rope with one hand, sat on his nose with some of my weight, and gutted the sheep with my free hand, all the while trying to make sure if the sheep and the tree departed said company they wouldn't take me with them to the bottom. At least gravity was working with me in the gutting process, and the ravens would be happy tomorrow. With the end of the rope around the sheep horns I climbed back up and then pulled the sheep to the top of the mountain by the rope. Now it was time to attend to Ed Jones' sheep.

Some have asked why I pack a rather heavy caliber on a sheep hunt such as the .375 H&H, which is regularly used on lion, Cape buffalo, and elephant in Africa. The reason is quite simple-- grizzly bears. I had a friend one time who was negotiating his way down a mountain with a load of sheep on his back in the darkness, when he heard something. He turned around to make out the shape of a grizzly following him. Since the grizzly is just about the color of darkness, he could only hear him shuffling along and breathing. It seemed to him the grizzly was getting closer by the minute, closing in on the raw sheep meat he had on his back. So he finally dropped his whole pack of meat for the grizzly and continued to the bottom of the mountain.

Now our night on the mountain would be spent with my .375 H&H by my side, and the sheep meat not too far away. With my "life insurance" policy by my side, I would at least sleep some. But where was Ed Jones' sheep? It had fallen with his first shot, but now it was not where it fell! We looked for quite a while, but finally had to give it up until morning.

The day broke beautiful, the view was astonishing, and we knew why we thought this was worth it! I found Ed's sheep about a ¼ mile away, lying on a rocky ledge in the sun. He had a red spot on his back where Ed's shot had just grazed him. After a second shot, the ram didn't move. If he had, he would have fallen

2000 feet into the gorge that had cooled me down on my first sheep hunt.

We got home that night with both sheep and the grandkids had to eat their words and sheep meat the next day. A fitting end.

So no sheep hunt is easy. They will test your will, your stamina, all your skills and common sense—and more. And that is why hunting these "lords of the high places" is more than just another hunt. It's a mesmerizing experience and unforgettable. I have noticed in the book of Romans that much of the world is in error, worshipping the creation rather than the Creator. I have discovered, in hunting the Dall sheep, a new appreciation for the Creator of this magnificent panorama and the sheep. It is almost universal to say that the dog or the horse is man's best friend, both equally proud of their allegiance to each other. But the sheep and the bear, I have suspected for years, are only tolerant.

HOWARD & FRAN--THE LOST ART OF LISTENING -- MAY, 1982

The old man stirred his camp coffee, getting all he could out of the once used coffee grounds, by adding a few more grounds. Then 72 year old Tom Goggins went outside his rustic log home on the Chandler River in the Brooks Range of Alaska to the nearby creek to haul water for the day's cooking and washing. It was May, a gorgeous spring day in the Brooks Range, one of the most beautiful mountain ranges in the world. Tom and his family had made this his home for many years, the children home schooled with A.C.E., a Christian school curriculum.

Tom was a trapper and gold miner near St. Mary's Gulch. Everything was on a small scale, just enough to get by, and get by they did. They would often go six months before seeing anyone but themselves, and they had no communication with the outside world. There were no roads, no electricity, no radio or TV, no running water except for the creek. Fish were sometimes in the creek and always in Big and Little Squaw Lakes. The nearest people, the nearest hospital lay 250 miles away in Fairbanks. His family could only be reached by small bush plane which could land 18 miles from his cabin on an abandoned gold mine strip. They would somehow have to get to the airstrip some 18 miles away if they were ever to meet a plane.

True isolation as this family experienced daily has to be a choice. A choice perhaps to enjoy nature and all its creatures without outside human intervention or interruption, to be dependent solely on the earth for your substance, taking gold dust from the creek to buy flour and beans and sugar and coffee. Your security is self-realized by each day's hard work, the nearest grocery store 250 miles away and Wall Street 5,000 miles. Perhaps the lure of striking it rich at St. Mary's Gulch and all the ramblings of the geologists of this area kept them there. They say this area is rich in gold, there is a fault that runs through this valley, and then there is Nolan Creek nearby, and others who have struck it really rich.

Tom Goggins' questions to all of us who might consider his lifestyle would be: "Is not life one of hope, of unfulfilled expectations, of not having to go to work for someone else for just eight hours, of finding treasures on your own as the earth gives them? Is it not recognizing the bears as they pass through, perhaps giving them names and knowing their habits? Is it not living where no other man dare?"

"It is here," he would say, "where one good unattended stack (stove pipe) fire can burn a cabin down in an instant and all your belongings with it. One casual slip across the rocks in the creek can result in a fall or broken bone; one glancing blow from the ax in the wood pile could open a life- threatening wound. A careless moment with the rifle or shotgun may become a life or death situation. Should an accident happen, those in the wilderness must deal with it themselves, as a doctor or dentist is perhaps six months away."

The decision to live an isolated wilderness lifestyle is not a decision made in a vacuum or made lightly in the overview of the alternatives. Almost every decision made in life has a philosophical reason behind it, even if that reason is unvoiced. A man cannot share entirely all the things that occurred to create his philosophy of life with the other people who come in contact with his vision or philosophy. Thus, one's offspring and all others "living the philosophy" must learn well the art of listening. There is always someone less directed, perhaps bored with his life, which is really a reflection on his philosophy of life, who will want to share yours, perhaps share in its benefits.

It was not surprising then when Howard and Fran came along; two city slickers recently from Fairbanks and who knows where before that. They made contact with the old prospector and asked if they could stay with him for one winter to learn the fine art of trapping and living off the land. Perhaps Tom felt his family needed the company, and he welcomed the slight intrusion into his domain. So Howard and Fran had to listen–to learn life as though from childhood in this pristine wilderness.

My grandfather used to say, there is a distinction between looking at something and really seeing the thing; a line between hearing something and listening. A mother with a newborn listens and sometimes hears the baby cry almost before it utters a peep. The father hears all that's going on and keeps right on snoring. To be acutely aware of your surroundings and listening is sometimes critical to life.

I once took a "would be" bear hunter into the field for the powerful Kodiak bear. Now this hunter was very afraid of bears, and I soon figured out the only reason he had come on this hunt was to kill one larger than his best friends. It was a macho pride thing only. His ability to live with the bear and fight with the bear on the bear's terms did not thrill him.

He told me on the first day out, "Now I don't like wounding bears, so I want you to get me real close before I shoot." What he was really telling me was that he was really a lousy shot. He was not prepared. He had purchased his big 375 H&H Magnum three weeks previously and certainly wasn't proficient with it. While in the field the first day, his rifle scope fell off on its own accord. We found the scope, re-installed it and sighted it in.

Then I made a stalk with him to within 30' of a 1400 pound sleeping brown bear. I told him to wait till the bear stood up because the grass was too tall to get a good view of the napping bear. The bear finally stood up and frightened him so much that he missed him clean at 30' and again broadside at 60'. Had he been by himself and the bear decided to eat him, the bear would have had a dinner. As it was, I let the bear run to his freedom, the would-be hunter cringing and crying inside for his cowardice and ineptness.

Howard and Fran would "hear," but not "listen." They had survived the whole winter and now it was spring. Tom treated Howard and Fran to a cup of camp coffee and began to explain.

It was obvious; spring was everywhere–snow was a melting, icicles dripping water on the back of your neck as you walked out the front door of the cabin. The sun had been gaining ground on its arctic course in the heavens and adding twelve or so minutes each day since December 21st and was now giving over twelve hours a day of honest warmth. It was a time of renewed hope in every creature from the greatest to the smallest. The long winter had been persistent, dark, and cold and would take its toll on all but the hardiest. But Tom, his family and Howard and Fran had persisted and were survivors in a real sense and were rejoicing in all the sun would bring.

Tom's explanations were in detail and had a serious note to them. "Spring in this country stirs everything," he explained, "the water, ice in the rivers as it breaks up, the spring flowers and all of God's living creatures large and small. This includes the grizzly bears," he emphasized.

"There are many bears in these mountains," he cautioned, "and they all come out of hibernation this time of year and pass right by the house here, following the creek down the valley. You see that hair on the corner of this cabin? It's from last year. I opened the door and an 8' grizzly was rubbing his shoulder on that log, and three years ago a grizzly almost tipped the outhouse over with me inside it!"

"Now for the next month," he continued, "I want you to carry your rifle everywhere, with the magazine full of rounds and one in the chamber with the safety on. I know you may think that's not the safest way to carry a rifle, but it is for the next month...trust me."

Howard and Fran listened intently. "You mean we have to carry that heavy rifle when we have to go to the outhouse? To get water from the creek or put clothes on the line?"

Tom confirmed that their observations were correct and then proceeded to warn them further that "all the bears were hungry when they wake up. Watch out about sow bears with cubs. Shoot a bear only if necessary." He told them where to shoot the bear and that even after a heart or lung shot a bear could still run 100 yards and maul them.

Howard and Fran's education had begun six months earlier and was continuing. But a student only learns if he "listens," if he has not merely "heard" but has "listened." "Listening" means one has assimilated completely the material and will act on what he has learned. Tom had something further to say.

"I bought a Honda 4-wheeler in Fairbanks last year, and Les is going to fly it in here next week. I'm getting too old at 73 to walk everywhere. I'm going to ride the snow machine 18 miles to meet Les day after tomorrow to get the 4-wheeler. I need you to go, Howard, to bring the snow machine back." So it was decided; they would leave Fran by herself with a rifle for a few days perhaps. Tom's wife and children would be nearby. It would be an exciting time for Howard especially, getting to see a plane and a new face for the first time in six months and a new 4-wheeler.

My calendar said it was time to make the flight--time to disassemble the 4-wheeler so it would fit in the plane, which meant the wheels and tires, plastic body and luggage racks would have to come off. It would then barely fit in the plane, always leaving a permanent scratch or dent somewhere on the plane. All the plane seats would need to come out of course, except the pilot's.

The destination was an unnamed abandoned gold mining strip near Big Squaw Lake, probably with some snow on it, a rut or two, brush growing up under the wings and of course very muddy. That's where these "Tundra Tires" come in handy again. With the Tundra Tires inflated to only 12 pounds, the plane would ride on top of the softest sand and most mud. There would have to be no wind from the side on this landing; keeping the plane straight in the mud would be tough enough without the wind. Lives and deeds were about to merge and lessons as well.

Tom and Howard had some more worn out coffee, along with a moose steak, dried eggs and sourdough pancakes for breakfast. Then they loaded their old snowmobile to the max. Each man had food, back pack and rifle, a forward look, and few parting words to the women left behind. Howard said his good byes--they would be his last. The pair started out, the snowmobile protesting like an old mule with too much on her back.

The snow had frozen from the night before and was hardened on the top, making going easy. Three miles into the 18 mile trip, the engine blew. Out here it was equivalent to a major heart attack--the machine would not live again in this life. Perhaps 500 years from 1984, someone will stumble upon this relic in this out of the way place on the tundra, proclaim it from another civilization, and write a book including it.

After analyzing their situation carefully, Tom said he would walk the 15 miles to the "airport" to meet Les. He instructed Howard to just follow the snow machine trail the three miles back to the house and Fran. Each went their separate ways.

The weather delayed my arrival at the strip till the following day, but Tom was waiting, his 73 year old frame bent with fatigue. A Honda 4-wheeler never looked so good to anyone! It was some struggle, but we removed the machine and put it together and stayed the night on the old gold mining strip.

On such occasions, I just sleep in the plane, my jacket for a pillow and my –60 degree sleeping bag my best friend. Supper consisted of creek water and a sardine sandwich, with a salted nut roll for dessert. My 44 magnum pistol lay next to me. The night delivered to me was star-studded, the northern lights doing their magic tricks in I-Max dimensions.

The next day we rose early, deciding to find breakfast at the cabin eighteen miles away and that good camp coffee. I drove and Tom hung on for his life, until three hours later the barking dogs announced our arrival to Howard and Fran. Fran came out from her place of hibernation and ran to greet us. As we dismounted, we asked, "Where's Howard?"

"I thought he was with you guys." Fran replied.

Tom and I looked at each other for some time, not saying a word. We both knew that if Howard was not here, we might never find him. His survival knowledge to handle even this Alaskan spring weather was about nil. His instructions had been so simple--"Just follow the snow machine track back to the cabin."

We decided to have our brunch and dry out over the wood stove; we had to study on our next move. The fear in Fran's eyes was all too obvious. She had that wrenching gut feeling, also knowing that Howard was too naïve, too inexperienced. He had no tent or sleeping bag, while the spring temperatures had dropped to just above zero at night. How could Howard have missed the trail? She remembered all of Tom's warnings now: "The bears are out, and I want you to carry your rifle with you everywhere for the next month--loaded, magazine full, and one in the chamber with just the safety on".

After several warnings to Howard when Tom had caught him not taking his rifle along everywhere, Howard had complained: "What do you think I am--just a big kid that you have to keep telling me to carry that rifle?" Fran remembered that Tom had said nothing more to Howard about it.

"Let's go call the state troopers," I told Tom. "We'll let them find Howard, but before we do, Tom, do you remember a red rag on the snow machine trail about three miles back?"

Tom probably waited five minutes, deep in thought, before he answered me in a hushed tone. "No," he said, "There shouldn't be any rag that far up the trail--no red rag for sure."

So thinking this a clue, we set out retracing our ride toward the plane 18 miles away, searching for that red rag and Howard. At about three miles, we could see the red rag at some distance laying on the trail, a beacon leading us to tragedy. Tom remembered some red long-handled underwear of Howard's which he had seen hanging on the clothesline from time to time, and this material matched. Without saying a word to each other, we knew what had happened to Howard. We looked in the immediate area and found a toothbrush and a pack of cigarettes. A gruesome story was unfolding, but we felt we owed it to him to look for him.

Looking back now, that was one of the most foolish of decisions--the idea that we should look for him with a 44 mag pistol in grizzly country. We were certain the bear had gotten him; it seemed the only reasonable assumption since so much of what had been Howard's was now scattered about.

His red underwear had been ripped, and the telltale piece left on the trail. I decided I would put my shoulder-holstered Smith & Wesson model "29" 44 magnum revolver with 8 3/8 barrel and target sights, loaded with factory 240 grain soft-nose ammo, on my shoulder and start looking for Howard. Now as I have explained, a 44 magnum revolver is not large enough--no more than marginal on a bear--even in the best of circumstances. But that's all I had. Tom had his old 30.06, and it was probably as old as he was. Even if he had offered it to me, I would not have accepted, knowing nothing of its reliability, accuracy, or quirks. There are no second chances with bear, and I would pack iron I was familiar with.

So Tom followed me in small, then larger and larger circles, searching cautiously and hopefully for a sign of or from Howard or for a fresh bear track, so I could gauge my adversary. The track would tell me the bear's age or if it was a sow with cubs. A good grizzly can swat the head off a man, kill him with one well placed bite, or shake him like a rag doll. A bear's attack is fast and furious--killing and disabling its victim in mere seconds.

All our searching produced nothing, so we headed back to the four-wheeler. On the way back, I found Howard's rifle, at the base of a tree, partially covered with snow, rusty. I showed it to Tom and opened the bolt. It told the whole story as far as Tom was concerned.

"I told him a hundred times, if I told him once," he lamented, "that he was to carry his rifle, the magazine full of rounds and one in the chamber with just the safety on." It was obvious to Tom that Howard had not listened, and it had perhaps cost him his life.

"Let's sit down and take a break and try to think like a grizzly bear," I suggested. "If I had just taken a man, where would I take him before I ate him?" Tom thought it a good idea, since a man getting his lunch also finds his place to sit down and eat.

Sitting there, we carefully looked around at all the terrain. Then I noticed something that caught my eye and stood up for a closer look, scouting around the base of the tree behind us. I could see some strange looking tundra flowers making a gallant effort to encourage the onset of summer, but growing at an angle while all the other flowers were growing as straight as though nature's level had been placed on each one. I pointed this out to Tom.

"Those crooked flowers indicate a drag mark. If we follow them, we'll find Howard!" With all the courage and some fatalism, I suppose, I started the path of foolishness following the bent over flowers. They led us to dense growth with little or no visibility, a perfect place for an ambush. My deodorant wasn't doing me any good anymore, but that was good--the more that bear had to smell, the better. Maybe he would leave me alone and run the other way!

About 200 yards in following the flower trail, the scenery changed abruptly. There in front of us was just a pile of dirt with bear tracks everywhere. On top of the pile of dirt was Howard's skull bone, his large arm and leg bones! Beside the bones were his leather-laced boots, his feet still in his boots with the legs bitten off at the ankle! Part of his belt and pants and hunting knife lay nearby. The bear had already finished his meal and had gone. We would leave things as they were for the state troopers to investigate. Fortunately for Tom and me, there was no attack--no rush to judgment by the bear. There wasn't anything for the bear to guard any longer because he had left nothing but bones.

But Howard's empty-chambered rifle told more than a story about his death. It also told about his life. He died learning the difference between hearing a command and listening to one. Adventure in this wilderness may only be presumed upon if you understand the danger and are willing to cope with the outcomes. Most men like to read their own maps—find their own destinations. Howard, like most men, was not willing to be mentored by one more experienced. And I had almost fallen into the same trap by going in to find Howard without sufficient backup in the face of the possibility that the bear could be there, guarding his fresh kill and me with only a 44 mag pistol. I, too, could have become an Alaskan bear statistic, because of Howard's inability to listen and "keep a round in the chamber with just the safety on."

Under the circumstances, was his life worth trying to save or find? I kicked myself for going in to find Howard with this pea shooter for my defense, but I guess Tom and I did the good Samaritan human thing. I might not do it again--follow a bear track to find Howard-- instead of Howard's tracks to find Howard. And surely if the bear had overpowered me in one second, could and would Tom, at 73 years of age, been able to help me with his rifle? Was he alert and fast enough to make his mark in time? It was the wise man, Solomon, who remarked, "Time and chance happeneth to them all." When it's all said and done, I'm sure God allows things to happen and that we, in our humanity, exercising our God given volition, also make things happen--good, bad and unfortunate. But one sometimes does crazy things in an emergency.

"Time and Chance"—a man can die quickly or slowly. Hopefully we all understand God's grace at the end to the point we can cope with it. In Africa, a man can be overtaken with malaria for years on end, with its chills and fevers and its nightmares, but, if one day the man sees the water from his kidneys is black, he knows he will never leave that place again, wherever he lives. He knows there will be long, tedious, very uncomfortable days ahead which have no real beginning nor ending. He will lie in his misery feeling the hours and minutes pass through his body like an endless ribbon of pain because time becomes pain for the rest of his life. Light and darkness in themselves, become pain; all the man's senses seem to exist only to receive more pain; to transmit to his mind again and again the ceaseless message that he is dying.

I had seen men, women and children die in this manner, and now I had seen Howard's demise. The African malaria mosquito lands on a person silently and, without medicines, he will die slowly. The grizzly bear no doubt descended on Howard in more or less a silent rush, not even giving Howard time to review the earlier instructions of Tom to him. The point I gather is, I don't know how life will end for anyone, but to know the grace of God to meet my end in dignity and in His presence is all important.

Fran did not take the news of Howard's death by the administration of the claws and jaws of a grizzly too kindly. Eventually the troopers came and saw to the details. Some time later, Fran approached me with a jar of ashes and instructions to throw them from the plane's window over Big Squaw Lake. That I did, and Fran went to Wisconsin, never to return to the "Great Land"—the place I have come to know as "no land for the timid."

The arctic is a harsh taskmaster and, in the sometimes bizarre dichotomy of character that defines the place, a siren of sorts--wailing out its warnings. As adventurers and hunters--once touched by the breath of the Alaskan wilderness, once surviving to walk away, once experiencing this barely imaginable land--it isn't the warnings we consider. The hunter will return, but it's no land for the timid.

Early on I observed in my native friends the subsistence value system—the necessity of living off the land, the ingrained hunting and fishing ethic so entwined that to miss a season of hunting and fishing for food would put this unfortunate soul in such a depression as to ruin his or her whole year. There is a vacant spot in all humans that can only be filled with the knowledge of God.   And another vacant spot exists, I believe, when one does not enjoy His nature.

A man doesn't come to any conclusion of enjoyment of either God or nature until he makes a conscious decision to want to experience both completely.   The white man sitting in his computer cubicle hunts for information continually to get ahead. The Indian and Eskimo do another kind of hunting, achieving the same effect, putting food on the table.   I just know that the computer nerd can't wait to go hunting one week out of the year— 'nuff said.

Truly, hunting in Alaska is an experience every hunter with an adventurous spirit should try at least once.   Arguably, as the license plate declares, Alaska is "the last frontier" left on the North American continent.   Finding all its good hunting and fishing spots would take a lifetime if you hunted and fished every day!

Imagine a land without fences, without "No Hunting" signs, without bounds, a land which seems to have no end, where the sun never sets.   Imagine only one hundred days between freeze ups, in which the lives of all things vegetative, showing life and color, are compressed by necessity into this time frame.   It's a land at times still and silent, resolute during those times when the temperature is -50 degrees to - 80 degrees, capturing your soul and body in its cold tentacles.

Enduring is the only option on the occasions when the snow blasts incessantly across the frozen reaches.   Hunker down and endure; read a book if you have one, because home is where you belong!   Make no mistake-- the danger is real, the land, the weather, and all its creatures, waiting for the unaware to make just one mistake.

THE 80 YEAR BLIZZARD -- SEPTEMBER 1997

The "unaware" part almost caught up with me a couple of years back while trying to put a moose in the freezer for the year. I was elated to be on my regular two weeks of hunting per year. Charlie, a 72 year old friend of mine, from Beckley, W Virginia, went hunting with Nathan, my 13 year old son, and me. We had landed on a runway which was really just a 1200-foot bare spot on the side of Monument Mountain, near the villages of Deering and Candle on the Northern Seward Peninsula. We set up our tents and began hunting.

It came out of nowhere--the worst blizzard in 80 years, the natives said. It would almost prove our undoing. Seeing new country is exciting, and hunting different kinds of game in that country is the stuff hunter's dreams are made of. Most of the sights and sounds and experiences will become part of fond memories. My wife tires of hearing me tell her of "Murphy", that fellow who introduces with quite some regularity, unpleasant surprises for the unready. But wild new country was out there, and we had to see it—to experience it. Experience it we did!

The blizzard blew at 50 knots for 24 hours, and a rather heavy snow left about four feet of snow on the ground and some great drifts. There were no eggs fried that morning, no coffee. We just hunkered down fully clothed in our coats inside our sleeping bags for 24 hours. Every two hours, I climbed out of my bag to kick the snow load off the tent to keep it standing. A jar beside my cot served as a "necessary", as it was too easy to get lost outside in the white-out on the way to the outhouse.

Twenty six hours previously, we had "called in" the moose my friend had taken. We had watched him coming to our lovesick cow call, thrashing the brush as he came. The pressure was almost unbearable as we watched his flashing antlers precede toward our fraudulent sound. How many deaths, how many wars have been started over time by the females of all species? Well, this one was no different--he was in love.

We barely had time to clean our prize for darkness was against us. We had to leave him a mile from camp, a "No, No." because of all the grizzly bears in the area. Then the blizzard came, the Arctic version of oblivion. The world might be standing on end, and then it might not! Your senses fail you.

When the blizzard finally exhausted itself, we went outside the tent to look around. So much snow had drifted that our Honda 4-wheeler wouldn't drive up the runway. We were a long way from any other people and must comply with the laws of nature. Without a shovel or snow plow, we had to tramp down the snow to the plane at the top of the runway.

Then we discovered that our moose had been claimed by a grizzly, but our noisy approach caused the bear to leave. The entire moose had been covered with a huge pile of tundra and dirt to protect it and to "age it" for a tender, tasty meal later. But our life was in the balance now, because the snow would stay, our one shovel was buried in it, the ATV would not go in the snow, and certainly the plane would not be able to move for any sort of takeoff.

One of our tents had been broken to the ground, as well as most of the cook's shelter by snow load. The plane had stood its ground, quivering in the wind, tied to earth by one strong rope.

You can never count on everything going your way in any of nature's surprising encounters. Our main objective was to get off that mountain--to stomp and push to the side enough snow to make a runway.

The wind had blown so hard, the aircraft itself was free of snow. But on a Cessna 185 fuselage near the rear, just forward of the horizontal stabilizer, are two little air scoops the size of fifty-cent pieces. The snow had blown into those two scoops and filled the tail cone with snow, putting the center of gravity completely out of range. There is no pilot check list that includes these scoops for inspection.

When we finally did make a run for it that evening, the tail did not come off the ground until the last 40 feet of the mountainside runway. Then it took full forward trim and down elevator until we reached 110 knots of airspeed. Eventually heat melted the snow, and it leaked out the back. Alaska had told us again that she was "no land for the timid."

All things being equal, one's chances of survival are directly proportional to his desire to survive. Equally outfitted with gear, adequate or inadequate, two humans of equal conditioning in a bad situation in the wild, the one with the greatest will to win, to survive, has the greatest chance of doing so.

The biggest problem among the white men I take into the wilderness is their orientation to calendar and clock. We self impose deadlines which cause the white man to get ahead in business over the traditional ways of the Indian or Eskimo, but deadlines are often his undoing in a survival situation. More hunters have been killed by "get-home-itis" than by any other means. In the Arctic, home is where you are when the bad weather hits. That wedding, funeral or board meeting isn't worth your life. "Let the dead bury the dead," we were told by One much wiser than ourselves.

It's like taking drugs from an addict when I ask that all watches be left in the airplane's glove box for the entire hunt. Time stands still for the fortunate as around midnight (for no one knows--the watches are in the glove box) they sit in silent darkness, listening to the caribou as they pass 50 feet away in migration--clacking their hooves and moaning to their young. The wolves howl in the distance, and, from across the valley, we hear the loud crashing of antlers of two bull moose in mortal combat over territory.

Above are the arctic Northern Lights, those eternal arctic dancers! The lights of many colors wave and shift, glow and fade, and then burst forth in color. It's haunting, beautiful, and will leave the most traveled sportsman humbled. And once that sportsman has taken in as much cosmic pageantry as his mortal soul can handle, the tent awaits. He is surprised at how few things one must have to make him really happy. This total, almost out of body experience, must be repeated again and again.

THE MEXICAN CONNECTION – 1997

That little clock keeps time –it rings or chimes when you set it, but it is a sad substitute for the sun hitting you in the face. But in Fairbanks, Alaska, on December 21st with ONLY three hours and 42 minutes of daylight, it's time to awake, to go on what is called "furlough" to the lower 48. I know it's not a real furlough, but a non-stop blizzard of activity, speaking engagements and making of many casual friends. A stern touch of reality overcomes the urge to just stay with the work and in bed. Sleep has fled, and I am defenseless against the future sunrise, so I'm up and grabbing strong coffee, the Bible, and day planner.

This will not be just "furlough." While I'm "Outside" (out of Alaska) I'll be going to Mexico, flying representatives of "Bearing Precious Seed" ministries to the inroads of this bordering country. I must not entertain too much discontent with my having to be on "furlough" for a year. I'm incorrigibly discontent to a degree in my present surroundings, knowing there are those to whom only my plane can carry the Christian message.

I am really an incorrigible wanderer, because all that I love is at and below my wingtips. The walls of my house hold memories and secrets and laughter. Life has been breathed into them, their logs returning warmth from the woodstove's efforts. Hands have turned the window latches; my children's feet and many feet of good friends have trod the thresholds, friends who have heard the cordial creak of our wood floor. And I'd like to stay, do a furlough here, shut off the plane, and hibernate. But memory is a drug that can hold you against your will, against the ability to do right and to hear what the "Master" said: "No man hath left father or mother or lands . . . ."

Besides, it will be easy to make this furlough into a serious and satisfying adventure. I'll call and see old friends and hopefully turn casual, frivolous relationships into long-lasting ones. We will sit and drink weak coffee (not mine) and discuss things that each has saved for the other to hear. I must not allow myself any misgivings or a moment's remorse; not the luxury of feeling young, nor the misery of feeling old.

As I leave Alaska for this year of "furlough," my main concern is that the heater in my house must stay on, or the water pipes would freeze, and a disaster would ensue. Someone responsible must look after the house, not just stupidly disregard my instructions while idly contributing a twig to the fire.

I sit there in the firelight and find my yesterdays mostly as good as anybody might want. I fondle my memories and see them all and file them away for my friends on furlough. Many of these friends have given sacrificially and rearranged their lives, like Joseph did for Mary, so that I could do what I do. Every fourth year or so, they expect the sound of my Cessna 185, and it always comes.

On the way I will stop by El Paso, Texas, and fly the bush of Mexico for a while for "Bearing Precious Seed." We will find remote places, small towns and ranches that rarely see an outsider. I will land in their pastures and on so-called roads and taxi the plane right into their town to give them Bibles. Carlos Demerest with his not-so-quiet personality will be so happy that I brought him. I'll ask him from the old Western movie, "Aren't you glad I brung ya'?"

I awaken much before dawn at such times (and it's very easy to awaken before dawn in a winter in Alaska) and look at the fading stars and Northern lights that are caught in the rectangle of my picture window. Outside is a winter wonderland of snow and frost, and a moose is wandering through my now-dead garden that he ate last summer, perhaps laying his claim in memory at least to another garden he will find here next summer. Little does he know I'm going to Mexico and won't do a garden this year.

I awake my family now and ask a simple question that every one answers but no one has listened to. "Are you ready to go?" When they finally are ready, there will be questions as to how all this will fit into the airplane. It's a six-place Cessna 185F and the rear seat is for children, but we now have big kids—two of them teenagers, and a dog.

The dog is a little bichon, a white canine powder puff, but he is a large component in the flight planning. That little white "worthless" mop would have to be on someone's lap for the thirty-three hours it takes to get from Alaska to the East coast. He would have to be walked, tethered, fed, and kept from marking his territory in the most inappropriate places, one of which was a gracious hostess's white lace curtains. He lifted his leg in utter defiance to protocol and just about ruined a friendship. If he would just tend to chasing cats, I could rationalize his presence more easily.

I must also include in this flight plan from Alaska to El Paso to Mexico my food stops for the seven of us. Here the dog's fare is simple--the same mundane pellets. There are long distances to cover in this land which is called "no land for the timid," and the times of travel will not coincide with our hunger pangs, so I arrived at a brilliant plan! I would have Jane make a large aluminum pan full of Mother's best old-fashioned bread pudding with lots of eggs, bread, raisins, and sugar--all the necessary food groups and dessert in one dish, which doesn't have to be heated and would last quite a while. If only I could get the rest of the family to recognize my genius!

On a certain day when it was 30 degrees below zero, we departed Fairbanks. We just knew we were heading south where the sun shines and this hope propelled us and gave us courage. I had forced my genius on them, and the hardest choice of each leg of the flight was who was going to hold the dog and who would hold the bread pudding in his or her lap?

It was our daughter Carol's turn to hold the bread pudding, to guard it with her life, the dog's nose twitching just inches away. The bread pudding made to Grandma's specs was extremely juicy with egg custard and needed to be kept level. For some reason, vibration perhaps, airplanes put people to sleep, and Carol was no exception. The pan tipped sideways as she napped and covered Carol's clothes with spicy sticky drippings.

Egg custard smells better than some ladies' perfume, so I didn't mind her being with me as a walking bread pudding advertisement. I only minded all that went with the clean up and the fact that, at age seventeen, she didn't seem to appreciate the humor in the whole episode. At age nineteen, Carol became a pilot for Peninsula Airways, a regional airline in Alaska, for which she flies larger more complex planes than I ever did. Not all our travels and incidents in the plane had turned her off to flying, but to this day, she refuses bread pudding!

That long trip through Canada seemed to never end, as did the bread pudding, but eventually we were in El Paso, Texas, a stone's throw from Mexico. The bread pudding pan somehow just disappeared from the scene, never to be found again. I wonder, what could have happened to it? It occurred to me that a consensus had been formed about the return trip and what would be served as refreshment or survival food.

"Bearing Precious Seed" prints Bibles and portions thereof, and I found their compound from the air on the outskirts of El Paso, Texas. The control tower has my plane on radar, of course, because of the drug runners using planes across the border. I radioed the tower that I would be landing the plane where no airport existed. I watched for cars on the gravel road, high-tension electric lines, and stop signs on posts higher than my wings, deep mud holes, and livestock. The landing was uneventful and taxiing into their parking lot received all the residents' attention, as well as the FAA's. I was legal, but at the same time suspect.

My Cessna 185 had very oversized tundra tires for unimproved landing sites, a STOL kit for short takeoff and landing capability, and dents under both the horizontal stabilizer and elevator where rocks had abused the lower surface—all of these a dead giveaway for a drug plane. The only difference was a large grizzly bear painted on the vertical stabilizer and the fact that I was into smuggling Bibles instead of drugs.

There is just something about teasing an over-zealous, "I got nothing better to do but look for trouble" bureaucrat. But I was in no trouble. I'm just a Bible smuggler. While his mind is full of questions about the plane, where did I drop in from, etc., I ask him one too. I have the right not to answer any questions, but I did have the right to ask any I like. "If you were to die today from any cause, are you sure you would go to heaven?" I think to myself, I'd give a penny for his thoughts just now, but a penny's worth was about what his entire mind produced.

The plane was parked in the front yard of Bearing Precious Seed right by the flagpole and under the watchful eye of the whole community. A few bystanders who were not even bureaucrats gave me that look--"we've never done it that way before." They could not help wondering why this "bull" had not followed the same "cow trail" that all the other "cattle" and "sheep" had followed. I was actually administering the first but necessary lesson that, once learned, would open up Mexico to BPS as never before.

I wanted them to know that I would be landing in cow pastures near small towns with no airfields, on ox cart roads that only burros and cattle traverse, and taxiing right into the village. This way we would see and deliver the Scriptures to people who otherwise would never see a Bible in their hand. They would all come out to see this crazy gringo who brought his plane to their streets.

Bearing Precious Seed had a number of buses used for mission trips to Mexico--some carrying people, some carrying supplies, and one just for cooking meals. In this part of Mexico, there is basically one paved road with many unmarked gravel roads leading to various "rancherias"--essentially small villages, and to larger towns and villages and some cases to a single ranch.

BPS was running out of new places to take buses because of the uncertainly of the roads. They might go fifty miles on a single lane road and find it washed out and have to back the bus all fifty miles to the main road, because there was no place to turn a big bus around. So my plan was to find new "rancherias" and villages this day from a lofty perch where oxygen is almost needed, and the one hundred mile visibility would give up the secrets   of   this   part   of   desolate   Mexico.

The air was heavy that morning in El Paso, the life gone

out of it. Ahead of me was a land that is unknown to the rest of the world and only vaguely known to the rest of Mexico. It was a land of grass and tumbleweeds and cactus and sagebrush. There was some forest, very little water, age-old mountains, but none tall enough to keep snow, stark and grim and foreboding as a moonscape—a land without much life, but a land teeming with life, but only a few people.

The air took Carlos Demerest, leader of BPS in El Paso, and me into its realm and enveloped us entirely, leaving us out of touch with the earth momentarily, living in space with a half-developed moon in broad daylight. Carlos loved the possibility of exposure to new people that no one from BPS had seen before.

Our distance above the earth while searching for the souls of never-before-seen Mexicans was such that we were not more than a passing murmur, a soft drone on the ears of the sleeping lizards 11,000 feet below us. To me the plane was alive, and she spoke to me and told me that the effort I asked of her was well within her powers. I flew so high and fast, she was starving for power, but the rudders and wings told me her willing muscles would carry me well on this mission. I was relaxed. My left hand rested upon the control wheel in easy communication with the will and way of the plane. Distance and time slipped smoothly past my wings with only a slight whistling sound.

We flew high to see the big picture and the largest towns and villages and then flew over them to put their G.P.S. coordinates on paper. Then I flew 20 to 50 feet over the "roads" to determine their compatibility with bus travel and, in all, we found nearly ninety new places that could be reached with a bus and entered the location in the memory of my GPS. Then the bus drivers could utilize a Global Positioning Satellite system in the bus as we had in the plane. They would be able to tell exactly were they were on any remote dirt road or how far one of those ninety towns was ahead of them. This was a significant thing for BPS, and it was the plane and modern technology that had won the day.

Day turned to night, signaling the end of a very fruitful day. Our last stop was a precarious landing on an oxcart path and some pasture and then a street. The airplane stopped only a stone's throw from a large horned resting bull that lay still but looked menacingly in our direction. I gave him wide berth while the chickens gave us the same.

There is a feeling of finality about the end of this flight through darkness back to the mundane world of dust and wind-blown trash and the slow plodding of men. It had been a very long hot day. As I cut off the fuel, the engine sighed into silence. I relaxed in the seat and slid back away from the controls. My ears and mind adjusted to the emptiness of the silence that engulfed me. "All I want," I would say to the waitress, "is a tall glass of Texas sweet tea."

THE BISMARCK CONNECTION – 1997

Flying through North Dakota is usually an experience that one hopes passes swiftly. It was 30 degrees below zero outside when I landed the Cessna 185, and the wind was 30 knots out of the Northwest. I wanted only fuel, a "pit stop" and some more altitude. My compass would point southeast to where God had more balanced the seasons. After all, the birds had enough sense to go south. As I paid my gas bill to a 65-year-old man whom I had known about the space of two minutes, his phone rang. It was the sheriff of Boulder, Colorado. He was calling this aircraft broker, a veteran of forty years in the business, about selling a plane.

The sheriff had a PA31, a Piper Navajo, with a Panther conversion (worth $150,000.00 just for the conversion alone). It was a beautiful plane, a twin engine, confiscated in a drug bust operation. No one in the sheriff's department could fly a twin so he wanted to trade it for a single engine Cessna Turbo 210. For some reason, the broker said to me, "Les, you may want to look into this deal."

I called the sheriff immediately and offered him the Cessna 185 I was flying, but he said "No," because none of his men could fly a tail wheel plane. I asked him to give me six days to find someone who would trade a Cessna T210 for my Cessna 185; then I would trade the Cessna T-210 for his nice twin engine plane. I explained to him that I needed this plane to smuggle Bibles into Siberia rather than drugs into the United States. I about dropped the phone when he agreed!

So I made six phone calls and found a man in San Marcos, Texas, who would trade my Cessna 185 for his T-210. The sheriff agreed to take that Cessna T-210 in exchange for the twin. The sheriff and the owner of the Cessna T-210 had never seen the planes they were about to trade for!

Now you may say all this was just circumstance, happenstance, and a fluke. But all three of us did the trade, and the sheriff loved the C-210 so much that he bought me an airline ticket from Denver, Colorado, to Mt. Vernon, Illinois, where the big twin was parked. While I possessed a twin engine instrument rating, I had never flown this type of aircraft before. That night I read the manual and flew it away the next day.

It may not be your miracle, but it's mine! This is not a common place thing. It is only common to men who view all things common, whose minds and souls have been dulled to all of those things attributed to "Providence." When all the pieces are put together, the whole is yours, and the pieces could not have been put together by yourself.

Now the drug lords had the money, and they had lavished their Navajo with all the best equipment, the best radios and navigation equipment. The sheriff took notice and removed all the radios and best equipment-- $17,800.00 worth--leaving me the option of sign language in rehearsing my next movement with the control tower. It was like fixing a Rolls Royce with bailing wire! A small hand held radio got me to my next stop for a missions conference where I spoke to thousands of college students, my last meeting before returning to Alaska with the plane.

Two days passed and the phone rang--that incessant phone--but it's okay when God is speaking through an airplane broker, a sheriff, or a long lost friend.

I hadn't seen this friend, nor spoken to him in more than twenty years. I had first met him when I was driving a semi-truck from Montana to Chicago to pick up a steel building. On the back of the big truck was a 1926 Chevy, all original, used regularly, and purchased recently from a second uncle for $50. (I sold that antique and made enough profit to purchase our tickets to Africa the first time over.) At that time, this guy was unmarried and intrigued to see me pull up to his church in a semi-truck.

When my phone rang, decades later he and his wife had a daughter graduating from Pensacola Christian College in Florida. I had been speaking to the student body where she was in the crowd. She heard this missionary speaker and remembered our picture staring at her for twenty years from her parents' refrigerator. She concluded that this had to be the same Zerbe and came to ask me. It was a grand reunion, even though she was not yet born when I had met her father-to-be.

Now her dad is on that incessant phone, and "Providence" is in the ring. He told me that he is the pastor of a small church that is about to merge with a larger one. They have some church funds that needed to be given to a ministry, could we make use of them? He would consult his people. This church group, never having met me, wanted to help me with the plane radios! "How much did I need?" they wanted to know.

A radio shop had assessed my needs at $17,800.00. They had $17,600.00! I jokingly told them that God was never $200.00 short! The rest came from another donation. Now I could navigate, communicate, and declare that a Potentate, without debate, had set my plate with blessings aggregate! Find your most capable computer or poker player, and you could never find the odds to compete with "Providence!"

SOME MIRACLES DON'T FLY –2004

I have almost come to the belief that real miracles these days are donations of benevolence from the heart of God through the hands of man. Such miracles that awe me are something too petty a plot to encourage talk with another. I have had numerous miracles surrounding missionary airplanes, but when I explain the miracle to someone there is usually only a grunt of some kind.

It's not their miracle, I guess, so what should I suspect is their lack of enthusiasm for my miracle. Is it that their walk with God or lack of it, merits a miracle? Could it be a jealous reaction to my "good fortune"? Is it that they don't realize that miracles are not really common place—else they couldn't be classified as such? Is it because a mind is too shallow to really appreciate a miracle for what it is—something fantastic from the hand of God? Perhaps their hearts are no different from the disciples who asked, "Who did sin, this man or his parents." Never seeing the bigger picture?

All I know is that few expressed real interest in a miracle that involved insulation. What could be more boring than insulation to work with or talk about? But in the Arctic, insulation is important! The hangar for my plane in Alaska had already been donated by a supporting church in Florida, a miracle in itself, but the hangar came without insulation. In the Arctic, a metal building with no insulation is an unheatable, cold building. I had no funds remaining for the insulation and no intention of borrowing any.

I called two brothers in the spray foam business for twenty years in North Pole, Alaska, to come and estimate the cost. I had planned ahead of time to ask them to hold that quoted price until next year. They spent an hour measuring everything and figuring, then handed me a quote of $15,000 for just the insulation! I was quite taken aback by the numbers and knew God would have to work a miracle for me next year.

At the very moment I read the $15,000 quote, my cell phone rang. My wife had called to inform me that a small church in South Carolina had sent a check designated "hangar project" for

$15,000! The provision was made for the exact amount to the penny! At the second of need! For mundane insulation!

Whether anyone else is happy for me or not, I will be happy with my personal miracles, a donation from Deity and Deity's people. Hip, hip, hooray!

THE CANADIAN RATTLESNAKE SWEEPER -- 1998

Alaska is home to many things, but snakes are not among the species that crawl through its trackless regions. The story of two rattlesnakes on the way to Alaska begins earlier.

Once there were some men in Houston who promised to buy some turbine powered aircraft for "Project Siberia." With turbine aircraft I could fly Bible educators, missionaries and school teachers to all regions of Siberia. It would be a daunting task, but they felt our plan was workable, and we were up to the task.

It certainly would have been interesting, taming the "evil empire" from this perspective, but it was not to be, as their foundation fell on hard times, and the planes could not be funded. But one of the gentlemen wanted to do something for me since our hopes for the planes were dashed. He informed me that maybe he could get me an air-ride 40-foot-long diesel bus that I could convert into a motor home, but "he would need a couple of days."

My concerned friend had seen a large diesel bus parked by a church and noticed that it was rarely moved from its spot in the parking lot. Now, he was not a member of this church, but he had a friend who was a skyscraper builder in Houston who had built the church--a fine steel building at a reduced price. So this second friend approached the pastor and asked him if they ever ran that bus.

"Not very often," was his reply. "We put a new engine and transmission in that bus, and brakes and tires too, and we've made only two trips into Mexico with it since then."

My friend then informed him that he knew a missionary that needed the bus worse than he did!

"Give me a couple days," he said, "and I'll talk to my men." My friend soon informed me that I was the proud owner of that bus—all I had to do was go pick it up!

I do believe in miracles, so I followed directions to an address in a city of around four-million people. When I found the pastor's office, I walked in, and he was on a long phone call. He merely looked up, asked if I was there for the bus, and said, "I'll be here awhile—here are the keys and title to it—have fun." On my way to the bus I did manage a smile and recognized it was just another miracle. "Is anything too hard for thee?"

On my way to Alaska in this bus, I went through Montana where my grandpa had homesteaded. It was a cool morning, the black asphalt being the warmest place on the prairie. Now there are a few things that I don't swerve to miss on the road, cats and snakes. The two species, along with the mosquitoes in Alaska, I am sure, are all part of the curse from the time of Eden.

The bus was cruising around 72 mph, and the two slow moving rattlesnakes on the side of the road were just a blur. Now I just happened to have a one gallon glass, empty pickle jar with me; why I don't know. It was probably the church folks who had eaten the pickles and left the jar.

It seemed like I had to back the bus up forever, but since the snakes were "cool" and not too spirited, they were soon in the jar with the lid secured. My pocket knife put breathing holes in the lid, and I placed them on the dash of the bus near the vent so they could be defrosted. It wasn't long, and they were warm and ready to strike anything that moved.

My plan was to give them to the school, so my children could dissect them in science class like they do the frogs and rats. In the back of my mind, I thought they might not make it past the border guards at customs, but they never asked about snakes, only hand guns and liquor. So I made it to the next town, where I had lunch. A phone call to my wife dictated I should make all haste in getting home, as all the toilets were not flushing, and I have this thing about the rates plumbers charge. Now it was a question of how fast the bus would run, and whether it would hold together for the next 1500 miles.

As I approached the bus, I noticed a man with some belongings sitting by the bus entrance door. He was friendly and seemed to know a lot about my kind of bus and claimed to have worked on them for several years. I thought he would probably be good company, as he had asked for a ride to 500 miles north where he had a job at an oil field.

Now I never pick up a hitchhiker, unless I have a hidden handgun nearby to take care of any emergencies, but I was in Tory land--a land still beholden to the Queen of England--and they now prohibited the carrying of handguns through Canada. I felt naked except for the snakes lying there now motionless in the glass jar, cooled by the lunch stop. My rider was intent on his new ride and didn't notice the snakes, until they moved in the jar once we got underway. The snakes were my handgun, and the man, I am sure, was wondering what kind of man had picked him up!

Well, it is interesting analyzing people. I had already analyzed my passenger; now it was his turn to wonder about me. Where did the snakes come from? Why were they in a glass jar, so precariously perched on a slick metal shelf by the bus windshield? Were they pets? Defanged? Was I a religious nut snake handler? Could he find another ride quickly, all the way to his destination? Why is he going so fast? Will I survive this trip? I would just look back and grin nonchalantly, making his ride all the more tortuous.

Now I figured a real man would not be afraid of a couple of snakes confined to a jar, especially a burly oil field worker. A real man would at least demand an explanation, a dialogue before death or departure from the speeding bus. I could see the color leaving his features, so I figured I would reassure him, let him know that this was not just a fast trip—somebody proving how fatal it is to be a fool. Snakes in a breakable jar on a slippery dash and stupidity; you can imagine the rest. My rider could imagine the rest, so I gave him a job and put him on alert. All he needed to do was keep the jar from hitting the floor! We headed for the horizon at 72 mph, the governed top speed.

We were now in the middle of nowhere, a situation easily found in both Canada and Alaska. My rider finally exerted a little manhood and asked me, "Why do we have to go so fast in the dark with rattlesnakes on the dash?"

I was so proud that he asked, but my answer, "The toilets at home in Fairbanks are stopped up," did not seem to appeal to him as the correct or truthful answer of any sane bus driver. But the answer was true, as I could envision backhoes and a half dozen men digging up the entire septic system!

I again encouraged his manhood by giving him a broom with which to keep the snakes at bay should they get out of the jar. Besides, I wanted to converse with him about eternity and his relationship to God, and I wanted him to keep me awake all night, or for the next 500 miles. This was not, in all probability good reason, but that's the way it happened. He assured me, with blue knuckles clutching the broom, that if he wasn't ready to meet God before, he was now!

I assured him that heaven had nothing to do with snakes, because one of them had started man's slippery slide into hell, and surely there would be none in heaven. I also assured him that these snakes were scientific snakes, due to be operated on in two days. A picture of my family and the teens who would shortly be carving them up seemed to calm him down quite a bit. But it was not for long.

Darkness had come, and there was some construction and road frost bumps typical of the arctic. I had not slowed in resolve or speed, and the bump sent the jar airborne--the snakes weightless and ready. The jar shattered, of course, and the two snakes were at my side and at his feet in an instant! I never slowed the bus which was humming along happily at the governor and 72 mph!

"Sweep! Man, sweep!" I said, as I opened the door to the bus.

He really had no choice, so he resolutely became, probably, the first Canadian snake sweeper in Canadian history. He took a sedative and left me alone to endure the night and his snoring, which was almost as scary as the snakes. The hours that marked the rest of the trip went on like the ticking of a clock that had no face and showed no time. But I arrived none the worse at my door, my wife greeting me in the proper manner.

"You look a little flushed," I said.

"The toilet won't flush," was her reply.

HANDICAPPED PARKING

"Life is not always fair, but it is always just." These words just rolled off the preacher's lips as though no effort was required, as though he understood "Providence" entirely, when in fact, only the God of heaven knows what's fair and just, and He is the only one able to administer it. Only He can be satisfied with it in regards to mere mortals. And God Himself, being the first hunter in Eden, could be the only One who would understand why one of His who loved hunting so much should fall out of a tree he was trimming and become paralyzed from the waist down at age eighteen years.

Deity does not stop loving us though we are seriously paralyzed, and so George Barry loved life and the rigorous sport of hunting, though permanently injured by the fall from his tree. He would not give up on what he loved. He refused to give up on life and all that makes it interesting. And so it was that George operated a 600-gun gun shop in Indianola, Mississippi, and operated it from a wheelchair quite successfully.

Barry's urge to be in God's creation and hunt His creatures for food for himself and friends was so overpowering that he found himself year after year hunting deer from a Honda three-wheeler by himself. He expended Herculean effort to find and shoot forty deer each year, clean the animals, get all the meat out, cut and wrap it, and get it into his freezer and to his friends. Solomon, the wisest man in all history was a hunter and said in Proverbs 12:27: "the slothful man roasteth not that which he took in hunting; but the substance of a diligent man is precious."

And as most men do, George dreamed of hunting in Alaska, but no one would take him. Hunting the "Great Land" usually requires hard walking over rough terrain--tundra, hummocks, rocks, water, mud, and quicksand (not to mention early snow)--that men with two good legs find difficult to negotiate. Wheelchairs don't go there, but that was his mode of transportation, period.

Then one day he called, and I could not refuse his plea to take him moose hunting. It was as though God had put "Moose Mountain" there just for George Barry with an inscription in the tundra reading: "Handicapped Parking." He would be the first to visit my secret "moose pasture," to put his useless feet in this grand arena. From the time George reached Fairbanks and my living room, the wheelchair became a non-entity, not at all a part of the equation. In the end, we would wish we had something to move him with.

Barry lived with his useless legs but their presence was but a whisper; they could not produce with vigorous ease as they had before. Moose hunting was in his craw, and nothing would dissuade him. It always starts out a pleasure to help such a handicapped, but determined man, fulfill his dreams. I would take him to a place on the northern Seward Peninsula, to the tundra, an endless and empty place, but a place as warm with life as the waters of a warm sea. So I took him under my wing and flew him to my moose pasture, where moose, grizzly bear, wolves, musk ox and caribou--750,000 caribou in this one herd by several estimates--so I thought this would be easy.

There are trails of the migrating caribou webbing the land like a spider web, the hollows and mountains trampled by thousands of them. Now and then, a grizzly bear or a musk ox appears plodding along on the horizon like a gray boulder come to life, and the adventure begins. There are no roads, no villages, no towns, no radio or telephone. There is no landing field here, but there is a top of the mountain, a patch of ground smooth enough to receive a plane if the wind is right and the pilot careful. I have landed there often, and usually I have seen caribou or musk ox in the path of my glide to earth.

The bears here have been bribed so often by the gut piles of the caribou we have killed, so as to make them in habit, sort of welfare recipients in the wild. But to approach these fur balls with claws and horns, however, would mean the sudden shattering of our kindly belief in the similarity of a teddy bear and the real thing, which goes much beyond their Hollywood-ian image. But since man still lives by the sword, it is a little optimistic to expect the bear to give up its teeth or withdraw its claws, handicapped as he is by his inability to read our "better" intentions about the immortality of bloodshed.

I am convinced personally, you see, that if this old bear could speak, he would say, "I am old and I shall die unnoticed, chewed to bits by another bear who wants my female friend. So just help me from the pangs of a lingering death and hang my skin on your wall as a token of my immortality." I'm sure old bears with battle scars, no teeth, and ivory claws are wishing this.

But today, I would share George Barry's somewhat reckless persistence in this pioneer tradition and be a hunting guide for my paralyzed friend to a 76 inch-wide-antlered moose near "Moose Mountain" on the Seward Peninsula.

Part of any aerial adventure in Alaska begins with a look at the maps and the weatherman's charts and predictions. Both will tell you lies. The available Sectional Maps currently depicting Alaska all bear the cartographer's scale mark of 1:500,000. One and one-half inch on the map is about 10 nautical miles. Moreover, it seems that the printers of these maps have a slightly malicious habit of including the names of towns, villages, and cabins which (while most of them did exist in fact as a group of prairie dog holes may exist) were usually so inconsequential as to completely escape discovery from the cockpit.

A cabin in a remote area, if a pilot and plane meet the earth due to unseen circumstances, is a most welcome sight. But many such cabins in Alaska are mere illusions, hallucinations of an airman's hopes. Time after time, I have looked for these, and, aided by my imagination, I would bank and swing lower over the suspected cabin until its outlines were sharp and clear, but, no, I was disappointed again. In the case of many cabins, they were just gone. These phantoms of hope lie everywhere on the Alaskan landscape; so I found it easier to carry my own cabin in the plane–a three-man dome tent and a few tins of sardines and pilot bread.

We were going west in the midday sun, and hot invisible shafts of air rose upward and exerted physical pressure against the Cessna 185's wings, lifting her in sudden motion as heat from a smoldering fire lifts a flake of ash. My friend, finding this incompatible to his stomach, buried his head in a large black garbage bag for most of the trip. So his remembering the exact spot where I would take him would still be my secret. He was not a flyer, but he was a hunter. It was sheer madness and pleasure for him at the same time, but after three hours of flight, we arrived at "Monument (Moose) Mountain."

I remembered once again that this is a "one way in, no way out" opportunity to land my Cessna 185. The mountain has at least a 7% uphill grade and once in a certain proximity to the mountain, you are committed to her like a good woman. Once you know her, there is no turning back. She is stately, and has her own beauty. She is a princess who hides gold in her thighs and you will want to return to her as often as you can, for she has a lot to offer. Her spell is unshakeable, and she is dangerous.

When you once know the obstacles, sizing her up with her errant winds blowing the trees as your only windsock, you fly right toward her, the nose of the plane diving right to the mountain's navel, adding lots of power in the flare and keeping power up to almost takeoff pitch to reach the top of the landable grassy area.

With the artificial sound of the plane no longer violating the mountain's serenity, the silence is deafening. No traffic, no horns or sirens, no radio or TV, no planes. Her silence is golden, but with all her heart, she is embracing you for a small season. Below her is a country laced with icy streams, and her valleys are alive with caribou, and her waters are chocked with artic char and salmon.

I set up camp then for my friend, which consisted only of a three-man tent, Coleman stove, some food and then assembled a homemade wheelbarrow I had cobbled together from a WWII stretcher and a four-wheeler tire. Tomorrow I would push him three miles to the 76 inch moose we had spotted. But the rough tundra would prove me wrong with her huge hummocks too large for even a large tire to trespass. This is a stern country somewhat high and cold and windy, demanding from those who would befriend her, the title of "toiler" and "brave heart" against the stubborn virginity of its earth. In my heart, I knew it was an idea whose time had not yet come; I knew the wheelbarrow would not work, and I would have to carry his 180 lbs. the three miles on my back to the moose. Passion at some point overcomes reason, and I knew this was one of those times. It was my friend's passion and my lack of reason that spurred us on.

The first day with my disabled friend made it clear that the wheelbarrow over the tundra would not work. Packing the tent, food, stove, and all other manner of camping gear, the three miles wasn't too difficult, but it was three miles back to the plane and then a second rough round trip with more gear. Then it was time to put his 180 lb. frame on my back and attempt to carry him the three miles to the moose. Hopefully, this is all going to be accomplished, and the big moose will be there when we arrive.

The moose had his harem of cows, so he should stay put, guarding his cows against all others who would intrude on his domain. At night, you could hear their antlers crashing and the cows bellowing, the bulls grunting as the battle for romantic dominance continued. There are no sounds like these sounds in the city, and I'm glad they are reserved for me to hear once a year. All this and more pushes me onward; onward to meet Mr. Murphy, the illusive con-man who shapes our future with uncertainties. I know I can't blame this on God, the devil, or my mother-in-law!

Twelve miles packing the gear, plus three miles packing a 180 lb. man and his nine-pound custom-made 70 caliber flintlock! Like the clothes that made the man in the city, it was this custom flintlock with a gorgeous cherry wood stock that set this handicapped mountain man apart in any setting. The moose were patiently awaiting our arrival, but our arrival almost never came. His 180 lb. frame on my 200 lb. frame was not working too well, but after many rest stops and two and one-half miles, I had to give it up. I knew any more fatigue and I would twist an ankle or worse, so I put my friend down and told him that big moose would just have to wait. "Les," he said, "I'll crawl the rest of the way and drag myself this last mile."

If a man will show this much determination, who am I to deny him his right to torture himself, to make a history and memory of this "hunt." Crawl and drag he did until his clothes were torn and his knees were bleeding. The big moose came into view around 9:00 p.m., his harem of cows standing as sentinels, watching our every struggle. And step back we did, hoping their sighting us would not spook them to yet another valley three miles over. This was a part of Alaska that was very remote and empty of man. No neighbors to help here – our struggle was entirely our own.

The next day dawned bright and crisp; a frost would make the blueberries soft today, but you could see for two hundred miles. A peek over a large rock revealed the moose were still there, and the wind was right so that I could make him pancakes and bacon and coffee without revealing our presence. But it was those legs that would not move. They had to be nursed and bandaged now and wrapped for the 600-yard drag down the hill, through the tundra, hummocks, the brush and rocks and boulders.

"Not tired of this hunt?" I asked him.

"Well, yes, at times I guess. But I'm on Monument Mountain now, and I have to have something to worry about, don't I? I can't just sit by on my porch in my wheelchair in Mississippi and watch the clouds go by."

I sat down on a hummock of grass and thought I might not ever have seen Africa or Alaska or New York, nor learned to fly a plane, nor learned to hunt or fix things, nor in fact, done anything except wait for something to happen one year following another. All we were doing seemed such a far step away from the warmth and flow of town life and the rhythm of flowing with it. This was much outside the things one knew in the city. No showers or heat. Just bacon frying and coffee perking--the scents wafting toward the nostrils of the bear and wolverine that came to investigate us.

Once I had heard a guide named Christian who was in my camp later remark, "I didn't come out here to rough it! It's rough enough in town!" I listened, but I said almost nothing. I saw in this crippled man sitting and unable to stand on this bare piece of ground, tinkering with his seventy-caliber flintlock, not a fool, but at most a dreamer, and I was merely an audience for his dreaming. His were solemn dreams, and in time he would make his dreams live. The day would unfold slowly so a good breakfast was necessary. Our trespassing on this domain of the moose was slow and sluggish, like a traveler loafing in the path tomorrow wants to take.

I was famished. My ankles were especially vulnerable on the uneven terrain. George would have to crawl to the moose, get the moose down, camp by the moose to hopefully keep the grizzly bears from getting the meat, while I went to get a friend to pack the moose and George back to the plane three miles away.

We made our approach slowly and carefully, and the 600 yards of distance took us about three hours to traverse. The tundra and brush were just high enough to deny this handicapped sportsman a clear shot at the moose, and the moose finally sensed him and moved slowly away to protective cover. The cows this time had failed as sentinels, but nature still had the upper hand. I could have taken the moose at any time, but I chose not to deprive my friend the opportunity of watching this magnificent animal walk his cows to yet another valley. It was time to go home and try next fall. It was time to crawl back to the tent and make a plan for getting my friend back to the plane and back to "civilization."

Somehow, the evening and morning were void of complaining from my friend, so I dared not. This was a world absolutely ours, but yet unclaimed by us. This world of ours on the tundra on Monument Mountain held no intermediate shades either of sound or of color. There were no subtle strokes in the creation of this part of the world. The mountains here were rich in silence, lovely with it, and one mistake could bury us here. I was sure I would have to get a friend to help me pack George out the three miles to the plane. The friend I had in mind was "Bear Whatley"– I supposed so named because of his general physical strength. "Bear" was strong, and it was time to call on him.

One side of "Moose Mountain" falls into a valley of rivers that also drains Granite Mountain, another landing site. Close to Granite Mountain, a natural hot springs flows from the ground. In times past, gold miners dug out a small pond, perfect to transform a weary pilgrim into proud, but wrinkled nobility. You can soak, sitting in this regal setting, up to your neck in warm water and shoot caribou and watch thousands of other animals go by to who knows where.

Now, I must make a run down the airstrip on "Moose Mountain" and make the three-hour flight to Fairbanks for "Bear." There was no difficulty in this except the downhill is so steep that once the takeoff roll begins, there can be no stopping without tipping the airplane over on its back. Caribou and musk ox and, once in a while, a moose detach themselves from their resting place and prance and dance and scatter danger in front of my craft; but the plane is accelerating going downhill quickly in a rendezvous with destiny. A Cessna 185 with a seaplane propeller has a tip speed just below the speed of sound and is one of the loudest single engine airplanes in the world. I was leaving this animal kingdom with vindictive fury, shattering the front lines of the animal legions and making a sort of conquest of their ancient sanctuary. But all it takes is one errant teenage caribou to dare my departure and I am "toast."

George happily stayed on Monument Mountain watching a world he had never dreamed of go by for two days while I fetched "Bear." Upon our return, we found George almost sad to see us, his return to "civilization" imminent. "Bear" meantime was packing George's large 70-caliber flintlock rifle, carrying it like a walking stick, up a steep place on the mountain, when a twig planted there by Uncle Murphy caught and snapped the hammer. Its report and, of consequence, its recoil drove the barrel of the rifle and its front sight through "Bear's" hand, cutting his palm deeply and critically, and broke the cherry wood stock as the recoil drove it into the ground. Now I had two emergencies—getting George off the mountain and Bear's hand, which demanded urgent attention! Something had to be done that day or "Bear" would lose his hand!

I ran the distance to the top of Monument Mountain and cleared some rocks and came up with a 400' "runway." It was slightly downhill which is fine, but a large boulder lay at its bottom, and there was a tailwind of about seven knots. You don't take off with a tailwind on a 400' patch of rough mountaintop – especially at an altitude where the air has fewer molecules and the propeller produces less thrust and the wings less lift. Everything they say that works in a standard setting is nonexistent in this stressful environment, but decisions have to be made and made soon or "Bear" will lose his hand to probably amputation or, at least, never be able to grip another rifle or pencil or fork in the same manner or with any strength.

My plan was to take him to Nome, Alaska, and let a doctor there fix him up. Intermingled with these factors are the best laid plans of mice and men mixed in with Sovereign help and man's plain stupidity. To be able to distinguish between who is the advocate of a certain action and who is the perpetrator of a less than a wise decision is sometimes difficult for a mere mortal. I know people who praise God for the successful passage of a string of traffic lights because they were late to some appointment and then almost curse the same God when one turns red. In fact, I have difficulty believing God had anything to do with their being late or the lights going their way.

The best we can do is ask God for wisdom, and I did, because the dark mossy mountaintop here blended with the dark charcoal-colored rocks and the approaching darkness would have the same hue. Just at dark, it was supposed, the wind would die down or cease, but it did not. And "Bear" standing there silently suffering, a man whose fate and possible death or probable loss of a limb was totally out of his control, exerted a pressure too much for any man with a conscience or observer of objective facts to dismiss. It was apparent to me that I must fly him off Monument Mountain this night, abandoning reason to the pressure of the moment.

I walked and measured the length of that challenging piece of earth and rock until my head was numb with memory. Memory – I would need it later when I pushed the throttle for take-off, or if I failed, for analyzing the scrap of aluminum just beyond the large boulder, dead center of the "runway." There are times I suppose when you must consider your life not more important than your friend's, and if you did, would make you less than a man and less of a decent human being. But also, how fatal it is to be a fool! Airplanes, rifles, the chase – and stupidity. Monument Mountain would show herself capable of a sardonic smile and would make clear to us all that she accepts new things, but allows no thing to escape her baptism.

The towns and villages of Alaska and Africa lack roads to unite them, and unlike the rest of the world, the airplane came before the road. And here I stood, one eye on "Bear" and his hand, one on the plane, now a glance at this rocky heap of stones and then a long glance at my handicapped friend whose fate none of us could guarantee.

The tailwind – it's the pilot's wish when airborne, but a curse when contemplating take-off. All the books are out there, the manuals describing in detail the specifications and performance of the aircraft and its ability based on a specific weight to beat the air into submission and leave the bonds of a more mundane world.

One wishes for mundaneness at times like these. There are factors to consider--air density, temperature, friction of the rolling surface, wind velocity and direction, the depth of holes and unevenness of the terrain, the size of the rocks, wind shear, weight and balance of the aircraft, air pressure in the tires which affect rolling resistance, the amount of fuel in the wing tanks, the initial flaps setting,. Should it be a tail up take-off or a three-point soft field take-off position? Would 400 feet suffice to clear that boulder?

It was time to stop testing memory or exercising emotions. It was time to become stoic and somewhat fatalistic without being careless. It was time to pray, unload any excess weight such as seats and knives and tools from the plane and our pockets. The earliest men here rode mules, used sled dogs or walked. I wondered now if we traveled any better. The sun was now disappearing, and soon that gray granite rock would blend so well with the rest of the mountain that it would become indistinguishable danger.

We sat there, "Bear" and I, in humorless silence warming the engine, insanity having claimed us for its own. A herd of caribou passed off to our right, now running in high step to erase from their memories the strange sound our plane made. I saw small shadows creeping from the rocks, and ptarmigan making flight to their nesting grounds, and I began to cloud my mind with home, a hot bath and hot food and my wife to greet me. It seemed futile to nurse any longer the notion of putting off this take-off with so much of the evening upon us. George probably was saying some pious prayer for us, as he sat there in his three-man dome tent not far away. I had left him the ELT from the plane as a consolation prize for being so forgetful, to leave his flintlock rifle with a cap in place.

The plane's tail wheel was as far back in the rocky landscape as possible, and we would arrive, if we did, in Nome, Alaska, with mere fumes in the tanks. I held the brakes and pushed the throttle to the stop, the tail trembling and lifting as the engine turned 2850 rpm, and the propeller tips reached for the speed of sound. The boulder was there as it always had been at the end of our take off run, but now appeared close in our windshield, ready to make good metal into scrap. The 20 degrees of flaps went to 25 degrees as I jerked the wheel back to clear the granite monument about to become our headstone.

The Cessna 185 did fine, but I had asked her to gain 3" of elevation she couldn't. The tail wheel hit the boulder in its center and snapped with a loud bang as it departed the plane, leaving a piece of it attached to the steering cables now caught by the wind and propeller blast and banging against the fuselage. The plane flew as usual, so we headed towards Nome and a medic. The Cessna had to be landed under heavy braking with the elevator trimmed high, the elevator pushed to its lowest position, and kept under power to taxi tail-high to the parking space. Beyond the broken wheel and the fork which held it, no damage was done.

The doctor in Nome took one look at "Bear" and, with a grimace in his voice, pronounced his inability to help him in the least; so we put him on a larger plane for Anchorage where he was mostly taken care of. Just a phone call away, since Nome had phone service, my dear wife Jane had a tail wheel and parts on the way.

Three days after leaving George on Monument Mountain to fend for himself, I returned to drop him a note stating that I would fly the plane to Fairbanks and pick up a Honda three-wheeler, previously purchased for $246, and return the following day. Then I would land in my regular place and ride three miles to pick him up. It all worked well except unloading the heavy three-wheeler by myself. That Big Red Honda remains year round on Monument Mountain and is a faithful workhorse packing out moose meat and caribou to the plane.

The big moose eluded George and never got quite close enough to put in the freezer. Somebody said, "That's hunting!" George came back the following year and got a nice moose and a caribou. Somebody said, "Now that's a hunter!"

We made it home without that moose but with a tale to be told on the third Tuesday of September, a brutally gorgeous afternoon brimming with cool clear air and the sweet scent of pine. On this glorious day, the brilliant sky was filled with banks of motionless white clouds as motionless as our weary bodies.

The Alaskan autumn is a season when the leaves change color and fall in three weeks, and when even the most foolish of men still stop to appreciate all that is set out before them-- the purple fireweed dying now on the stem and flocks of geese, swan and sand hill cranes calling their way South to a warmer winter. I thought to myself, but never voiced the thought that my Eskimo friends in Barrow and I probably had a deficiency in one part of our brains and therefore our brains could not match that of a goose!

BACKSTRAP BREAKFAST - ROAD KILL CAFÉ - 2001

Try to find Loup City, Nebraska, on a map sometime without consulting the city locator page in the back of the atlas. This exercise may help you to find more unnoticed towns, and more to the point, their unheralded farmer Americans who are the salt of the earth, who deliver to us corn and beef and soybeans. America could survive but one month were it not for these that feed us. The earth has those that till it, the ones who first deserved the characterization of "down-to-earth people" or "salt-of-the-earth people." These are also some of the finest Christian people of all the ones I know, born humbly and unnoticed, living, by some standards, somewhat mundanely, but with meaning and purpose. They are somewhat reserved and plain-spoken, and without saying, truly good Americans.

Such are the people of First Baptist Church of Loup City, Nebraska. It is partially their gifts and prayers that sent me and my gift of wings and the Gospel to the needy in Alaska -- and before that Africa. These people really do care about people they have never seen, and they care about me.

It was my turn to visit them, to say thank you, to renew old acquaintances. I was their featured speaker as well, and they put me up in perhaps the only hotel in Loup City. The city is a picture of a small town, for none of the unsavory qualities of a big city exist here. Old farmers live here, some retired, but others too wise to give up work--the ethic that drives them. The same ones gathered each day for coffee and perhaps breakfast at the same café. They talk of potatoes, the price of corn and cattle, and the new combine or tractor someone had purchased.

The waitress would bring their food, never having taken an order, except for one distant farmer who was not a regular, and each one was called by his first name. It would be a sin when passing another "pick-em up truck" on any road not to raise a hand from the steering wheel to wave, or not to block the road for awhile talking of the disc and the price of fuel these days. These folks want to talk, not that they have to, but because when alone on the landscape, there's no one to share it. The farm is there, and owning it makes the farmer feel bigger than he is, but farms can bite and give the sting of death if too many bad years lead to a foreclosure. Talk is the cheapest thing around, so they talk.

The man of the city, who drives a car that never seems to get dirty, may greet you if he is confronted, but will walk away with vanity in his heart to get in his chariot and drive to the next car wash. Since I was known in Loup City, but only showed up to say "hello and thank you" once every five years or so, I was sometimes a captive audience, an audience for their previously told life stories, but as yet untold to me. None of them ever groped for glory or a headline or ever tried to become prominent – only to be left alone without government interference to farm as they wished. Their down to earth stories told the history of heartland America and never seemed dull.

The farming community I knew in Loup City attended church. Deity was not their second thought, but their main thought. I was more than once admonished to "Pray for rain, Les, pray for rain," and I would sometimes respond and tinker with their theology by reminding them that God sends rain "on the just and unjust alike." But they would still pray for rain.

In Loup City on Saturday evenings, the proverbial sidewalks were "rolled up," and a silence in the streets ensued that was deafening. Everything was closed, the door of my motel, stores, and restaurant. Because it is my firm belief that "coffee drinkers make better thinkers," I was up early Sunday morning for that cup "good to the last drop" and some serious study before I got behind the pulpit. But the restaurant in the motel was closed, and so were all the rest. It was as though even the dogs could not bark on Sunday morning in this sacred hour. Sunday had become a disaster for this visiting speaker in the motel, as the only noises being heard before the preacher were the meadowlarks. But the good people of the church were unaware of my plight.

I had plenty of time, so I drove the car they had loaned me to the nearest "big" town quite a few miles away. Sure enough, the same scene greeted me, but I was early enough to make it yet to another smaller town of which I was sure would greet me with the same silent stare. I began to wonder if a raven would have to feed me, so I prayed silently and with very little urgency the "protein prayer" which is much, I suppose, like the "rain prayer."

"Dear Lord, I could use some coffee, two eggs over-easy, well-done hash browns, buttered toast with blackberry jam and some thick-slicked country bacon. Oh, yes, and some half-and-half for the coffee, strong enough coffee, Lord, so I can't see the bottom of the cup."

I am incapable for the most part of doing more than looking on with awe at it: the workings of Destiny. Had I not been raised in Africa as a little white-black boy, had I not hunted and cleaned and ate animals from about age seven, had I not developed as a result a better taste for protein than oatmeal, had I not learned early on that a knife is to be razor sharp and is one of the most valuable tools and weapons known to man, and had I not chopped off chickens' heads and helped butcher beef and, for the last twenty years, put a moose each year in the freezer, the following scene would have meant nothing to me and would still mean nothing to probably 99.99% of all Americans. The question is an old one. "Why did the chicken cross the road?" Now it was, "Why did that deer cross the road in front of that farmer's pick-me up truck just ahead of me?

Now I'm supposed to be on "furlough," whatever that means. Does it mean that I should be on some kind of rest, maybe even pampered, and rarely have to make my own breakfast? Or does it mean that I wear the furs I've collected in Alaska around my ankles? Or does it mean that I get no rest, traveling to forty churches in a year or more and thousands of miles, spending more than comes into my wallet, and then go back to my work? It generally means the later. But the Loup City people make this a fun trip, and being fed by the ravens or a deer in the ditch is not a foreign thought to me. When a moose in Alaska is stupid and becomes the victim of vehicular homicide, the troopers phone charitable agencies to salvage the fresh meat from the road kill. The old road kills, however, are for the ravens, you know – it's the fresh they must bring me!

I drove about one-half mile past the deer and then returned. The farmer had only slowed, but his pickup, not being severely damaged, disappeared over the horizon. I searched for the deer on the side of the road; it had not gone far before collapsing.

It was time for breakfast. I always carried a razor sharp folding knife on my belt, and then it was in my hand cutting the deer's throat to shorten by perhaps a day its suffering. The scene on this Nebraska landscape that Sunday morning had to be at least strange to the average passerby. Fortunately, it was only God and a farmer and his wife who put their turn signal on to stop, but decided for some reason not to. I certainly was not unfriendly and would have given them some.

Here was a missionary pilot in a white shirt and tie, and slacks and dress shoes in the ditch beside the road, standing over a dead animal and holding a bloody knife in his hand with a grin on his face! I suppose looking back, it was fortunate for me that no game warden, state trooper, or legion of social workers had passed by at the same moment, or I would still probably be in a straight jacket in Ward 13 in Kearney, Nebraska's best hospital for the slightly touched.

It was all bloodless and quick. I only touched the deer's clean hair on its back as I cut it away from the backstrap. Next, I cut a small sapling close by, peeled it, and sharpened a point on its end. Then I cut backstrap steaks, four of them about 3/8" thick, and put the stick through the steaks while still on the animal.

Looking around, I saw a windbreak of trees in a field and crossed a barbwire fence. There was an abundance of dead wood in the windbreak, and, in five minutes, I had a roaring fire. I held the green stick over the fire and in 10-15 minutes, the steaks were done. I ate them off the stick.

In all this adventure, I had not one drop of blood on me and had never touched the meat, except with my knife and teeth. The only thing missing at this roadside café was a little garlic and salt and pepper. One of each in small quantity now rides with me whenever I travel the West. The hardest part of the whole affair was crossing the barbwire fence and answering the question from one at church, "Did you enjoy your breakfast?"

THE ALASKAN "RIGHT TO LIFE"

The history of mankind is tragedy. Unlike the animal world, man has a hard time finding his place, his order. The rules the animals have written through instinct remain constant; the rules of Homo sapiens seem to change daily. We have the capacity to know God and emulate the devil.

"Life, liberty, and the pursuit of happiness..." You may not have any rights when it comes to your Sovereign God, because He has all the rights. He will decide if you come into being, the direction your being takes in life (subject to certain decisions you make in life), and the end result, or the future of your life. That's because God is Sovereign.

But when it comes to men in relationship to men, there are certain inalienable rights that God has given them. All of God's creatures claim a right to life. The fire ant will bite you fiercely, if tread upon; the eagle will swoop with tenacious talon. The she-bear will chew all potential enemies of her cubs to bits of shredded flesh; and any mother of mankind, once her child touches her breast, is equally committed to its protection. As in much of man's world, might makes right in the animal world. Your dinner or your offspring is his, if he can take it from you.

The animal world has not degenerated enough to want to destroy its young while in the womb, but animals don't place a value on money or any means of exchange. Only in man's world has the "value of money" caused the parents to pay to have their own child killed before it naturally exits the womb. Thus, man becomes the absurd one in the world of living things. The "doctor" kills for money, then sells the babies' parts of which the "doctor takes the profits." The mother allows it because the fetus will cost her money and inconvenience in the long term.

The male or boar of the bear species, as well as the cat family, will eat the young if not closely protected by the sow. It appears that human men are worse in the treatment of their young, for they also will pay a lot of money to have their offspring prematurely terminated. Maybe the next step in this digression is for the female homo sapiens to allow her baby to be born, then not protect it; so that the male can freely eat it, which would be cheaper than paying a "doctor" to kill it. All this doesn't make any natural, animal, or human sense, and no moral or common or monetary sense.

In the community of men called the Christian community, who would say generally that they oppose the destruction of the unborn, and even classify it as murder, there are certain questions that must come to bear on their common and moral senses. Do they really understand the value placed by the Creator on innocent human life? Do they really understand their male responsibility to see that all innocent human life is protected, even if it costs them their own?

One time I asked a game warden who was "checking us out," about an Alaskan law which states that if a bear is stealing from the hunter a freshly taken moose, the hunter may not kill the bear to protect "the moose." For some unexplained reason, it is no longer the hunter's moose. The bear, which is doing what comes naturally in his domain, now has "rights" to the moose. So I asked the game warden where he went to school. When he told me a certain university, I asked him if, in that university, they taught all students that man is just a higher form of animal, without a soul and spirit, setting man distinctly apart from the animal world.

"Yes." he answered.

Then I asked him, "If a fox gets in a fight over a piece of meat with a wolf, who wins?"

"The wolf," he said.

"And if a wolf fights with a bear?"

"Then the bear wins," he replied.

"So, if I'm just a higher form of animal, and I get in a fight over a piece of meat with the bear, what is so wrong if I win?" I queried. Of course, he had no answer.

Likewise, the average "Christian" male, I'm convinced, is just as profoundly blind and stupid, because his Christian mind set should help him understand, but his unwillingness to answer, "Who is my neighbor?" emanates from his materialistic, self-preserving, yellow spine. If this is too strong a language for you to digest as an average person, then ask yourself these questions: What does the Sovereign Maker of the universe and mankind have to say about it? What would Abe Lincoln and all the forefathers have done? Have you ever discussed this issue in your church openly or have you only heard comfortable rhetoric from the pulpit that demands no action? Have you ever given your dollars to any cause to help educate the public and stop this national tragedy?

A preacher once asked me this question for which I had no answer. Since then I, myself, have asked at least a hundred others and received no answer. I now pass this on to you for your answer.

What is the difference in the demonstrated efforts of two groups of people and events, who only lived at different times in American history? Consider the actions of the Boston Tea Party. All good Americans revere those men as patriots, who because of a tax and money issue, disguised themselves, and under the cover of darkness, without taking human life, threw the British tea in the harbor, destroying private property in the process to prove a point about taxation without representation. In the history books and in our minds, they are patriots-- men who set the tone for the Revolution. Again, what they did was in disguise, under the cover of darkness, and destroyed private property to prove a point about the issue of money or taxation without representation.

The question was then asked, "What is the difference between them and another group today who, in disguise under the cover of darkness, put a bomb under an abortion clinic, destroying private property, but to prove a point about the issue of life?"

It would seem that the issue involved here is the issue of innocent life, an issue supremely more important than the issue of money. "So," he said, "logically, morally, and from any other argument, we either have to take the Boston Tea Party heroes out of the history books and classify them as thugs, or elevate the fellows who would destroy the abortion clinic."

"In both cases no human life was taken, so only private property is at issue." "You can't have it both ways," he said. His point was, if you say the Boston Tea Party guys were okay when their issue was taxes and money, then you would logically and morally have to elevate the destruction of the clinic to a higher ethical level than the tea party episode, because innocent life is the issue.

Christians today are extremely uncomfortable even discussing these issues; let alone acting on them. Alaskans have always said they pride themselves in the right to life, liberty and the pursuit of happiness. And many would say all animals have rights, even the mosquito to some are sacred, all the while allowing in their thinking the late term taking of an obvious life of their own species.

Are we then really any better than the cat or bear family in our thinking and actions? When millions of dollars are spent each year in America to protect animal life and millions to destroy human life, one wonders at the possibility of the insanity of us all. Hitler after all killed only 6 million, while America has killed 50 million babies. If you were God, how would you judge America?

And on top of it all, insult is added to insult as preachers preach "to the choir" that abortion is murder when their own federal tax dollars are being spent to support the abortion industry. Does that not make them accomplices to "murder?" So the madness in the world in general is being assimilated and accepted by the Christian world.

THE BEAR THAT STOLE OUR TROPHY –1991 –
TAKING DOMINION

Speaking of life, there is possibly no creature on earth that defends its young and its own more than the grizzly or brown bear of Alaska. Self preservation among this species is extremely high on the list of its priorities. On one occasion (and I have had many occasions to observe and be confronted by these 1500 pound carnivores), a large boar took over both our hunting camp and a nice set of moose antlers, which we had temporarily left attached to a large bull moose carcass not more than 300 feet from our tents.

We were north of the Brooks Range of mountains in Alaska, on a remote river bottom of the Chandler River, and I had already flown the meat from the moose to safety at Coldfoot Truck Stop, the "Northernmost Truck Stop" in the world. This moose would feed the family for the next year with 350 pounds of hamburgers and 400 pounds of steaks and roasts. But we wanted to have the antler set to remind us of this hunt or, at least, make a hat rack or overhead lamp. The bear could not be seen, but his tracks went right through our camp and straight to the moose gut pile. We had to assume he was guarding his meal, totally aware of our presence just 300 feet away.

I told my preacher friend with me that I would investigate the situation, but would probably get charged and possibly killed by the bear, somewhat secure in the fact of Scripture that man had been given dominion of the earth and all its creatures. My preacher friend weighed very carefully my plan to retake the moose horns from a big bear we couldn't see because of dense brush, the command to take dominion, and the complete folly of such a plan. I followed by giving him a choice of either staying put, in which case if I, the pilot, should get eaten, his chances of ever seeing civilization again would be quite slim indeed. The other choice I gave him was to go in with me and help me if the bear ever got on top of my human carcass. I told him I would rather have him mistakenly shoot me and be accidentally killed by a friend, than on purpose by an enraged grizzly bear, intent on taking dominion of his part of the world. My friend also agreed that he would not shoot under any circumstance unless I shot first.

With this catch-22 dilemma casting shadows of grave doubt on his whiskered face, we proceeded to follow the bear's tracks toward the gut pile. I hadn't gone far when I determined that the brush was so high that we would never see the bear in time, and that anything nature would have to offer us would be useful in this situation. So we walked out until we were in the clear part of the graveled river bar and proceeded to throw stones into the bushes, at an unseen bear that even yet may not be on the moose carcass.

All our actions were to no avail; there was not one sound from that direction. Still I had this gut feeling that the bear was there, awaiting his opportunity. I told my friend that we would make a wide circle and look for a clearer area to approach the bear which I was sure was there. We soon found an open area that would come to within about 100 feet of the carcass.

Now, in situations like this, you must think like a bear; be aware of his plan. The bear, if there, had heard a loud aircraft land, two strange beings talking, approaching, going back, and now circling. If there was a bear there, he would be extremely nervous and agitated that something or someone had the nerve to challenge him for his meal. After all, every creature in his domain runs from him in terror, but these newcomers had the audacity to approach.

I told my friend that our plan would be to approach and stop in the middle of the clearing, guns ready, 100 feet from the "imaginary" bear. My theory was that this was like a crow in a tree. You may walk under the tree and, as long as you don't look up, the crow will stay put. Look up and he knows he has been discovered and will fly. Upon our stopping in this clearing, the bear, I thought, would either run away, stand up on hind legs to investigate us, or charge us. I was correct.

Instantly, when we stopped walking toward the moose carcass, the bear roared and started his charge. All you could see at first was brush moving and branches parting as he closed ranks at 35 MPH! You can calculate how long it takes to go 150 feet at 35 mph! In those few seconds, you have to think of your family, your stupid "take dominion" mentality, getting the rifle up, aimed and the safety off, and the fact that running away now is totally useless! So stand side by side we did, rifles in the direction of moving brush, awaiting our fate.

The great bear came into view about 50 feet away and made one leap towards us that covered over 9 feet! As I watched him in that eternal second, I saw a bear that changed his mind in mid-air. Never had anyone or thing stood its ground before him as we did. When his huge paws hit the ground on that last leap, they were skidding to a stop, dust flying, and, in the same motion, he turned and ran straight back to the carcass. Our heart rates at this point were probably off the charts, clearing my plugged up arteries from the bacon consumed at breakfast!

How does one interpret a bear's thoughts in that eternal second? Is it by a different look in his eye, ears coming forward which had been laid back, and the slight lifting of his head? Or is it something else? Was there a slight uncertainty in his stride? Could it be, since life is at stake--his or mine, that the bear really does figure out in that eternal second that I do have dominion; that with one ounce more pressure exerted on the trigger, I will send him to "bear heaven" before his time?

Could he possibly sense that something would soon bite him as he'd never been bitten before? Something like a Pre-64 model 70 Winchester in a 375 H&H caliber that the British designed for stopping Cape Buffalo, elephant, rhino and lion?

As it turned out, the bear won that day. The bear lived, and the bear kept the moose carcass and antlers. In a real sense, he had had the last word!

Now whether you like it or not, whether you will really admit to yourself where your steak and hamburger comes from, it will not alter the fact that since Adam's transgression, everything in God's creation is hunting something else. If you don't like hunting, then you must come to terms that God Himself was the first hunter, first for Adam and then for an animal skin to cover him.

Hunting a wild animal pits the man out of his usual element and into the animal's element, therefore giving the hunted a great chance of escape. With a McDonald's hamburger, we raised the animal in our element on purpose just to kill it. So from logic you can't dislike hunting and have your hamburger too! Many Alaskans view it as part of our inalienable rights to life liberty, and the pursuit of happiness. With great relish, they reserve their severest criticism for the McDonald's head in the sand mentality.

We must give credit to man for his desire to make all his kills of animals quickly and cleanly. But in the animal world this is not so. The beloved wolf is one such example, literally crippling its prey and then eating it slowly alive. An African mother busy planting her rice, who leaves her baby sleeping under a tree, unaware that the soldier ants have found it, will return to find its eyes and all of the softest parts of its flesh eaten first. A cat will often throw a live mouse in the air again and again, waiting for its slow death. And a killer whale which is capable of killing all but another whale quickly, will toss a seal again and again into the air, tormenting its pray long before it consumes it. Just go out tonight and grab another steak for the grill, folks!

THE BEAR THAT WOULD NOT GIVE UP

Now I hesitate to point out that not all human attempts to put meat on the table end with a clean kill. Personal experience bears this out. On one occasion, I had another gentleman with me who attempted to kill a 9 ½ foot bear from 75 yards with his 375 Holland and Holland Magnum. It all should have been over with one shot because it was well placed, with a caliber large enough to kill on both ends--one at the barrel and the other at the hunter's shoulder with enough recoil to shake any fillings loose in his head!

My friend shot four times, each a lethal injection of "lead poisoning." He then reloaded and shot the bear three more times, each shot finding its mark, but the bear appeared to be just as charged with energy after the seventh shot as he was the first! This surprised my friend to such a degree that he dropped his rifle on the tundra and exclaimed that his rifle scope must have been damaged or his personal ability poor!

I assured him this was not the case and encouraged him to reload and keep shooting, but this slight delay gave the bear opportunity to run for dense cover. Once in this cover, all bets are off. You as a sportsman must go in after him and, therefore, put yourself at great risk indeed. The ball is in his court, and, even though mortally wounded, he would probably still have enough strength to eat his last meal--you!

The bear had a small creek to walk through--about 5 feet deep and 10 feet across, then an 8-foot embankment before reaching the safety of the brush. Rather than wait for my friend to get his act together, I decided I must finish the bear. My shots were all perfect from a knee rest, but after each shot in the shoulders of the bear, he would merely fall back into the creek with a big splash. Very quickly, he would present me with another shot as he stood straight up once again and put his front paws on the top of the embankment for a leap to "freedom."

Well, this stunning show of strength and endurance finally prevailed as my hapless friend was watching dumbfounded. Then I was out of ammunition, and the bear escaped into the brush. All was silent except for the breeze, the incessant cries of a seagull, and the rush of the salmon creek.

Once we had calmed down, I told my friend that to wait 20 to 30 minutes before looking for the bear would be prudent. Surely then, we would find a dead bear. So I ate a Snickers bar and reminded myself that the bear had had the last laugh. After 30 minutes of working up the courage, reloading and reminding ourselves that WE were supposed to have dominion of the animal world and of this situation, we started to follow his tracks up the creek bank.

Once up the steep bank, we were on his level, not knowing where he was, but seeing where he had been. With one sweep of our eyes, we could see the one inch alder brush he had bitten off, and a cleared trail of brush some 3 feet wide going 20 yards into heavy cover. At that same moment, we saw movement at the end of that dark tunnel, and it was coming towards us! I was in front, so I raised my big 375 H&H magnum in the direction of the 1400-pound bear.

Now one must use precisely the right equipment in such a time as this. First, the cheapest part of your hunt or survival experience is the right weapon and ammunition. Never take a knife to a gunfight! It's best to buy the best ammo with bonded core slugs that cost around two dollars apiece and then buy the shell casing, primers and powder and a hand loader. Then hand load correctly or some nasty surprises could be in store.

Also, one must use the equipment with enough frequency to feel sure of your mastery. The binoculars must not give eyestrain or fog up. The boots must be waterproof and comfortable; your clothes layered and comfortable; your knife razor sharp; and for bear situations like this--specialized shooting practice.

Before a hunt, I go to a local remote area and hang a paper plate on a tree 100 yards away, then one 75 yards away, 50 yards, and 25 yards. This simulates seeing a bear at 100 yards, which is about where I want to start shooting. Any closer and he would eat me before he expires, even with many perfect shots. Not farther away, since one shot usually will not be sufficient, but not too far away for a follow-up shot. I must hit the 100 yard plate, the 75, the 50 and, finally, the 25 yard plate in succession in a total of 11 seconds. I may hit the plates anywhere, proving a certain amount of control.

If a human runner can run 100 yards in 10 seconds, and only obtains maybe 18 mph, how fast can a bear run 100 yards at 35 mph? I must hit that bear all four times in an area that counts, or else do like grandpa said, "If you can't run with the dogs, stay on the porch!"

All of this is freehand shooting. No props. And I must consider other possible factors. It's raining. There's water on the scope lens. A mosquito is buzzing around my nose. I'm on a side hill. I haven't had time to get my gloves off. I'm not sure where the barrel of my buddy's rifle is. My glasses are fogging up with my heavy breathing. The safety is on and I must take it off. My scope must be on the lowest power. My mother is not here, and I hope my guardian angel is working overtime helping me take dominion! Oh yeah, and my underwear should not be of the white variety, as I may be ashamed to take them home!

"Now for the rest of the story." At 20 yards, the bear filled the scope! He had already absorbed 11 rounds of 375 H&H, 300 grain slugs at 2,750 feet per second, delivering around 5000 foot pounds of energy, entering the bear at .375 diameter, and then going through him, making a hole the size of a coffee mug. It's "kind of like" sitting in a dentist's chair, as the younger generation would put it.

As he charged, my 12th shot went right beside his massive head, through the full length of the bear. At that point, the bear realized that I was going to take dominion; so he turned and ran the opposite direction. My 13th round then entered a private area known only to doctors, veterinarians, and such that for some reason has been named the "Texas heart shot." With this, he went down, but got back up and ran away into the tall grass.

I told my friend, as I hurriedly reloaded, I would try to run him down while the bear was in the "run-away-mode," lest he have time to go into "I'll hide-and-wait-for-you" mode. We hadn't pursued more than 15 yards, when I could smell him. I stopped and finally saw just his eyes and ears above where he was hiding behind grass and pile of brush. He knew that he had been discovered, that his seconds were numbered, and that the 15 feet separating us was close enough to make his move.

Those giant shoulders came up first--the powerful shoulders with the characteristic hump, muscles rippling with enough power to tear my head from my shoulders with one swat! When the big 375 H&H thundered the 14th and final time, the bear fell 10 feet from my gun barrel! We had prevailed! We had taken dominion--but barely!

What is important is the story of the rifle, a 1937 Winchester model 70 in. 375 Holland and Holland, the story of the bear and me. This is what creates the fabric of our souls—living life with passion with all of God's creatures. This old gun in my safe waits patiently, keeping the dreams and the dreamer alive. I'm reminded that all men die, but few men really live.

THE BEAR WHO ATE CABINS FOR LUNCH

I once received a report from some Native Alaskan friends that a grizzly, a professional cabin dismantler, was in their area. Would I please come, locate the bear, and destroy it?

We landed the plane on the river bottom and fried up some bacon on the gravel bar. It's illegal to bait grizzly bears in Alaska, but you can fry bacon anywhere! Now this bear had a memory, and he liked cabins and their contents. This cabin had been entered through its side, then all its contents "examined" by the bear. Even the rafters were broken, almost collapsing the roof.

The bear came that night, licked up the bacon grease, but we never saw him. So the next night, we wrapped an orange florescent paint can with bacon and left it in front of the cabin door. Sure enough, he came and ate the bacon and chewed up the can. The can was so pulverized, the pressure put orange spray paint over a wide area!

Somewhere on the Melozitna River, there is a florescent orange bear. If we could have found him, we would have done more than take his picture, but we never saw him again. Maybe there were cabins which he now preferred with fewer surprises than this one.

BILLY BLOOM – MAY 2003

There are men that I care to associate with whose successes are easily anticipated, and there are men whose failures surprise no one, and then there are those individuals who achieve great success in spite of great challenges.

Billy Bloom cleaned swimming pools in Phoenix and hunted. Bob Boutang was an Alaskan state trooper who was now retired and loved to hunt. Billy wanted to hunt brown bear with me, and Bob would join us for the last three days. You can't live in Alaska and not hunt or fish, and you can't clean swimming pools in Arizona and not want to come to Alaska to hunt or fish.

Billy Bloom was handicapped, but only in his body – his mind was clear, his aim precise. He had fallen from a boat and was trapped under it, the propeller taking one arm and one leg. His arm he could partially use and he used it completely. His leg was made of what looked like wood, but was really the latest technology in prosthetic legs.

Billy had several animals already safely recorded in the Boone and Crockett registry of world record class animals and needed no instruction on how to use his 375 H&H magnum. Most men do need instructions, and I give it to them in a realistic way, because a hunt for the Kodiak bear allows for no mistakes. Ability to shoot well and presence of mind are only two of some very necessary ingredients for success.

Most men don't hunt or come in close contact with big brown bears very often and, therefore, cannot appreciate their cunning, speed, agility, tenacity, and ferocity. A large brown bear can weigh 1500 pounds, stand around 11' tall. With one swipe of his mighty paw, a bear can take your head literally off your shoulders or disembowel you.

Most authoritative observers say that a bear can be running 35 mph on his second step, and, if that's true, he can run the 100-yard dash in about half the time as an Olympic runner. With 1500 lbs. of rushing madness coming towards you at 35 mph, there are no mistakes allowed, no hesitation, no missing the moving target. A man making mistakes here might as well save the last round for himself, as there is little time for prayer. You had better be caught up on your prayer life before you go hunting these beasts.

With the exception of Billy Bloom, I would say to everyone that some practice was in order before they travel into the bears' domain with a handicap the bear would almost certainly take advantage of. My test of a hunter was this: I would put a paper plate for a target on a stick at 100 yards, one at 75 yards, one at 50 yards, and the last one at 25 yards. Then with his back to the target, the hunter would turn around and shoot free hand at the plates with no rifle rest, while I timed him with a stopwatch.

Starting with the farthest plate at 100 yards, the hunter would have to put a hole in each plate, ending at the 25 yard one, in 11 seconds. Hitting the plates anywhere counted, but missing one would start the whole process over again. With the heavy recoil rifles necessary for bear hunting, a hunter was using a rifle that "kills at both ends" and could soon start flinching with each shot, like a child who put his fingers into an electrical outlet. If this should happen on a second or a third try, I would say nothing and just resign myself to having to shoot the bear for him.

But no such schooling was needed for Billy Bloom, and besides, Bob Boutang would be there as well. Bob could make molehills out of mountains, and we would share the responsibility of getting Billy Bloom a bear. Bob, who became a Christian in my presence, could pass off as incidents true stories that a less modest man might have enlarged to a story, "that deserved to get better in the telling." His reputation living in the company of and hunting the big bears is approaching legend.

Billy Bloom was highly impatient as each rainy day came on the Alaskan peninsula and stopped our glassing for bears. We decided to get in the plane to move camp closer to the base of the Pavlov Volcanoes, a twin set of volcanoes, one still spewing steam out its uncertain crater. Near its base, we went with the plane, landing on its volcanic bed of ash.

Earlier I had flown the plane in a 50 knot wind to the lip of the volcano at 8,000 feet, and by turning into the wind, I could hover like a helicopter 50' above its lip right next to the steam which billowed past my wing. But we landed on her flanks and parked near a salmon stream and sat each day on a small hill just up from the stream where the bears fished. We sat in the beds they had made, where they would take their fish to eat in peace. We had just 50 yards to a small clearing where any bear checking out the stream would pass. Day after day we sat, testing Billy's patience, he testing ours.

One day a 100 mph wind and rainstorm came through that lasted two days. I sat on a milk crate, with my back against the wall of the tent to keep the wind from destroying it and rolling us down the hill, my feet in 10 inches of water. I sat in that one spot on that milk crate for the better part of 26 hours. I began to wonder about the sovereign command giving man dominion of all creation. If this was dominion, then my choice was to be a bear rather than a man. The tent we were in had been christened a "Hurricane Hut," by the manufacturer, but its claims were hollow in this wind-driven place.

It was the last day of the hunt and the last five minutes, when one of the largest bears ever taken in Alaska walked into the clearing 50 yards away. Bear! Hunting! Hurricane winds! My early childhood and now a plane had brought me to expect excitement – a release from routine, a passport to an adventure that I thought probably no man desired. But life was better today, and I had made it so with the location, the bear and my good cooking. God made the day, and it was a best day in the life of Billy Bloom!

Billy Bloom was told to shoot until that bear quit moving. Nineteen rounds later of 375 H&H magnum shooting 300 grain bonded core bullets at the maximum speed hand loading allowed, the bear went down for the count. Billy's ammunition was all used up on the sixteenth round, so I loaned him three of mine.

The bear was truly a record-book bear weighting around 1500 lbs., measuring 11' and with a bear track that a hunter could stand in with both feet. I knew as I packed out that 160 lb. hide on my back that the bear population would soar in the area. This big old bear, a dominant boar, the oldest ever taken in Alaskan history (as we learned later from Fish and Game), would never eat another cub. His 30" skull and attendant teeth would soon grace Billy Bloom's office.

Bears! Alaskan safari! Hunting! Surviving nature's worst! Taking one of the largest and the oldest bears in Alaskan history, clear water from a spring, good food, good plane, good friends, good weather to see you to the house, a passport to adventure, a release from routine, a perfect start, a rough middle, and a perfect finish! I imagine that one day the lion will lie down with the lamb, and I with the bear and put all this in my proverbial pipe and smoke it. I think that I am blessed – enjoying life to the fullest.

Now it's good to be home, and what she couldn't accomplish easily with her hands, she attempted with soft words, and I suppose that I will stay awhile and wait for the bears to grow. Then I will go myself again to find a larger cub-eater than Billy's.

EVERY DOG HAS HIS DAY – 2007

It was a cold day in February in Fairbanks. We live about eight miles out of the city in a log house on two acres. Cut from Alaska white spruce that were once 100 feet tall, the house was built in the "Scandinavian scribe" method, each log scribed and hand-fitted to the other. The result was a piece of art to be admired by any wood craftsman.

The doors were all hand-made as well, with two layers of tongue and groove pine with a foam board of insulation sandwiched in between. This door warped a little in the dry, cold winters and sometimes closed well, but other times could be pushed open easily, if we were not careful that it latched into place. I never expected I would have a dog problem.

My wife was out late this evening at an American Sign Language class and had not yet returned by ten P.M. I was at the kitchen table writing thank you notes. To my immediate left leaning against the door frame is a lever action 22 Winchester rifle used on a regular basis to keep the squirrel population down. Ever since those pesky rodents chewed their way into the attic a few years ago, and they tried to make a nest in the insulation near the stove pipe, it's been open season on squirrels. To my right on the log wall hangs a Browning 22 magnum pump rifle with a scope on it for long range squirrels.

Jane, an animal lover, would like to have a friendlier relationship with the animals in our neighborhood. She liked to put out bread scraps and seeds for both the squirrels and birds. And she would give left over leftovers to any dogs that wandered by. Grudgingly, she laid down rules for me and the boys when we started shooting the squirrels. My wife's requirements were to do the job with precision so as not to cause "cruel and unusual punishment," to use one bullet per each animal to save on ammo, and to get rid of the carcass so she could not see it in the yard and so that our dog would not find it and roll on it.

I love dogs, many of the species being friendlier and more forgiving than humans. They never hold grudges for very long. Some dogs are bred to fight and kill; such is the Pit Bull. My wife's dog is a small, fluffy white lap dog—a Bichon Frise—named Andy, but I have nicknamed him "Bear Bait."

Suddenly, at 10 P.M., Bearbait came alive from his snooze on the couch, running to the front door and barking his head off! On the other side of the door was a deeper "Woof-woof!" Through the small diamond-shaped window in the door, I could see the problem—a young pit bull in his prime, trying to get through the door at Bear Bait. I had never seen this dog before, and didn't know his temperament.

Now, I am not personally afraid of a pit bull. He is just another dog that I could kill anytime with the knife I always carry, even though he might be locked onto my other arm with his jaws in the locked position. But, I decided I would teach this pit bull a lesson on property boundary lines, but not without my 22 magnum in my hand. I was about ten feet from the Browning when the door sprang open and the pit bull met a snarling Bearbait in the entry hall. As Bearbait backed toward the kitchen, the pit bull clamped onto the neck of the smaller dog and made his way towards the kitchen.

I now had the Browning in my hand as the pit bull ran by me, knocking the garbage can over and shaking Bearbait like a rag doll. There was a lot of noise and Bearbait was bleeding. As the pit bull passed, oblivious to my presence, I kicked him in the side as hard as I could, spinning him around 180 degrees! It made no difference. He was intent on killing this miserable Bearbait who had claimed this house as his kingdom.

Then I grabbed the pit bull's collar in one hand, lifting him almost off the ground, hoping that if I got him off balance, he would let Bearbait go. The strategy failed. Quickly, I shot the pit bull in the spine, paralyzing him. Still he held the smaller dog in his jaws, claiming victory even in his own death. A large pool of blood was forming on my wife's new kitchen flooring, so I grabbed a roll of paper towels to arrest its flow to all corners of the kitchen.

Another 40 grain slug to the pit bull's head, and he expired, finally letting Bearbait go. I carefully cleaned up every drop of blood from the new kitchen floor. While I was driving out to go to the dumpster with the dog in a garbage can, Jane arrived home. "I'll be right back," I told her.

By midnight, I was in bed asleep, but Jane was still downstairs in the kitchen. She screamed when she heard a tap on the door and saw a face in the diamond-shaped window in the door. It was the owner of the pit bull from several streets away, looking for his dog. He could see that our lights were still on and inquired, "Have you seen my dog—a pit bull?"

"No, I haven't. Have you called the animal shelter?" was her reply. I had not told her, as I was tired and wanted to go to bed. Knowing her love of animals, I didn't want her to feel bad late at night. Or give her something to dream about in her sleep.

The owner was back on our street again, searching for his dog from house to house, thinking he might still be in the neighborhood.

"How long have you been missing your dog?" I asked.

"Three weeks," was his reply.

"If he's been missing that long," I said, "I'd just go get me another dog."

He seemed satisfied that was the best solution to his loss. Bearbait lived with some stitches and scars. It was a sad day for all concerned, but something that had to be done.

THE THREE AGNES (ES) IN MY LIFE ---2003

It is not often that a man can have in his life three accomplished, daring, and distinctive women all at the same time, and have the women's blessing at the same time. They all have the same name, but other distinctions are very pronounced. Let me explain my "womanizing."

The first and most important Agnes in my life doesn't like the name given her, would make as perfect a wife as any man could have dreamed of, is a fabulous housekeeper, cook and organizer, the best children's story teller on the planet. She put up with four children and put them through school in her own house, is well traveled, and a straight-A student, has written several children's books, and in short, is a dozen Martha Stewart's all rolled up into one, without any of her vices.

She is immediately liked by all who meet her, and settles into any conversation with an unassuming attitude of a mother hen who has been there and done that. She likes fried chicken, this Agnes I claim, and makes cinnamon rolls with enough goo and nuts to delight the sweet tooth in anyone. So at age 57, my love is deeper than ever for an older woman who is now 82 years of age. I know my mother would probably have a few words for me about how I have just described her, but "her price is far above rubies." Her name? Agnes Loraine Zerbe, better known as just Lorraine Zerbe, wife of Ludwig Zerbe.

My "womanizing" continues with another very fine lady, one Agnes Moore. She is an Athabascan Indian, whom our kids "adopted" as grandmother, who is of noble ancestry and has all the knowledge I need to have to enjoy a long life in the wild country of Alaska. She is in a senior citizens' home called the "Pioneer Home," but is free to come to our house anytime we can fetch her. She has a son who is a good minister, and she has wisdom that is sometimes hard to extract from her shy disposition. But like an expensive lady's perfume, her fragrant, yet whimsical, personality takes you in as her spell binds and commands attention – to learn – to see her world from another, but valid Native Alaskan perspective.

She can pick blueberries in a bear's patch of fruit-laden tundra and make a moose head soup or bone marrow soup that any king would appreciate, if only the soup's ingredients were not known to him. She has spent much time on Arctic rivers, catching, trapping, tanning, and producing some of the finest furs and beadwork that takes the finest artistry to a new level.

She wants to go caribou hunting with me this year. There are few like her who would almost get sick if she would have to sit out a hunt, or at least be mentally handicapped in some form, if she had to remain indoors at this time of year. She would be like a she bear with cubs to feed that was caught in a trap.

She now walks with a certain gait that speaks well of her ability to tramp upon the hardships and inequities of life. Some of her life before Christ had its ill-fated moments, but she has a smile now and a confident step. She will always be a valued friend, a true unmistakable pioneer in the most unobtrusive sense. When she's in hunting camp, her complete pioneering personality is in full bloom.

Every wrinkle in her weathered face speaks of a certain piece of wisdom I should experience and cultivate. She is without pomp and ceremony, but no Honda four-wheeler is worthy of bearing her dignity, but a four-wheeler is all she desires for transport, and my company is all she desires today. We shall slay a caribou together, and Agnes and I shall have caribou bone-marrow soup and a good fire to warm our shins and a story for the grandchildren.

Like my mother, Agnes Moore has as many facets as a cut stone, but each of these facets shines brightly with individual brightness. Both shall be remembered as great pioneer ladies who faced hard tasks with irresistible will – and accomplished them all. And both at times, I think, faced the harder tasks of being a husband's wife with less will than patience, less aptitude than loyalty to their husbands' callings, but responsible to a great extent for their success and genius.

Agnes Moore will be awakened by my rustling around with the coffee pot at around 5 a.m., when the morning is still part of the night. I will find her with her head and frail body buried deep in a 60 degree below zero North Face sleeping bag waiting for shooting light. "Your coffee is served, Madam. Was it one or two sugars you like?"

If you were to fly over a new but relatively barren part of Alaska in the dead of winter, and you caught in your peripheral vision a green palm tree, as green as a piece of quality jade against the white of the tundra, you might continue flying for a while, the tree violating your sense of harmony till it made you swing around on your course to take a better look. That's precisely how I found my "moose pasture" of the last eleven years. I have returned here year after year to bag my quota of moose and caribou. I fly three hours in my plane at 150 mph to get there, and I'm convinced that I'm the only human to have set foot here.

Alas, how deceived I was, how oblivious to the fact that someone else has been here, has circled this arena of splendor, has hunted and fished here, passed and stood on this very hill I so proudly claim as my own. After eleven years of hunting this remote scrap of earth and seeing no other human, this time I discovered the third Agnes and her husband Chip Hailstone and 6 children--Eskimos living the traditional lifestyle off the land.

Agnes sees that we have killed caribou and offers to help skin and cut it up. Surprised, my hunting buddy and I are glad for the help in this tedious task. Agnes puts her young baby on her back inside her jacket and zips it up snugly, so the baby can be secure, but still breathe. Soon she was up to her elbows covered in blood. Then Agnes offers to stew some of the fresh meat for us, too. We were impressed with her friendly spirit and confident ability and wanted to learn more about this family.

In her life there was no time spent at the doctor or dentist, no trip is necessary to the Department of Motor Vehicles for tags and title, no tracking or record keeping for the IRS, no bad news from the TV or radio will pierce their ears. Breakfast, dinner, and supper will just happen whenever it is ready, but no one will worry about it except the baby, but lunch for him is ready all the time.

In Agnes Hailstone's world, everything is handy if you are in the right place and just reach out for it. Everything can be made into something useful in the native fashion, into something that someone needs. Hers is a practical love for her family, not one that collects trinkets from Wal-Mart to be displayed so that everyone that comes through her doors can observe them.

The earth upon which Agnes Hailstone her family tread is often damp or snow covered and pitted with footprints of game that followed a web of trails that seem to lead nowhere, but always to water, leaving the pungent smell of their droppings and bodies in the crisp arctic air. The river they live on some of the time, the place of their largest cabin is narrow, but vibrant with the songs of a few hardy birds. Its banks are dotted with bright flowers that scorn the sun. She can count on this flowing testament of provision as she can her husband, children and dogs. Who needs, much less wants the government's help, when all the help and love you need is there for the taking or asking?

I was so impressed with the character of the third Agnes and her family that I invited them to fly five-hundred miles to Fairbanks with me for a week's visit. What a delight for this wilderness family to stay in a large warm home, will all the comforts—running water, washing machine and dryer, and more! In exchange Agnes gave me a piece of art she had created—a walrus tusk carved (scrimshaw) with a picture of a herd of caribou and an Inuit hunter.

Bad weather stretched their week to three, but the guest house was still theirs over Thanksgiving. Then the family came to church with me, and Agnes wanted to know for sure that she was going to heaven. I felt privileged to know these hardy people and to be able to minister to them.

They are true nomads of the North, living 100% off the land and accepting no welfare. I publish these details of their life, so you can know them too:

January and February -- Trapping and hunting wolves, beaver, arctic fox, caribou, and musk ox. Gathering wood for heat, hooking trout, sewing skins, carving ivory -- scrimshaw.

March -- Traveling by dog team or snow machine is better with more daylight, more hunting, sewing skins, repairing skin boats, trapping, seals come out, shee fishing starts, tom cod.

April-- Move to Kobuk lake spring camp, shoot seals in the ocean, all the birds return, weather warms up. Shoot skinny male caribou for drying meat, bear dens start to drip water and wake bears. Geese come when ponds stay thawed all night. River floods, trap beaver, muskrat, otter, shoot ducks (children's job)

May -- Spring camp at Kiwalik spit

June -- Shoot seals and make sealskin floats for walrus hunting. Move to summer camp. Ocean breaks up, Oogruk (bearded seal) hunt, salmon netting, ocean birds— gather eggs & featherless birds. Greens start to appear such as musru, onions, surro. Wood gathering, hunting black bear.

July -- Some ocean hunting, pink salmon fishing, white fish, gathering greens, Caribou skins good for clothing and lean meat, collect salmon berries and featherless duck, lots of Dolly Varden fish.

Aug—Caribou hunting for lean meat, fish silver salmon. Wood gathering, black bear hunting, catching young geese.

Sept-- Caribou hunt up Kobuk River, fishing at the Kiwalik spit.   Dig musro & onions; gather grass, geese swans ducks.

Oct -- Freeze up -- catch Tom Cods, hunt seals at spit, herring catch, and whitefish under ice, sewing, and scrimshaw.

Nov -- Move up river, set traps, hunt caribou, trout fishing, and sewing

Dec -- Same as Nov -- Try to keep warm. Repair tents, sleds, snow machines, train new dogs to pull sled, repair rifles ad fishnets. Read books, home school children.

Oh yeah, home school children. Chip and Agnes wanted their kids to live the nomad traditional lifestyle not suited to regular schooling. The State of Alaska helps families in remote areas with home school, even sending in a traveling school teacher every month to check on whether the kids are getting their lessons done.

THE KGB CONNECTION -- 1992

I was off to Nome, Alaska, a most interesting place on this earth—a place drawing man here because of gold in the mountains and streams and in the sand in her beaches. I departed early this morning in N1688R, my trusty Cessna 185F, her engine turning 2850 RPM, and the tips of her sea plane propeller turning right at the speed of sound, announcing to all of Fairbanks that it's time to rise and shine.

Five hundred and twenty miles is really no distance for me today in this plane. I would be counting countless lakes, beaver dams, moose, caribou, bear, and white swans and Canadian geese as they go south. I would be passing hundreds of hills and mountains with gold hidden inside and small rivers and creeks--if there were only places to land. Should the weather be lousy with ice in the clouds, then the trip would seem endless--it depended on so many things.

Today was perfect; I could see Mt. McKinley easily--150 miles away. I would look at her again, all dressed in white; I'd fly near her flanks and gaze in wonder once again.

I gauged my best friends to some degree by what they think of the "Mountain"—the tallest in North America at 20,320 feet. If they remarked in some fashion; could not move their eyes as we passed by, or pointed to some new thing about her majesty; then I knew they could be a tireless friend—tireless of the mountain and perhaps of me. I think of all humans who never look more than once, who don't appreciate something so magnificent, if they can take the Mountain so lightly, they probably will me too.

I had no friend with me today, so I would enjoy the Mountain singularly, wondering how many people trying to climb her treacherous slopes she had swallowed this year. Some they never find in this mountain of mystery, always intriguing, but never wholly solved. She was as uncompromising as any sea, as ruthless as any desert and without temperance in her harshness or in her favors. I could not pass by without uttering a word, even if to myself, or to take a picture. Competitors in conquest have overlooked her vital soul and have tried to conquer her for conquering sake.

"Why do you climb it?" they are asked.

"Because it is there!" is the reply.

But all have retreated down her slopes, the mountain itself just being there, emanating true resistance to conquest.

I was on what should be an interesting trip. It was 1992, and the Soviet Union was falling apart. For the first time in seventy years, the Russians would allow Eskimos from Siberia to visit their Eskimo relatives in Alaska. The grand occasion was called "Hands across the Sea," and I was interested as to how these indigenous people get reacquainted. I landed in Nome where the reunion would take place and intruded into the Eskimo world.

I noticed only Eskimos at first, dancing to their walrus and seal drums; telling a story with every move of the dance. But I also noticed about a dozen well dressed men sitting in the back of the audience, and, at first glance, I determined they were Russian. Who else could they be except KGB agents sent here to keep order and defectors from crossing over permanently to the USA?

In keeping with my personal philosophy and following my instincts, I walked in the direction of my fears and introduced myself.

"Hello, my name is Les Zerbe, and I live in Fairbanks, Alaska. I came here to see the "Hands across the Sea." You guys must be KGB, sent here to keep these people from defecting. And you guys must speak English, or they would not have sent you here."

My bold statement took them by surprise, and they hesitated to answer, so I continued, "I plan on coming to Siberia in the future for church work soon. I'd like to get to know you guys, so if get in trouble over there, I'll know somebody to help me get out of trouble."

They loosened up a bit and gave each other that KGB smile as though to say to themselves, "This guy is harmless, so we can talk some." They had to sit there and keep watch. They could not order me away as they were on American soil, and I regarded them as my captives, held hostage to at least conversation. We eventually exchanged cards, and I flew back to Fairbanks, via my moose pasture on the Northern Seward Peninsula near Koyuk, but closer to Granite Mountain.

Six months went by quickly, and notices went up all over Fairbanks for the first ever Russian Rock Concert with Russian rock star entertainers. I decided to go, not to see the "artists" or listen to the "music" (because I don't consider them to be artists or their gross sounds to be music). Instead, I figured correctly that the same KGB would be there since they spoke English, so I walked right up to them again and reintroduced myself. They were somewhat taken back, and later told me they thought I must be the CIA following them around. I assured them that I had lived in Fairbanks for over 12 years, and I had an idea for them.

"These rock stars are about the most worthless people in the world," I said. They nodded in agreement. "If they run away from the Soviet Union, it would be Russia's gain and our loss," I told them. Their smiles all around told me they agreed on this as well.

"Why don't you gentlemen do this," I suggested, "Pick out one man in your group who has the lowest seniority and make him stay here by himself to watch these crazy people. Then the rest of you come with me in my van. I'll take you to all the best stores in Fairbanks, and then I'll take you out to eat somewhere."

It all came together in short order, and away I went with eleven KGB agents in my van to see Fairbanks. In our travels around town, I saw a sign advertising a 300-table gun show at the gym on the University of Alaska campus. I did not tell them where I was next going to take them, but I couldn't think of a more desirable place to take these former sworn enemies of the USA than to a good, old Second Amendment gun show. I paid their way in, and the history lesson began.

The KGB agents thought surely that our government had done this to impress them. I assured them otherwise and explained the Second Amendment to them, that this was a cherished and necessary freedom. I showed them from my pocket-sized Citizens Rule Book, containing the founding documents of our republic, that weapons in the citizens' hands were not so they could go hunting and not so much to protect themselves against Russians, but to protect ourselves from our own government.

When this concept began to jell and take root, I thought for awhile that it would be the eleven KGB agents who would defect, to seek a life enriched by the notion that people could somehow govern themselves, and that dictators would not be tolerated.

Our day went well, and then some early plans were made to invite the Russians over to Fairbanks for an air show. Eventually it all came together, and the Russians brought their Mig 29's and several other aircraft for an air show in Fairbanks.

During the cold war, I would have gladly dumped Russians out of my plane, but during the air show I really had the chance to do it! But these Russians had parachutes—their crack parachute team-- and were part of the air show. This was followed up by a good number of Alaskan airmen flying their private planes to Siberia on a goodwill tour.

I realized that, like the Africans, the Russians had no understanding, had never experienced, could not dream it, and had no documents to support the notion that "all men were created in the image of God and had certain inalienable rights." To get these KGB agents to realize that all our documents--our Declaration of Independence and the Constitution, and all their relevant effects on the nation--had foundation in the common law as derived directly from the Holy Scriptures, would probably take at least the seventy years it took them to crumble under communism. As for the African who had malaria, it would take the right medicine and a long time to cure. I can only hope I had been part of the cure. At the very least, it had been entertaining and educational.

WINTER FLIGHTS NORTH OF THE ARCTIC CIRCLE -- DECEMBER 2006

Missionary flying is without question the most rewarding kind of flying possible for a mere mortal to experience. It is so because it is mere mortals you are servicing and helping, only they don't have wings—a way in or out; their existence hanging in delicate balance. There is an anxious hope in each missionary's breast that all will go well with the plane and its pilot. In a way, the best of all worlds are at their fingertips and mine, because they could be compared to the richest executive in America. The difference is that the missionary is working with the most valuable commodity in the world--its peoples. And the missionary has at his beck and call his personal plane and pilot, just as the business executive, but his product line lasts forever if his general audience will accept a one time gift of "Good News."

Some missionary flights are merely support flights, flying supplies of all kinds to some very remote locations. Five hundred miles in Alaska can be no distance in a plane, or it can be from where you are to the end of the earth. It depends on so many things, one being the Arctic darkness 24 hours a day in December. If the flight is to be made at night, it depends on the depth of the darkness, the height of the clouds, and the ice or snow they hold, the speed and direction of the wind.

Today will be a night flight, because that's mostly what I have to work with today. It will be a fourteen hour day of darkness regardless of how good the planning and weather is. This trip from Fairbanks to Wainwright up near Point Barrow will take about four and a half hours one way with a dangerous load behind me consisting of one heavy coal furnace, one gas engine snow blower, many groceries, some paint, laundry soap, survival gear, and seven five-gallon cans of aviation fuel. My ears will listen to nearly nine hours of droning sound which, I hope and trust, remains uninterrupted.

It's up at 5:30 AM for shower and breakfast. The news says the Iraqis are still killing each other another world away. The plane has been loaded the day before and rests under the stress of a very heavy load in a warm hangar. To me she is alive and is silently protesting these harsh demands on her engine and airframe. She is more than just a resonant, guttural voice of exhaust and pounding pistons –she is more vibrant and articulate than mere wires, spark plugs and a propeller beating the dense arctic air. She speaks to me in certain tones now, saying, "I can do this if this missionary really needs the coal stove." And he does. He has been collecting coal off the beach since summer because the price of heating oil is so high.

I fly at 150 MPH. I fly high—northwest for 4½ hours, over the Brooks Range and Gates of the Arctic National Park, with 10,000 foot peaks reaching out to pluck me from the sky. On my first flight here in the early 80's, the flight was somewhat more challenging.

It was the same flight to Wainwright, Alaska; the difference was that there were no working navigational aids there then. Five minutes after being airborne from Fairbanks and going northwest, there was a feeling of absolute finality when considering the end of such a flight after 4½ hours of absolute Arctic darkness. The scheme of life in Fairbanks lived moment by moment-- with constant human voices, cell phones, all the hours of roaring sound of active city life--ceased abruptly as the control tower passed me off to the solitude of the darkness of the territory north of the Arctic Circle. The cost of aircraft insurance at least doubles while flight is endeavored above this line. Planes and their pilots are swallowed in these desolate regions and the Civil Air Patrol won't come looking for you when the temperature dips below -20 degrees F.

On the first flight in December to this northwestern coastal village with a prospective missionary, I followed a compass heading and used a stop watch to time our destination. As usual, the pilot weather briefer with a sardonic smile had told us all should be well with the weather for that flight. When it comes to Wainwright, I don't really think weather truths can be comprehended.

Upon our uncertain arrival at 800 feet above the surface, only a faint glow of the village lights appeared, and the runway lights about 100 feet apart could only be seen one at a time. I made two passes over the village in a blinding snow storm, with 50 MPH winds blowing the snow across the runway. Each time, I was not quite lined up with the second and third lights of the runway. The third time, I put the wheels on the runway's pavement, which I could not see due to blowing snow.

My rollout was only about 50 feet, because the plane flies its slowest on landing at 50 mph. Since the winds were 50 mph in a slight cross wind to the nose, I was much like a hovering helicopter. A closing of the throttle eased the motor to an effortless hum, but I had to hold the brake continually and allow the wind to blow me slowly backwards to a parking and tie down spot.

The darkness was punctuated by the headlights of almost every snow mobile in the village! They had all shown up to see the plane wreck! My missionary passenger soon found a Christian family and a tiny motel where we stayed the night. The missionary couple with eight children moved into the village, staying that first year in an abandoned Eskimo house. Any water left near or on the floor would be frozen in the morning.

Was that flight a close call? Close only counts in horseshoes and hand grenades. Did Daniel have a close call in the lions' den, Jonah in the whale, Esther before the King? I think not. My question to Deity is, "Why me?" "Why do I have to make this flight?" The Arctic darkness is intimidating enough. The 50 MPH winds and snow are pelting me to frozen insanity, and, here under faint northern lights, Wainwright seemed to lack even human warmth, a community without laughter. It is perhaps that this kind of survival existence on a dark Arctic night immobilizes the muscles that help one to smile. Or perhaps it is because the dead cannot be buried until the summer thaw.

That was to be the first of several Baptist missionaries I would regularly fly to Eskimo villages. I am always glad to come to the North Slope of Alaska and happier yet to leave.

One time I flew to Wainwright, and spent a day or two there waiting for an elderly evangelist and his wife to conduct a meeting. The missionary there had showed up at the airport with his only piece of transportation, a used snow machine with a sled behind. It was 30 below zero, and the wind was blowing snow in 30 mile per hour gusts across the runway. That poor old preacher and his wife nearly froze to death in just that half mile ride to the house.

I was informed I would have to push my airplane just ten feet ahead to be able to plug in the electric heaters for the plane. What the Arctic demands is a 100' extension cord with a three-way plug, a silicone 200 watt oil pan heater, an electric battery pad under the battery, an 1800 watt electric hair dryer for inside the engine cowling, and an 1800 watt electric heater for inside the plane to preheat the instrument panel, in addition to fabric covers to fit the wings, windshield, prop, and tail. To fly north with the night in December is no easy task. Almost everything you touch is a potential close call in the making! That dark night on the Wainwright airport was no different.

I pushed the plane about ten feet forward on what appeared to be a flat snow-plowed hard packed surface. The nose wheel found the only hole in that parking area. The hard packed snow over that hole was as deceptive and uncertain as Bill Clinton was while testifying.

The snow pack collapsed; the nose wheel disappeared, allowing two of the three propeller blades to touch the ground with the tail jutting high in the air. Had I taxied under power the remaining ten feet, the whirling propeller would have been bent and the engine damaged! I would have had to overhaul the engine!

Was that a close call? I think so, except for the fact that we had really committed ourselves to His safe-keeping before we turned the key.

While I lifted the nose up and out of the hole, a village policeman with a four-wheel drive pickup and a long rope pulled the plane by its landing gear. Later leaving Wainwright was not easy either. I burned out three electric heaters trying to preheat the plane. Then I had to "jump through several hoops" to borrow a kerosene space heater belonging to the school district, which lasted just long enough to get the plane started and to burn the paint brown on a previously white engine cowling.

I left those lonely missionaries to their frigid existence and took off with the evangelist and his wife, a four and a half hour flight back to Fairbanks. There was wind enough as usual for a short takeoff. After a long climb, N3968Q found the stars at 12,500 feet. The North Slope and the Brooks Range Mountains soon slid unseen beneath our wings, and we were thankful for the lusty song that engine made. Then a hundred miles ahead, the city lights of Fairbanks glowed an eerie greeting. The Arctic air was so cold and had received me into its realm, the night enveloping me entirely, out of touch with the earth and any comfort, living temporarily in a vast space with the stars and a sliver of moon.

I continued south, feeling the need for some sleep, but not from exhaustion as much as boredom. What contributes most to my loneliness in flying vast arctic countryside at night is the absence of any signs of life for hours and hours. On occasion, I see a trapper's light or his snow machine light or the light on his forehead he uses to guide his dog team. He is as unaware of me as his tomorrow's worries. He is a sign of life and hope in this vast wilderness.

The glow of Fairbanks is ahead and I plot my descent as carefully as possible. I will pick up ice on the way down, and who knows how much? I calculate and choose to go down through this storm of clouds at 1500 feet per minute, ice building up with each foot of descent.

My windshield now covered so I cannot see out the front, I must quickly cover the heater duct for my passenger to force more hot air up the defrost duct. It works to a degree, and I have 1½ inches of clear windshield to see through. For hours now, I have been sliding across a surface of white clouds as if I was Santa's sleigh running on fresh fallen snow. My descent through this white and seemly endless sea of snow and mist and ice is about to end.

I head for the brightest spot in Fairbanks, still really unseen and merely hoped for. I'm below the storm's belly now and the bright lights below are the property of the Dodge dealer on the east end of Van Horn Road. I slide past the dealership, descending, squinting in the darkness through the 1½ inch slotted view of reality.

I search for three gravel pits over which I must fly in succession and at a certain compass heading and altitude. Now, I turn both landing lights on. I'm looking for three reflectors at the end of this unlit runway. Cowl doors closed, flaps at 20 degrees, prop control full forward, mixture knob adjusted for this power setting, trim adjusted nose up all the way, set the stop watch to monitor 5 minutes at engine idle to cool the turbocharger, airspeed at 60 knots indicated, and make sure I take the craft past the unlit windsock where the runway snow has been plowed.

I'm lined up, the stall warning horn protesting the declining airspeed. I'm down and well. I taxi to the hangar and bring the engine to idle. With the plane idling and cooling the turbocharger, I step outside in the very cold air, accelerated beyond comfort by the propeller blast, and open the hangar door. Back in the idling plane, with a burst of power, I taxi into the hangar.

This was a trip I had done many times before. To most pilots, the whole trip would be classified as a "close call." I had simply rediscovered an old path in the sky and wandered there and back. All I can say is, I know this plane and my limitations and that mountain range and that unforgettable glacier. I'm only left with a question: "Did I tempt or trust God on this fourteen hour flying day?"

WE DO FLY THESE DAYS –1997

We do fly these days, but we have not conquered the air. God's nature as found in Scripture says it "snows on the just and the unjust alike," or something like that. Nature is now proceeding again to test me, permitting me the use of her skies and its forces in direct proportion to how much I understand of her. It is when we pilots presume to know Nature's whims to assume intimacy with her, that a harsh reality of her capabilities against the pilot and his craft is clearly defined in one corrective moment. In a way, is it really too much to think that, despite all those pedestrian centuries which came before us, we should now in a century have learned to fly? We may have learned, but there is much more to learn.

Most missionary pilots are aircraft mechanics as well. The well-wishing of an airplane mechanic to a pilot who is not one is not to be taken lightly, but I am my own airplane's mechanic, my own contact with reality. It's the oil and dirt on my hands, my extensive tool box, the aircraft manuals carefully adhered to, and the trouble light--only these--and a prayer for wisdom keep this scrap of tin in the air. But this scrap of tin has careful design to it.

The world likewise evidences careful design. To say that God did not create every last thing in the original world and its universe is to believe the possibility that some aluminum and steel in some universal tornado put together random scraps that, when settled, became a Cessna 185 F or a Boeing 747!

As my own mechanic, I have only myself to blame for not following the designer's manual for understanding its design and maintenance program. So many people refuse reality, living a lifetime, and at the end of it they understand more about all those around them than they know about themselves. They never watch or learn about themselves, because they don't want to be lonely. We read books, watch TV, and care for the dog or cat, all trying to avoid ourselves, the yearning to dispel loneliness as natural as life itself. And so we fly scraps of tin to take the "Good News" to lonely peoples, seemingly ignorant of their Designer or His design for them at all.

Fairbanks International Airport– Destination Fort Yukon, eight miles north of the Arctic Circle. Today, I'm flying my miracle Piper Navajo, the drug bust plane, a gorgeous thing with a Panther Conversion for higher performance. It had all the amenities because drug dealers have the money and inclination for speed. This cabin class twin had airline quality radios, 350 HP on both sides, four blade "Q-tip" propellers, additional fuel tanks, a Shadin fuel management computer, and a good auto pilot. It would cruise easily at 205 MPH.

I had a load of native people aboard in total darkness and snow so heavy that it was an indefinite ceiling of about 300 feet. It would be a simple IFR flight of 45 minutes. With the run up complete and everything checking out, I pulled onto the active runway. I could only see one set of runway lights, which meant forward runway visual range was down to about a hundred feet, as I began the take off roll.

In some way, I have overlooked some portion of this complicated airplane's maintenance, as now one engine is apparently quitting on me! Now in total darkness and heavy snow at an altitude of 300 feet, I feel the craft refuse its burden and begin a slow descent to somewhere. It is the actual silence of one engine and the suddenness of it that stuns me. But I don't have time to feel fear; I can't allow myself to feel anything! I had been trained for this moment, and fiddling with emotion now would only slow things and complicate whatever was next. I think the denial of natural impulse is what is meant by "keeping calm," but impulse must also have reason when flying a stricken plane on its way to an accident site.

All I can do now is observe my hands maneuvering quickly, and know that, while they are moving to push the control wheel forward to gain some airspeed, pulling the malfunctioning engine's lever to feather the propeller, lowering the landing gear, and calling the control tower, I can't see 500 yards away! I'm landing straight ahead, hypnotized by the needle of my altimeter and the faint glow of runway lights somewhere beneath me.

In one sense, it seems a terrifying abandonment of all logic and reason and sanity to direct an impotent craft toward a shortening, unseen runway. My mind, instincts, and soul reject it, but I must follow the letter of the law I had practiced so many times before in simulated practice, and, for some reason, my hands don't shake. I can only observe with a kind of stupid disinterest that my hands, although practiced, had also been guided by Deity. There was, in the end, no sign that Fairbanks was aware of our leaving or quick return or that she cared.

NO PLANE, NO GAIN

Flight, as best as it can be known by man, can be no more enjoyed than in the world of "missionary flying," shrinking greatly the pressure of having to get there by road and getting there safely and rested. The Gospel is not put where man does not put it. The airplane takes you to the vital souls of a continent where souls of men are dead and distant; whose wisdom comes in simple terms and sometimes appears to be nonexistent in modern terms. In

Africa, as in Alaska, a hundred miles is but one step in a country so big; it is truly a journey to the edge of the sky.

Beyond are villages still sleeping in forests or on reservations--villages peopled by those who are vaguely aware, if at all, that because of a plane and the message of Christianity, their lives may soon be forever changed. To some degree, I have lived the life of a transient. I have lifted my plane from small village airstrips for perhaps a thousand flights, but I have yet to feel her wheels and wings lift from the earth to the air above without knowing the uncertainty and exhilaration of a great adventure.

My father before me and I have walked to some remote villages, built an airstrip, and watched the plane change the society. Sure, the people involved were the real agents of change, but God, as with the staff of Moses is using the animate to make connection with the inanimate. The essence of progress is time, and the plane gives us much more of time and, therefore, progress.

Yet, some consider a plane a luxury, a rich man's toy, but these are the facts. A Cessna 185 or 206 could be purchased in 1974 for a sum of $28,000. These craft can carry six people, plus baggage, at 160 mph for 5 ½ hours and go in a straight line to the destination (unless you are enjoying yourself zigzagging). At times, I would have to fly in the tree tops of the jungle, the tops of the tallest trees being in the clouds, or in the Mountain passes, the Mountains being in the clouds. I acquired the name "Zig Zag Zerbe," but I saw creatures and country others only dreamed of in flying this way.

The same Cessna purchased in 1994 for $28,000 could be sold for $150,000 in the year 2000. Since I am an A & P (airplane and power plant) mechanic, the engines cost me an average of $6,000 to rebuild to new engine tolerances. I would run the engine 1,400 hours before overhauling the cylinders, and then run the engine to 2500 hrs. Therefore, going 160 mph for 2500 hours is the equivalent of 400,000 miles of travel for around $10,000.

Since I'm going straight line--missing all the crooked roads, the stop signs, the West Virginia Turnpike, State Troopers who stop people for going 56 in a 55 mph zone, and the drunks—I have to add about 100,000 miles to the 400,000, totaling about

500,000 equivalent car miles. Besides the fact that my hard asset has increased in value tremendously over time, I have also traveled 500,000 miles for $10,000, as compared to at least three automobiles purchased in the same time, each costing, let's say $30,000 (each.) and saved thousands in hotel and meals. Therefore, I have $90,000 of worn out automobiles worth very little except to a junk yard dealer.

So much country is lost to the traveler who has trees on both sides of the road--his vision blocked to that of a cattle trail. With an airplane, one can see the country in panoramic vision, and, do so many things, as I have done--land in a meadow for a nap and lunch, land on the Alcan Highway on the way to Alaska, taxi up to a restaurant to have coffee and a cinnamon roll, land on a remote beach and watch the walruses, and see three polar bears, more red than white, gorging themselves inside the carcass of a large whale. With a plane, one can land on a volcano, on a gravel bar, on the exposed part of a river bottom, and with skis or floats landing sites are limitless.

You don't have to worry about passing someone or someone passing you--in short, "air-rage" need not overtake the aviator. But most of all, an airplane enables you to meet people in areas that have not been touched by the message in the Bible. Had he been born subsequent to the Wright brothers, the Apostle Paul surely would have been an aviator or would have flown with one. "Not where Christ was named –to whom He was not spoken of, they shall see; and they that have not heard shall understand." Romans 15:20.

In the Cessna 185, I can land on a steep-angled curved beach covered with washboard sand, park in the tall grass out of tide's way and take the largest Sitka Black tail deer ever taken by rifle on the Kodiak Island. I can deliver the mail and paychecks to remote villages, the good and bad news, or the medicine to cure a disease. Likewise, I can fly the expectant mother to the maternity ward, the snake bite victim to the doctor, the body to its funeral.

I can fly the lantern fuel to those who would have light, the dignitary to the political rally, the petitioner to the Governor,

Christmas presents to the remote homesteader, the Bible to the waiting Russians. I can transport the groceries and relatives to the remote missionary, the tourist to the best scenery in the world, the Eskimo teenager from their inaccessible village to Kako Bible Camp, and the 2,000 lbs of salmon to my house from the camper's fisherman father who puts a net into the river for me.

I can deliver the lumber, paint and all manner of building materials, plus laborers to their mission project, the missionaries to their conference. I can fly the hunter to my private moose pasture for our winter's meat, a sled dog to the Iditarod Dog race and the wife to see her husband cross the finish line.

Has my argument for the airplane been made yet? If not, I can mention more of its potent potentials. Whatever the greatness of airplanes over all other forms of travel, the animate object is to serve the inanimate. The airplane has, as it were, a soul almost of itself, but its use is for the souls of men.

In Africa, as well as in Alaska, people learn to serve each other. They live on credit balances of little favors that they give and, most likely, one day ask to have returned. Many "modern" or "civilized" sections of the world are empty of real men, but full of "nice" ones, where "love thy neighbor" is just a pious injunction and not a rule for survival. In Africa or Alaska, if you meet someone in trouble, you stop and help him, because another time he may stop for you.

It is the geography that often makes a man more civil. In London or New York, two of the most "civilized" areas of the world, the people are hardly very civil, not even greeting or looking at each other, each willingly oblivious to the other's existence. Not one store is inexpensive here, the sky and the earth meet like strangers, and the sun is as dispassionate as the hand of a man who is unsure of his male gender. But now it is also the geography, the countryside. This Alaska and Africa have not yet been entirely found; they are unknown. Most of their areas have just barely been dreamed.

Someday, should I conquer my fear of endless ocean and need a forced vacation; I may take a tramp freighter to Africa once again. It's a choice of fourteen days on the sea or fourteen hours in the air. Like all oceans, the Atlantic seems never to end, and the ships that sail on it are small and slow, completely at her mercy. These ships have neither speed nor sense of urgency; they don't cross the ocean, they just live on it until the land comes into view. Such a voyage will bring either sanity out of rest or insanity out of boredom.

All this in my life and more has happened, and if some of it was hard for me to believe, I had my log books, my maps, my box of papers, receipts, ticket stubs in hand and pictures to prove it to myself. I have always practiced the philosophy of going toward the world, in the direction of my fears. My great fear would be that, someday, I would have to wait while the world comes to visit to me. A greater fear yet is to be unable to think fast enough, push the throttle, move the ailerons, or push the rudder peddles, but instead to only watch the world fly by.

THE LAST GREAT RACE ON EARTH

THE DOG RACE---

We're all in the race of life. Some people run the race by the rules; some don't and go to jail and sit life out. Jezebel in the Bible did not run the race by the rules and the dogs ate her as God had said they would. Lazarus ran the race by the rules, the dogs licked his sores, but he went to heaven while the rich man did not. God gave us His word, the Bible, to show us how to run life's race.

THE DISTANCE—1149 MILES!

To the young person, life is too long. To the older, it's too short. God says your life is but a vapor, and none of us are assured of tomorrow. The question before every person is, "if I were to die today, would I go to heaven when I die?" God says with His forgiveness of sin through Christ, we can go the distance and get help to life's finish line by His grace alone. The Bible clearly teaches that our good works, "my parents were good

Christians," or "I think my good works out way my bad," will not get us to heaven.

THE DIFFICULTIES ---

Life is full of difficulties, some larger, some smaller, than the difficulties one finds running the last great race on earth. Satan has ruined so much of what could have been good, so that life now seems too often to be filled with insurmountable difficulties. But to have the peace of God, knowing our sins are forgiven, that God's promises are sure, helps us through life and takes us into God's presence when we die.

THE DISTINCT MARKERS

It's so easy to get lost running this great race. Nome can seem so far away when you miss a marker and start wandering in a blizzard. This can cost you the race, or cost you so much time as to bring you in last. You know life is like that and who has the right to put the markers where they are if it isn't God? God says in Romans 3:23 --"For all have sinned (missed the mark) and come short of the glory of God." God also says, "The wages of sin is death." So we don't want to miss or overlook the markers that are there in God's Word that mark the most important race. These markers are clearly set out for us in the Bible; just read it.

THE DESTINATION – ALL PEOPLE IN EVERY CULTURE ARE IN THE RACE OF LIFE. EVERYONE KNOWS:

1. There IS a God somewhere.
2. There is good and evil.
3. There is life after death.
4. *There is reward for the good and punishment for evil*

There is nothing better after eleven days and nights of hard running to see the lights and finish line at Nome. It means the end of an exhausting race, recognition for something well done and rewards, a name recorded, relaxation, and the wonderful

company of many others who appreciate what you've done. God says to one who runs the race of life with Christ as Savior: "Enter thou into the joy of the Lord."

Paul said in Phil 3:14-- "I press toward the mark for the prize of the high calling of God in Christ Jesus."

Hebrews. 12:1—"Wherefore seeing we also are compassed about with so great a cloud of witnesses, let us lay aside every weight and the sin which doth so easily beset us, and let us run with patience the race that is before us,,,"

II Timothy 4:7-- "I have fought a good fight, I have finished my course, I have kept the faith.

Ga. 5:7-- "You did run well: who did hinder you that you should not obey the truth.

THE BIBLE SAYS THERE'S ONLY ONE WAY TO HEAVEN

Jesus said, "I am the way, the truth and the life: no man cometh unto the Father, but by me." John 14:6

NOBODY ELSE CAN SAVE YOU. TRUST JESUS TODAY!

"That if thou shalt confess with thy mouth the Lord Jesus, and shalt believe in thine heart that God hath raised him from the dead, thou shalt be saved." Rom. 10(

1. Admit you are a sinner. See Romans 3:10

2. Be willing to turn from your sin (repent). See Acts 17:30

3. Believe that Jesus Christ died for you, was buried, and rose from the dead. See Rom. 10:9-10

4. Through prayer, invite Jesus in to your life to become your personal Saviour. See Rom 10:13

What to pray:

"Dear God, I am a sinner and need forgiveness. I believe that Jesus Christ shed His precious blood and died for my sin. I am willing to turn from sin. I now invite Christ to come into my heart and life as my personal Savior."

If you trusted Jesus as your Savior, you have just begun a wonderful new life with Him. Now on the race of life:

1. Read your Bible every day to get to know Jesus Christ better.

2. Talk to God in prayer every day.

3. Be baptized, worship, fellowship, and serve with other Christians in a church where Christ is preached and the Bible is the final authority

4. Tell others about Jesus Christ.